595

EVERYBODY WINS:

Transactional Analysis Applied
to Organizations

EVERYBODY WINS:
Transactional Analysis Applied to Organizations

Dorothy Jongeward

Interpersonal Relations and Communication Consultant
Director, Transactional Analysis Management Institute

and Contributors

ADDISON-WESLEY PUBLISHING COMPANY
Reading, Massachusetts • Menlo Park, California •
London • Don Mills, Ontario

ISBN 0-201-03318-6
  CDEFGHIJ-MA-79876543

PREFACE

Every organization faces not only the task-oriented problems of getting the job done, but also those problems that have to do with people dealing with people. As a consequence, a rising consciousness grows across the nation concerning "people problems." Training departments, management development departments, and people in organization development have all turned to the behavioral sciences for answers. It was not until recently that the behavioral sciences had something practical and usable to offer.

One of the most effective approaches now available to help us understand people and the dramatic scripts people live by is Transactional Analysis (TA). Transactional analysis as developed by Dr. Eric Berne was originally a method of psychotherapy. However, his new and exciting constructs have practical application and meaning far beyond their use as a therapist's tool.

Transactional analysis is an intelligent, thinking approach to understanding the motivations and sources of human behavior. Almost anyone can learn and apply its basic principles. Not only does it offer a basic method of understanding communications between people, but it also offers a blueprint for change.

It is a most appropriate interpersonal relationships tool for organizations because it is a nonthreatening, practical, interesting, and often fun approach to learning about people. In addition, transactional analysis helps us understand how the scripts of an organization can be analyzed and changed. Such an analysis is a fresh approach to organization development.

This book was motivated by the already many successful applications of TA to organizational problems. This is an advanced book and is not intended to teach the basic principles of TA. Other works are more useful to accomplish that goal. (See Appendix A for a complete bibliography and information about the International Transactional Analysis Association.)

My contributions in Part I are based on my own experiences in business, industry, and government. A new concept which I've found most exciting to share is on organizational scripts and how they can be analyzed. In addition, I have included a comprehensive section on games, since at this time little is written about how people adapt games to the organizational setting. Other emphasis is placed on effective management styles and effective interpersonal relationships. Everybody *can* win.

A further purpose of this book (primarily Part II) is to bring together a variety of comments and programs from people throughout the country representing different kinds of organizations which are using TA. The contributors are primary sources who are pioneers in the field of applying TA to problems in the market-place. As editor of this book, I am in no way endorsing those programs that appear here which I have not consulted with.* They are here to give the reader insight and information about some of the current thinking and applications of TA to organizations. In addition, Part III relates TA to other management theories and practices in supervision.

TA also helps us understand how the scripts of an organization can be analyzed and changed. It is my hope that organizations which seek healthier scripts and healthier interpersonal relationships will create a climate of growth and development for the individuals working in those organizations. How else can individual goals and organizational goals mesh in a healthy and mutually rewarding effort?

Organizations are concerned with people, productivity, and, for the private sector, profits. It is the premise of this book that happier, more responsible employees contribute to the vitality and success of an organization. Effective workers produce. Everybody profits. Everybody wins.

Acknowledgements

I wish to extend my thanks and appreciation to those people who contributed their time and energies to this book, and to those organizations which backed them up by sharing their transactional analysis programs. I also wish to extend my thanks and appreciation to my secretary, Glenda Robinson, for all her fine and often untiring assistance.

Pleasant Hill, California   D. J.
August 1973

---

* Those programs I have consulted with are the Bank of America, Pan American World Airlines, and the Career Women's Seminar for the U.S. Civil Service Commission.

CONTENTS

3 GAMES CAN BE STOPPED MANY WAYS

4 TA CAN HELP DEVELOP EFFECTIVE MANAGEMENT STYLES

5 TA CAN IMPROVE INTERPERSONAL EFFECTIVENESS
   (Bank of America Study)

13 A TRANSACTIONAL ANALYSIS OF McGREGOR'S
THEORY X-Y by Marylynn Goldhaber, M.S.W. and
Gerald M. Goldhaber, Ph.D.

14 THE TRANS Ⓐ CTIONAL MANAGER: AN ANALYSIS
OF TWO CONTEMPORARY MANAGEMENT THEORIES
by Lyman K. Randall

INTRODUCTION

*One cost analyst complained, "I thought my job
would be dealing with figures, not people.
What a surprise!"*

*A stewardess puzzled, "I just don't understand
why people do some of the things they do."*

*An electronics executive lamented, "I thought
my skills at engineering would be all I needed.
Now all I do is engineer people — without half
the training."*

*A teacher mused, "I'm not teaching geography.
I'm teaching people. My biggest problem is just
keeping order. Why didn't anyone prepare me for
this?"*

Such frustrations over "people problems" are common in today's organizations. It's often not only the "job" that frustrates us, but also the problems of relating to people and fulfilling our own human needs. Such problems are a reality in organizations to people trying to get new ideas across, feeling suppressed over a policy that seems arbitrary, unable to resolve a problem of job performance, investing time in unrewarding activities, and feeling powerless in the face of organizational structure. Jean Paul Sartre in his play *No Exit* purports that each person's real hell is other people. Perhaps with better people-skills each of us can increase those moments when other people seem "heavenly."

TA HELPS SOLVE PEOPLE PROBLEMS

We are living in the Age of Aquarius. Knowledge is no longer coveted by the chosen few who call themselves experts. Anyone who can read can gain expertise. It is fitting and appropriate at this time in human history that a model for behavior and human interaction has come along that can be used as a blueprint by almost any person who can understand its words. Transactional Analysis (TA) is an exciting and fresh perspective of human behavior.

1

Insights into one's own personality and into what makes other people tick can help any of us improve our relationships with people. In addition, it may help some of us reevaluate our own life goals. We can ask ourselves, "What am I doing out of past compulsions? What parts of my script are unfulfilling, unrewarding, and perhaps even tragic in terms of my real possibilities?" The same questions can be asked of organizations.

Transactional analysis is a practical and useful interpersonal relationships model for organizations because (1) it is easy to learn, (2) it gives a positive communications tool that is practical and almost immediately usable, (3) it helps to increase a person's on-the-job effectiveness because of better self-understanding and greater insight into personalities and transactions, (4) it may help solve personal and family problems, (5) it gives a common language for people working together to attempt to solve their own communication problems, (6) it is a nonthreatening approach to self-evaluation, and (7) it offers a method for analyzing not only people but also organizational scripts.*

TA is no panacea. However, it is a powerful tool which can help people and organizations work together to become and remain winners.

---

*   This is an advanced book and is not intended to teach the basic principles of TA. It is suggested that the reader first read *Born to Win: Transactional Analysis with Gestalt Experiments,* and a list for further reading is provided in Appendix A.

Part I

TA APPLIED TO ORGANIZATION DEVELOPMENT

1

ORGANIZATIONS HAVE SCRIPTS

One editor complains, "Our organization has been the leader in its field for over 30 years. Why can't the group upstairs see that now we're floating on our reputation? We haven't captured a new market in 10 years."

An insurance salesman exclaims, "This is an exciting place to work. The company is stable, yet we're always going after a new market, trying new things. I've never had an idea put down."

One wholesaler laments, "Our sales are deteriorating. Top management seems asleep when it comes to new ideas. I've quit making noises. Nobody listens. Nobody seems to care. I really feel discouraged about working for this company."

Why do some organizations seem stuck in the mud? Why do others seem vital and moving? Why do still others seem as if they are dying on the vine?

Just as individuals have scripts, so do organizations. The lifeline of many organizations resembles the lifeline of a person. Investment analysts often reflect the following pattern when depicting a company's progress: (1) at first a rapid growth rate, (2) a stabilizing and leveling-off period, and then (3) a decline and possible demise of the organization.

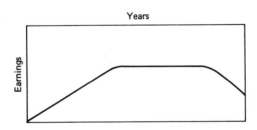

Organizational scripts include the ongoing program for the success, failure, or "treading water" story line of the company's progress. This story line may depict a comedy, a saga, a tragedy, a farce, or a dull, plodding drama going nowhere. Making up such an organizational script is a cast of characters, their dialogue, the themes they are carrying out, the climax which the dramatic action moves toward, and, finally, the conclusion. Where does it all end up?

Such scripts also include the institutionalized injunctions and permissions regarding expectations from all levels of employment, the built-in rewards for approval and status along with the built-in punishments, and the formalized lines of communication — which are all too often downward.

Organizational scripts dictate sex roles, grooming expectations, touch patterns, personal conduct, working hours, etc. They are the dramatic patterns which give an organization its identity and which eventually determine its destiny.

Some organizations seem destined for success just as some people do. Some organizations seem destined to fail just as some people seem destined to fail. In both instances it is the capacity to change that will determine the survival possibilities.

ORGANIZATIONAL SCRIPTS ARE OFTEN RELATED TO THE FOUNDERS' SCRIPTS

It has been my observation that the most powerful force in forming the script of many organizations is the personality, will, and script of its founder. How that individual operated, how that person related to others, what life goals he held, what Parent tapes he followed are all likely to be eventually solidified into what is commonly called *company policy* — both written and unwritten. Once these dramatic patterns are set, they often remain in spite of a turnover in personnel. This is particularly true of many large corporations in private industry today.

The power of company policy is often directly related to the power of the individual who founded the company. Many of today's large organizations were started decades ago by one strong person — most often a man. That individual may or may not have related to his employees in a basic Parent-Child fashion. However, it is likely he did.

One organization was founded by a strong, authoritarian man who struggled to the top of the American economic system in spite of his "old country" poverty. He managed from a strict Parent position and built a sound firm. As a consequence of the success of his style, he surrounded himself with other managers who wielded their power in the same manner. After his death, his management style became part of the organization's script. When this Parent management style became inappropriate, the management scripts were unable to change. It took many years before a leader who operated from a more Adult approach was accepted. In the meantime the organization suffered from discontent, high turnover, and bad mouthing from employees.

In other organizations authority lines are so heavily laden with Parent-Child transactions that company policy cannot be effectively changed until the "founding father" dies. For example, *Forbes* (February 1, 1973) describes the late head of Distillers Corp.-Seagrams as a man whose "word became law" and whom no one questioned — not his sons in the company, his employees, or his outside directors. As a result, *Forbes* says, the father (founder) became more and more "out of touch with the industry," and either he was not told or he refused to hear the truth about his company's position. He remained unaware of changing markets, and it was only when he died that change could begin to take place.

In such cases, it is likely that the Parent-Child relationship between management and employees still exists to some extent — if not at the top, in some departments.

Still other organizational scripts change when the founding fathers retire. In many cases the decentralization of authority occurred almost simultaneously with the retiring of the established leadership. In some of these instances change could occur only when the father figure no longer returned to the building.

In such instances it may take time before the personality of a new leader begins to effect a concrete change in the script policies of the organization.

For example, one large organization following old-line policy sent out a memorandum (1969) that women could not wear pant suits to work and must follow a strict dress code. They sent yet another memorandum that men could wear sideburns only if cut at "police" length. These memorandums caused much uproar and belligerence among employees. The punitive Parent policy activated rebellious Child ego states. Women came to work dressed in circus-like costumes. The organization leadership was quite embarrassed when it realized that there was really no way to enforce such dictates, especially since the dictates were not rationally related to the safety, productivity, or effectiveness of the employees.

Unless there is some Adult reason for a restriction in personal grooming or dressing patterns, attempting to establish such regulations resembles a punitive Parent establishing arbitrary rules because "that's the way it's always been."

These occurrences were the residuals left over from the beginning of that particular organization. They are examples of management investing time in arbitrarily maintaining past scripts on appearance and costume. In the past the dictates of the employer were law, and people wanting to keep their jobs had to follow them. Such a position of power resembles the Parent saying, "Do what I say, or else."

At the same time this was happening, the company mentioned above committed itself to a new program for the deprived and underprivileged. This program educated and prepared people for employment. It was innovative, socially responsible, and very successful. There were no previous scripts around this subject. Such ambiguity is typical in many organizations that are now experiencing a transition from one script to another.

Oftentimes managers both young and old remain committed to the old organizational scripts. If so, they may not examine patterns that brought success in the past in the context of the realities of today's world. Such a situation usually creates tension and a resistance to change.

Some founding fathers, even years after their demise, sit like ghosts at today's conference table, wielding an eery influence over present decisions.

Still other founders set up their organization to self-destruct when they die. They delegate no authority, share few responsibilities, covet the records, and literally leave things so that no one can take over effectively.

For example, a company founder in London developed a special formula for a certain stone. Statues still stand made of this unique material. However, this man took his formula with him to his grave. His organization dissolved and no one to this day has unlocked his secret.

SOME ORGANIZATIONAL SCRIPTS DIE HARD

The Parent tapes of 9 to 5, or the 8-hour day, have enjoyed years of sacred worship. For example, many cities that suffer traffic jams daily seem reluctant to examine the possibility of staggered commuting hours. The concept of what hours people should work only now begins to break down. Many organizations are trying the 4-day, 40-hour pattern as discussed by Reva Poor. [1]

Other organizations are even braving the idea that some employees would function more effectively if they came in at 5 A.M. and left earlier in the afternoon. Some people work better at night, even though this is not a requirement of the position. For many managers this is a blasphemous affront to the way things *should be*. For others, it does not meet their practical needs.

The scripts of most organizations automatically cast women in low-level jobs. As a result, 76% of Federally employed women are at the lowest GS levels 1-6. Under the pressure of Executive Order #4*, which obligates organizations to establish Affirmative Action, many organizations are reevaluating former sex stereotypes in jobs. Women are being prepared for managerial positions that have not been open to them before. Men also can now aspire to being secretaries, nurses, telephone operators, and grammar-school teachers.

What women should do and what men should do has been arbitrarily set for decades. Many men are automatically cast as climbers who are expected to go up the ladder as far as they can. Consequently, many risk being stuck at their level of incompetence — the Peter Principle. [2] They are thought of as unmanly if they want to stay put in a job they really like. As a result, few companies have policies which allow a man to advance financially while staying with the position he does well.

It is my observation that scripts often are more rigid in departments within a large organization that have been in existence a long time. Such patterns are entrenched with time and are often unyielding. New departments, however, may be relatively free of the old patterns. For example, in the case of sex-role expectations in one organization, the legal department, which was old, had a difficult adjustment to make when the first woman lawyer was hired. So did the customers of the legal department, to say the least.

In contrast, the data-processing department, which was relatively new, was fairly well integrated in terms of male and female employees. In fact, one department head told me, "I don't see what all this fuss is about women getting ahead. In our department we have nearly 40% women." Even here, however, only a few women were in management. Most were in lower-level jobs.

Often the scripts of the organization must change before change can be realized for individual employees. If the system is locked in to a set of patterns that are not dealing with present problems, people in the system tend to become apathetic, frustrated, or rebellious.

In addition, just like individuals who are following their scripts, in a locked-in situation, the energies of management are expended in maintaining old scripts rather than keeping up with the times. Diversions of energy, such as suppression of creative problem solving, suppression of customer reactions, production of a soon obsolete product, selling and advertising something useless or harmful, etc., all destroy an organization's ability to function in the reality of the current and coming markets. They are perpetrating their own inevitable obsolescence.

---

* Executive Order #4 requires all companies doing business with the Federal government (as prime subcontractors) to establish Affirmative Action programs.

For example, a company that spends its energies maintaining a near monopoly may ignore, and thus fail to meet, the needs of customers. If the monopoly is broken, in the face of competition and the demands of a coming age, profits are bound to go down. In a competitive situation, the customer makes the final decision.

A different pattern, but the same basic problem, occurred in a management consulting firm which had been long established in its field. This firm functioned with participants in a strict Parent climate. Even so, their methods worked for many years. In a recent session, however, their commitment to past patterns was more than evident. Trainees were to adjourn to different section meetings. A trainee suggested, "Let's all go to the section we want the most." An old line trainer responded, with indignation, "We've always *told* our participants which section to attend."

MERGING ORGANIZATIONS HAVE MULTIPLE SCRIPTS

As corporations merge, the plot thickens. Scripts become multiple and vastly complicated. Sometimes there are tradeoffs in terms of scripts as to what the company actually ends up acting out. For example, in one company the merger with a larger organization allowed the advertising department much more freedom and creativity. This immediately improved the quality of their advertising. However, the smaller organization had a nation-wide reputation for excellent service. The company with which they merged had no such commitment to customer service, thus this script was tampered with, much to the consternation of the sales force.

Many superstructures such as city, state, and especially Federal governments would be most difficult to analyze in terms of "founding father" organizational scripts. However, even then, occasionally there is a department that bears the strong stamp of resemblence to the person who has run it. One example would be the FBI and J. Edgar Hoover.

MOST ORGANIZATIONS HAVE SACRED TRADITIONS

Even if a "founding father" script pattern cannot be identified, all organizations will tend to have "corporate Parent" sacred traditions. Like sacred cows, these traditions are adhered to without objective evaluation — status symbols such as location, written and unwritten policies, behavioral expectations, roles expected by management, roles expected by subordinates, roles expected by men and women, the company picnic, the gold watch at retirement, plus all those dramatic commitments that make up a script. Once these regulatory expectations are started and adhered to by the majority of the group, they are hard to undo, even though they may inhibit the functioning of the organization.

One organization clung to the belief that it was possible to function in only one particular city. The management in the organization could not bring itself to move out of this city, even though there would be obvious tax advantages, space advantages, fewer commuter hassles, and equal transportation opportunities. The compulsion to stick to a script is often stronger than reason.

Another organization went through a difficult ordeal because its new building faced the wrong street. It would no longer have the prestigious address that had been enjoyed for many years. Adhering to such symbols even in the face of facts is often destructive to the necessary adaptations for the survival of an organization.

In addition, leadership in flux is a new pattern for many organizational structures, just as it is in many modern families. The principle goes against previous scripts dictating superior/subordinate relationships which are locked in. In the old scripts one person is often expected to seek the approval of another in a fixed way. Many such old pressures come to bear on individuals as they seek to change the organization's scripts.

While some organizations will die like the dinosaurs because the environment no longer supports them, others will look for greener pastures.

MANY PRESSURES AFFECT INDIVIDUALS IN ORGANIZATIONS: An Exercise

It is an interesting exercise to examine the complexity of negative and/or positive pressures which are felt by the individuals within organizations. What are the various expectations and pressures brought to bear on the individual within your organization? (Refer to the figure on the following page.)

Identify as many outside pressures and expectations as you can from your organization: people, policies, performance demands, conflicts, personal and family life, etc.

Which of these are realistic and necessary?

Which of these are inhibiting and arbitrary?

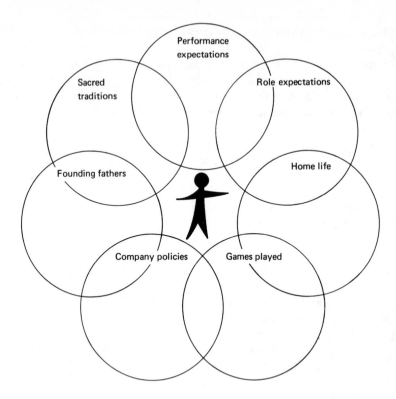

Which of these keep a person functioning below potential?

Which of these encourage growth and development?

Which of these encourage productivity?

How many people past and present are you trying to please?

How many people do you expect to please you?

How is the person's personal life influenced by these pressures?

All transactions are two ways. Individuals bring their personal scripts to organizations. They also can assert pressures toward their environment. Of openness Gardner writes:

More significant than his receptivity to the external world is his openness with respect to his own inner life. He does not suppress or refuse to face his own emotions, anxieties and fantasies. [3]

On independence he says:

The creative individual has the capacity to free himself from the web of social pressures in which the rest of us are caught. He doesn't spend much time asking "What will people say?" The fact that "everybody's doing it" doesn't mean he's doing it. He is capable of questioning assumptions that the rest of us accept. [4]

List the pressures that individuals can assert toward their organizational environment.

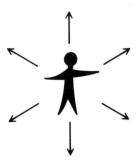

What negative script elements can an individual assert in the organization?

What positive script elements can an individual assert in the organization?

Which do you assert?

What are some of the effects on productivity concerning these outer/inner pressures?

IS A BUILT-IN AGENT FOR CHANGE POSSIBLE IN ORGANIZATIONS?

One reason that the Constitution has survived as long and as well as it has as an instrument of government is that it has a built-in method for change. Albeit, such change is very difficult. This was exemplified in the years of struggle American women endured in order to obtain the vote and again in their recent struggle for the Equal Rights Amendment. However, change is not impossible.

Human personalities have a built-in possibility to change even though many never use it. Gardner writes:

One of the clearest dangers in modern society is that men and women will lose the experience of participating in meaningful decisions concerning their own life and work, that they will become cogs in the machine because they feel like cogs in the machine. [5]

By activating and using the Adult ego state, people *can* get in touch with their old programming and make new decisions about life goals, primary transactions, the games they play, etc. They can decide against being cogs.

People in organizations can also change unsatisfactory or outmoded policies if there can be a built-in agent for change within the structure of the organization. Can a team be aware of current reality and serve in the sense that the Adult ego state serves in the personality, updating information and making new decisions and new choices?

Within organizations, can the process of foresight itself be institutionalized?

The process of change is a function of organization development (OD). For some, however, the functions and goals of OD have been confusing or unclear. Applying TA to OD helps to clarify OD's role. It's purpose is to analyze current problems and develop methods for appropriate changes. Understanding organizational scripts clarifies what needs to be changed within the organization.

Just as people may need to know their past histories in order to understand how they traveled to where they are, so do organizations. In addition, by applying the principles of objective evaluation, decision making, and goal setting, organizational scripts can be changed. Currently, many cultural and organizational scripts respond with change only in the face of force or violence.

Warren Bennis [6] purports that organization development is itself a response to change. Its purpose is to develop educational strategies that would change the attitudes, beliefs, and values which make up the structure of an organization. Such structural change would in time allow an organization to adapt to new markets, new discoveries, etc. Lyman Randall writes:

The focus of OD is on the difference between what we are and what we are capable of becoming. Individual and organizational change are directed toward narrowing this gap. [7]

The principles of transactional analysis can facilitate this journey.

What kinds of things must be understood by management if self-renewal is to be part of a more viable organizational script?

How can organizations examine and evaluate their present scripts, determine what is possible to change and what change is needed, and then take the necessary steps to bring it about? A transactional analysis approach to organizational scripts can help to define the problems so that there is a higher probability they can be solved. Such a procedure facilitates management by objectives.

ORGANIZATIONAL SCRIPTS CAN BE EVALUATED: An Exercise

TA offers new ways of evaluating the structure and future success of organizations. It also offers ways for you to see your own relationship to your organization more clearly.

With your organization in mind, work through the following exercises and questions.

1. Think of your organization as a person. If your organization were a person, what kind of person would it be? (Some organizations are so large that it may be more useful to deal with only your department, team, etc. You may wish to do both.)

2. If it's possible, recall the founding person (or persons) of your organization. How powerful was this person?

   Is there a picture of this person on your wall?_____ If so, what are its positive effects?

   its negatives effects?

   Describe the essence of this person's personality in three adjectives: _____ , _____ , _____ .
   Are any of these adjectives related to (1) above?

   What were the policies established by this person?

   What policies are still adhered to?

Are they appropriate to meet the needs of today?

Often founding fathers were innovative in their time, but their policies have become rigid. Many times people feel "stuck" with attitudes that seem irrelevant today. If you are in an organization that still reflects a person, ask yourself: What would he/she do in the situation we have today? You may find a creative answer.

3. What would the ego state portrait of your organization look like? Would any of these fit?

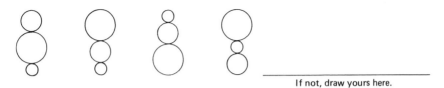

If not, draw yours here.

4. How would the above affect *your* ego state portrait as a worker?

Draw yourself in relationship to your organization, using various ego state sizes.

5. How would your customers picture your organization?

6. Does your organization assume any social responsibilities?

How do you feel about this?

7. Is your organization a healthy place for people?_____
   What are the arbitrary or punitive requirements made of
   employees?

   What are the nurturing activities towards employees?

8. Are there non-job-related expectations of the employees in your
   organization (i.e. status of spouse, dress, or appearance codes)? If
   so, what are they?

   Are they reasonable?

   How do you feel about them?

9. Does your organization have a theme (i.e. staying on top, plodding
   along, trying hard, making it big, going down hill)?

10. If your organization continues doing what it's doing now, where
    will it be in 5 years? in 10 years?

    Where will you be in relationship to this organization?

11. What was the last major decision made by your organization?

Was this decision based on the full facts of today?
Was it based on inertia from the past?

For better or for worse, were there any company "ghosts" sitting in on this decision?

12. List as many of the sacred traditions of your organization as you can.

Which of these are rational?

Which can be changed?

Which need to be changed?

Is anything being done about it?

13. What did your organization fail to do this year that it should have done?

    What did it do that it shouldn't have done?

    Can you relate these actions to organizational scripts?

14. List 8 characteristics of an organization that you see as *winning* characteristics.

15. List 8 characteristics of an organization that are likely to be *loser* characteristics.

16. List 8 major characteristics of your organization.

    How does your organization stack up? A winner?_____
    If so, how?

A loser?_____ If so, how?

Some of both?_____If so, how?

17. If your organization has a losing streak, how could it be changed?

An effective tool to figure out the dramatic patterns within a working group has been developed by Thomas C. Clary.* Clary's three-act dramatic approach to the organizational script is a useful tool for the very small organization that may be comprised of under eight people as well as for segments of superstructures.

Thomas Clary has contributed the next section of this chapter. If a working team works through this three-act drama, the dramatic patterns, role expectations, and games played can be discovered and worked on by the group. It is hoped that the group may end up writing a happier conclusion to its organizational drama.

SCRIPT ANALYSIS IS A NEW APPROACH TO OD

by Thomas C. Clary

A Diagnosis

Organization scripting is the OD diagnostic process we will use to determine where organization change is necessary and desired. Only

---

* Thomas C. Clary is an associate with the National Training and Development Service for state and local government, Washington, D.C. He previously taught at the University of Oklahoma, where he introduced transactional analysis as an executive development technique in management courses for the U.S. Postal Service. He trained in transactional analysis at the Western Institute for Group and Family Therapy at Watsonville, California. He is a certified member of the International Transactional Analysis Association.

Clary has a Bachelor's degree in Business Administration from Pace College, New York City, a Master's degree in Public Administration from the University of Oklahoma, and he is now a Ph.D. candidate at the University of Oklahoma.

He has published numerous articles in the area of transactional analysis as a management development technique.

after making this determination can members of the organization commit themselves to dramatic changes that will cause a rescripting process which brings autonomy from old traditions, policies, or procedures — the script.

Since the script of an organization is much like the script of an individual,* it can be viewed in the terms of a dramatic stage production which the organization is compelled to play out.

Act I of a play establishes the setting, introduces the major characters, and explains the premise of each for their future actions.

Act II is the action phase with the conflicts, nonconflicts, or problems, whatever they may be, that spell out the plot of the play.

Act III is the resolution of the conflicts and problems so that the play is brought to a finale. The organization diagnosis follows this format.

The Process

Under certain conditions, an internal OD person may act as the facilitator, but it is usually advisable, at least in the beginning, to have an external person act in this capacity.

This program is designed to be conducted within an organization only. The participants may be the entire organization membership, a horizontal slice of the organization hierarchy which would preferably include top management, or a vertical slice of the organization hierarchy which also would include top management and might go as far down as desired.

If the group is as small as 8 to 12 participants, it could remain intact. If the group is larger than 12, it should be broken down into subgroups of 6 to 12 persons. A spokesman should be selected for each subgroup. He or she would report to the entire group when required.

When data collection is required, individuals should be given time to write down their own thoughts and then proceed with the group or subgroup doing a brainstorming session. Not only is this expeditious, but it is also less threatening in the initial phases of the exercise.

This process may take from one-and-a-half days to five days. The shorter the time, the more important it is that the participants be well grounded in transactional analysis. For example, require preworkshop reading of *Born to Win* by James and Jongeward.†

The facilitator will find it easier if he or she finds a way to relieve anxieties of the participants in the beginning. A number of different methods can be used. Some examples: Ask them to state what they like

---

*   See the beginning of this chapter and, for a more detailed explanation of individual scripts, see Eric Berne, *What Do You Say After You Say Hello?* (New York: Grove Press, 1970).

†   Reading, Massachusetts: Addison-Wesley, 1971.

best about themselves. How did they feel when they came into the room? What ego state were they in? On a one to five scale, what are their expectations of this workshop? (Keep the sheet recording this data and compare it at the end with what they feel were the results of the workshop.) Have participants make a public contract as to what they want out of this workshop for themselves and for their organization. (Be sure these are concrete and possible achievements.)

YOUR ORGANIZATION
A SYSTEM EXAMINATION IN A THREE-ACT PLAY *
USING TRANSACTIONAL ANALYSIS

Prologue

The prologue provides a further method to relieve anxieties without any great threat to individuals. The facilitator in small groups (or the spokesman in subgroups where there are larger groups) should record the group's reaction to the questions on newsprint (a flip chart). This gets the participants in the mood to think about their organization.

1. What were the original philosophies and policies in the organization that have now become traditional and sacred?
2. Who was responsible for setting these?
3. For what purpose were these philosophies and policies established?
    a)   What were they expected to accomplish?
    b)   What was the purpose given?
    c)   What do you think was their *real* purpose?

Let's look at an example.

1. *Traditions.* Bosses are very paternalistic in giving excellent benefits to employees in an effort to keep unions from penetrating the organization.
2. *The beginning.* The founder had this same philosophy.
3. *Expected.* This policy was expected to result in happier and more productive employees.
4. *Given purpose.* The given purpose was to create an organization which was like a family.
5. *Real purpose.* The real purpose was to keep unions from organizing the employees.

---

* The use of a three-act play for this purpose is the original idea discussed and developed on the telephone between Laurence D. Smith, a New York actor, and myself.

This gives the background and sets the stage for what the organization is today. In practically every case, the organization continues to play out the script that was set at its very beginning or perhaps even before it came into existence and was still a concept in the minds of its founders. Eventually it forms its own personality.

ACT I. Setting the Stage

Participants may be asked the questions in the total group or be furnished the questions below to act on in their subgroups. The answers must be recorded on newsprint for all to see and retained for future reference. The facilitator should not be limited by the questions and thoughts here, but may want to utilize other exercises of his or her own design to augment this data. Remember, the purpose is to set the stage for the organizational drama by identifying the physical setting, the characters, their roles, costumes, the premise for their actions, and their internal and external conflicts as they affect the organization or as the organization affects them. Awareness of what is going on may vary among people within the organization. This is the place to attempt to capture what awareness exists.

Some of the questions that should be asked are as follows:

1. *What is the setting?* Assume you are watching a play of your organization. The curtain goes up. No characters are on stage. What would you see as far as the scenery, props, and general stage arrangement?

   Participants may be asked to draw what they see either in small groups or individually to share later with the total group. After the physical setting is drawn, have them add the major characters. The spatial relationships and interaction may serve as a good beginning for the next question. Participants sometimes draw the hierarchy of management, sometimes plant setting, sometimes their relationship to others in management, etc.

2. *Name and describe each major character involved.* This will vary with the organization, but the number would be kept down to a workable size. If possible, only deal with characters representing those present. During the interactive process this will help people to talk *to* one another, rather than *about* one another. All participants, including the "character in question," will give their description in adjectives or phrases so that they can be recorded on newsprint. Continue the recording of the information for each character as required in items 3 through 5.

   The brainstorming technique is helpful in getting participant involvement and it is not regarded as so threatening a situation as it would be if each participant had to confront the other initially.

For example, let's consider two persons in our organizational drama: Joe, a department head, and Mary, Joe's boss' secretary. Joe is described as a person who is easy to communicate with, dedicated, open about problems, and a frustrated policeman. Mary is an efficient secretary, congenial, but not always easy to approach.

3. *Determine the premise for the action of each character,* i.e., from where each is coming. What does each like most about himself or herself, and what does he or she like least? What are the expected, desired, and real roles played, and what are their effects? How do the costumes or dress of each identify the various roles, both observable and nonobservable.

To continue with the previous characters, as examples: first, Joe comes from an autocratic background. He likes himself as a hard worker, but doesn't like his continuous worrying self. His expected role is to be a participative type manager; he desires this, but feels insecure and plays a very safe type of manager, which causes conflicts for him and confusion for employees. He is comfortable only dressing in a suit, white shirt, and tie because that's the way bosses should dress. He feels very uncomfortable in any other dress, even though it may be encouraged or permitted. Mary fantasizes much of the time because she feels she is overqualified for the job she is in. She likes the fact that she can speak for her boss, but dislikes the fact that she worries about the job away from the office as much as while she is there. She is very formal with her boss and very authoritative with others. She dresses in a very "ladylike" manner as she thinks a secretary should.

4. *Identify apparent internal and external conflicts of each character and their effect on the organization or the effect of the organization on each individual.* What are the forms of recognition, positive or negative stroking, or a lack of any within the organization? What is the effect of technology on the organization? Does the organizational setting or location have any effect on the situation? What are the various good and bad feelings about the organization? We determine these and outline various demands made on individuals. Then determine what the pressures are and what the feelings present are as a result of these demands.

For example: Joe is uncomfortable giving and receiving positive strokes. He feels particular pressures of his own autocratic background as against the external pressures of the organization and this encourages him to be less autocratic and to treat employees more as equals, with due recognition to each. He feels pressures from outside citizens because, as head of an investigative department, he must be harder on himself than on others to comply with every regulation in absolute detail in order to set an example. He feels the polarity of his family and organizational demands which contributes to added pressure, worry, and guilt.

Mary, a widow, seeks her strokes at the office, but seldom gets them. She compensates by worrying about others within the organization. She feels her friends both in and out of the organization make demands on her because of her position. She enjoys this and at the same time finds it difficult to cope with the pressures.

5. *Explain the extent of awareness of each character about the situation.* An excellent method exploring this is through the Johari Awareness Model.

Johari Awareness Model

This model consists of four quadrants which represent the total person in relation to other persons. The basis for division into quadrants is awareness of behavior, feelings, and motivation. Sometimes awareness is shared, sometimes not. An act, a feeling, or a motive is assigned to a particular quadrant, based on who knows about it. As awareness changes, the quadrant to which the psychological state is assigned changes. The following definitions and principles are substantially the same as those in group processes. Each quadrant is defined:

1. Quadrant 1, the open quadrant, refers to *behavior, feelings,* and *motivation* known to self and to others.

2. Quadrant 2, the blind quadrant, refers to *behavior, feelings,* and *motivation* known to others but not to self.

3. Quadrant 3, the hidden quadrant, refers to *behavior, feelings,* and *motivation* known to self but not to others.

4. Quadrant 4, the unknown quadrant, refers to *behavior, feelings,* and *motivation* known neither to self nor to others.

The authors of this model explain that there are eleven principles of change.

1. A change in any one quadrant will affect all other quadrants.

2. It takes energy to hide, deny, or be blind to behavior which is involved in interaction.

3. Threat tends to decrease awareness; mutual trust tends to increase awareness.

4. Forced awareness (exposure) is undesirable and usually ineffective.

5. Interpersonal learning means a change has taken place so that quadrant 1 is larger, and one or more of the other quadrants has grown smaller.

6. Working with others is facilitated by a large enough area of free activity. It means more of the resources and skills of the persons involved can be applied to the task at hand.

7. The smaller the first quadrant, the poorer the communication.

8. There is universal curiosity about the unknown area, but this is held in check by custom, social training, and diverse fears.

9. Sensitivity means appreciating the covert aspects of behavior, in quadrants 2, 3, and 4, and respecting the desire of others to keep them so.

10. Learning about group processes, as they are being experienced, helps to increase awareness (enlarging quadrant 1) for the group as a whole as well as for individual members.

11. The value system of a group and its membership may be noted in the way unknowns in life of the group are confronted.*

For example, Joe is open to the extent that he likes to talk about his problems and is generally aware of his behavior, but his strong adherence to traditions and fear of change make it difficult for him to commit himself to change.

Mary is aware that she is a re-actor rather than a pro-actor. She is not open for fear of being hurt and covers this up by acting for the boss instead of herself.

ACT II. The Action

The stage is set. The characters are known. The roles they play have been established. Act II is ready to begin. This is the interaction phase — the conflicts, nonconflicts, and other problems that may exist.

---

* For a more complete explanation of the Johari Awareness Model, see Joseph Luft, *Of Human Interaction* (Palo Alto, California: National Press Books, 1969).

The players know their scripts and fall into the roles established for them. Discovering these interpersonal actions reveals the plot of the play or the organizational script which is imposed on the actors.

1. *Show how each conflict, nonconflict, or problem comes about, based on the information discovered in Act I.*   One example is that individual conflicts form the basis of interdepartmental conflicts. A department head such as Joe feels he is being thwarted by the secretary, Mary, in presenting his case to the manager. His insecurities and previous comments by the boss that he is too autocratic make him fear going over her head. Therefore, in the organization, many of his responsibilities are assigned to other departments.

2. *Explain how each character is trying to work through these conflicts or problems.*   By more awareness of the situation, the manager realizes for the first time what is happening and sees that the organizational conflicts are affecting production. Joe has become apathetic. Although the manager and Mary are unaware of it, Mary is displaying an unfavorable image of Joe.

   By looking at the data revealed during Act I, the participants can begin to see other conflicts, such as channels of communication splitting responsibilities between departments, purchasing procedures, customer relations, salary structure, and even unhappiness with a ritual like the annual company picnic which all are expected to enjoy.

   From this information one may now begin to see the unfolding of the plots of the organizational drama. Ask yourself: Is it a tragedy, a comedy, or perhaps a farce?

   Is the plot of the organization to further the organizational games such as "Big Brother is Watching You" or "We're Only Trying to Help You"? Like individual games discussed in the next chapter, organizations become identified with the games encouraged by their structure and script. In fact, the organizational setting and an individual who did not play the game would find himself or herself ostracized. After reading the next chapter on games, use Appendix B to diagram an organizational game that you are a part of in your organization.

ACT III. The Resolution

At this point participants may begin to feel they are so much a part of the organizational script that there is no hope for change. As in the classical three-act play, there is a resolution — there is hope — change is possible with commitment. This act discloses how the organizational script can be changed if there is a desire and a commitment.

In Act II we saw individual conflicts melting into the organizational conflict. Changes in Joe's and Mary's personal attitudes and behavior might help *them*, but it could have little if any effect on the organization. However, if the organizational script is changed, it will affect every member. The script can only be changed if there is either commitment from the top voluntarily or commitment is forced from lower in the hierarchy. The changes must be important and dramatic. For some, they will probably be traumatic. These questions designed within a TA problem-solving model can bring about a rescripting process.

1. How can the conflicts or problems brought out in Acts I and II be resolved? You may want to go back and identify some of the sacred traditions.

   a) Participants should be encouraged to get into a Child ego state. Brainstorm some solutions. Brainstorming is an ideal way to achieve this information, so that participants get in the Child ego states and give possibilities that are as wild as they can imagine, without fear of criticism or judgment from the Critical Parent. The purpose is to be totally idealistic, "pie in the sky," the wilder the idea the better, even if it sounds impractical. Some questions to ask before the brainstorming session might be: What do you wish would happen differently? What would you really like the organization to be? If, by magic, anything could be changed, what should it be? Examples of changes: change organizational structure so that it is horizontal rather than vertical; do away with organizational charts; eliminate company-wide rules and regulations; create an ombudsman; encourage risk taking without fear; eliminate status and titles; require no educational credentials or classification testing for hiring; change working hours based on individual desires, eliminate seniority system, etc.

   b) Have participants shift into the Nurturing, Loving Parent ego state, and the feelings of the Creative Child, and present possibilities on how the ideas expressed during the brainstorming session could work. These are the advantages.

   c) Shifting to the Critical Parent ego state, participants should now give all the restraining forces that would prevent these ideas from happening. These are the disadvantages.

   d) Observe all of the data collected during these preceding sessions in the Adult ego state and make probable action steps and decisions, for example, "We will not change the organization structure," or "We will make a change from a highly structured organization to a less-structured organization," or

"We will study the situation further," which results in a bureaucratic cop-out.

2. If there is a commitment to make certain changes, a plan is necessary. The following questions and suggestions should help formulate that plan.

   a) What is the biggest problem in your organization?

   b) Describe how the changes are really important and dramatic rather than just minor or evolutionary changes.

   c) How would the changes make the organization any different than if the changes were not made?

   d) How will everyone in the organization know when the changes have been made?

   e) How will making the changes keep the organization from returning to its original script?

   f) What mechanism is in the system to provide for the review of changes for effecting needed dramatic changes in the future?

3. Commitment to certain changes should evolve. Individual participants should then volunteer to assume the responsibility to follow through on each change. Objectives should be set as to what each is going to do, that is, each person will coordinate with others to firm up the action steps. Each should have a specific date as to when the task will be completed. Another person should be assigned to check with each person on how the project is coming. This makes the scripting workshop a continuing endeavor.

Final Curtain

If the play is successful, there will be applause. The applause should not be for the facilitator, for the person who is the director has faded into the background. The applause is for the actors — the participants. But applause is not the only measure of success. After the play is over, the performance must stand up to the critics' review, and the box-office (stockholders or taxpayers) will determine the length of time it plays.

Excitement is naturally high at the end of this intensive session. Take advantage of the situation. Let the participants determine where to go from here. Guide them toward a feedback session within four to six weeks to check on how close they are toward meeting their objectives.

Have the individuals pair up and instruct them to call one another within two weeks and explain to each other what has been done differently as a result of the workshop.

At the beginning each individual made a contract as to what he or she was going to accomplish both personally and for the organization. Now is the time to review and update this contract. The public recitation transforms the desire from a New Year's resolution to a definite action step he has declared to all of his colleagues.

Finally, have the participants evaluate the experience and compare it with their expectation expressed at the beginning.

THE END

SUMMARY

People individually follow dramatic life plans that are usually programmed by the injunctions and permissions received from significant parent figures. Organizations also follow dramatic programs — some successful, some failure-oriented, some going nowhere.

For better or for worse, some organizations still function under the impact of the persons who founded them. The founder's attitudes and expectations often solidify into the organizational script. Such scripts may be difficult to change, even though the founder may have been in the forefront of change in his or her own lifetime.

Even if the founding person is difficult to identify, an organization is still likely to worship sacred assumptions that may not be relevant for today's corporate life.

TA offers ways of looking at organizational scripts which can help management objectively evaluate the present patterns and make decisions for change.

Changing organizations means changing their scripts.

FOOTNOTES AND REFERENCES

1. Reva Poor, *Four Days, Forty Hours* (Cambridge, Massachusetts: Bursk & Poore, 1970).

2. Dr. Laurence J. Peter and Raymond Hull, *The Peter Principle* (New York: William Morrow, 1969).

3. John W. Gardner, *Self Renewal: The Individual and the Innovative Society* (New York: Harper & Row, 1965), p. 36. Reprinted by permission.

4. *Ibid.*, p. 36.

5. *Ibid.*, p. 59.

6. Warren G. Bennis, *Organization Development: Its Nature, Origins, and Prospects* (Reading, Massachusetts: Addison-Wesley, 1969).

7. Arthur C. Beck, Jr. and Ellis D. Hillman, editors, *A Practical Approach to Organization Development Through MBO-Selected Readings* (Reading, Massachusetts: Addison-Wesley, 1972).

2

GAMES COST ORGANIZATIONS MONEY

*A social worker retorts, "Well, I was only
trying to help you!"*

*A staff person blames, "If it weren't for the
old man upstairs, we'd have this project well on
its way."*

*A stewardess complains, "I don't see why all
the weird things always happen to me."*

*A company lawyer gleams, "This is the fourth
time he's botched up a job for us. We've got him
cold this time."*

When people play games, they do things like: fail to come through for others, pass the buck, make mistakes, complain about and dote on their own sorrows and inadequacies, and catch others in the act. Psychological games can be a powerful force in preventing people and organizations from becoming winners.

Every game has hidden agenda. People playing games are not really talking about what it sounds as if they're talking about. The hidden motive discounts the players. Someone collects negative strokes. Someone gets hurt. Real problems go unsolved.

GAMES LIMIT PRODUCTIVITY

Structuring work time with psychological games not only decreases the problem-solving capacities of the organization, but also inhibits full productivity. People who otherwise could be productive divert their psychic and physical energies into their games rather than getting the job done, making the decision, or solving the problem. Awareness focuses on past events rather than the current reality of the work scene. If the reality of a situation goes unperceived, problems go unsolved.

Games played in organizations are not necessarily different from games played at home. People play games wherever they are with people. This chapter, however, (1) deals with what motivates game playing on the job, (2) illustrates extensively how certain games are acted out in the organizational setting, and (3) demonstrates how some games can be broken up. Further comment on breaking up games follows in Chapter 3.

GAMES HAVE MOTIVATING FORCES

Games appear to have "advantages." However, most of what occurs in a game is destructive, at least to some degree. Naturally, the intensity with which people play games varies, just as the intensity with which people act out scripts varies. Some games gain social approval. Some are more serious, so are hidden. Some are played for keeps and end up in prison or the morgue.

Games are a way to fill up time. Structuring time is a basic human need. If time is not structured, people suffer boredom. Boredom encourages physical and mental deterioration. *People bored with their jobs are more prone to game playing.*

The need for strokes (any act of touch or recognition) is also universal. We all need strokes to survive and negative strokes are better than none. People get strokes from playing games, even though these strokes are negative. For example, a person who plays a game of *Stupid* does stupid things and collects put-downs. Each time the game is played, the player reinforces a negative stroke pattern learned in childhood, adding to a collection of "stupid" psychological trading stamps. *If the work environment is void of positive strokes, people have more need to play games.*

Games reinforce our psychological positions. We base our positions on experiences which lead to decisions. Decisions made by a small child — a child too inexperienced to make accurate judgments — are likely to be irrational and distorted. Powerful motivators to scripts and games are (1) a person's self-image — an imagery focused through the eyes of a child, based on reflections given by parent figures — and (2) learned expectations toward others. Games always strengthen a sense of I'm not-OK and/or You're not-OK. People who take the position "I'm stupid," begin to act stupid. In this sense, such people are stuck maintaining their own status quos. *Company time can be used to reinforce old negative self/other concepts.*

Games assist in avoiding or regulating intimacy. While people engage in games, they avoid authentic, honest, or open encounter. Some organizations discourage openness and honesty. *Authenticity on the job can be foiled by game playing.*

Each time we engage in psychological games, we reinforce the sense of identity and destiny that is characteristic of scripts. Games will always help to fulfill and further the negative elements of a person's script and of an organization's script. In addition, the organization can be the place where individual script events take place. For example,

Harried Executives may depress or kill themselves with their work. The organization, following its script, may give positive strokes to *Harried* players.

ORGANIZATIONAL SCRIPTS OFTEN ENCOURAGE GAMES

The dramatic expectations and patterns of organizational scripts may foster certain games. For example, a hierarchy structure encourages games like *If It Weren't For Him (Them)*. Individuals or groups within an organization who play this game blame someone else either above or below them for problems. It is a way to pass the buck. Players of such games render themselves pure and blameless by placing the responsibility on someone else. *See What You Made Me Do* is still another blaming game. However, people play it to blame their *own* mistakes on someone either up or down the ladder.

In some organizations, in order for employees to follow the upward mobility patterns set by the organizational script, they must develop a strong sense of competition and undercutting rather than teamwork and cooperativeness. In such cases, in addition to the blaming games, games that catch people up or point out their mistakes are likely to be prevalent. *Now I've Got You, You S.O.B.*, *Blemish*, and *Bear Trapper* help to fulfill these organizational dictates. In *Now I've Got You* someone ends up being caught for having made a mistake. In *Blemish*, tiny, inconsequential mistakes are pointed out. In *Bear Trapper* the trap falls on an employee who may then have to decide whether to stick with the organization or to seek employment elsewhere.

Some organizations, rather than stroking cooperativeness, stroke and expect employees to play the undercutting games. In addition to those games mentioned, organizations may encourage the one-upsmanship style games. Employees may feel compelled to act these out in order to "get ahead." This climate encourages *Let's You and Him Fight* and variations of the game *Mine's Better Than Yours*, such as *I'm Closer To The Boss than You*. These games need be only slightly adapted as a person moves up through the hierarchy structure.

The investment in time and energy in a traditional hierarchy communications system is one of the reasons why, in many organizations, lateral communication is the most difficult and the most ineffectual. In addition, communication lines rarely move upward in a positive way. Movement upward is more likely to be hostile, rebellious, or revolutionary. The scripts of organizations with these patterns will tend to have a long history of communication lines moving primarily downward.

In addition, some organizations are acting out rescuing scripts. If a rescuing organization has a vested interest in perpetuating itself, the problem it sets about to rescue is likely never to be solved. Typical organizational games in this situation are *Ain't It Awful*, *See How Hard We're Trying*, and *We're Only Trying to Help You*. An example of this is the organization that wails about poverty and then does another study, instead of trying to alleviate the poverty. An organization like this is often ineffective in helping those who come for assistance. For example, if people needing jobs complain about bum steers, they may hear, "Why we're only trying to help you. Things are tough. Don't get upset with us." These games remain more entrenched if the clients have few alternatives for seeking help.

If a rescuing script is to be maintained over a long period of time, it stands to reason that the victims can't be allowed to improve their lot. After all, who would there be left to rescue?

The next section illustrates how individual games are adapted to the work setting. Many of the games will also fit into the demands of the organizational script. As you read through the following games, be aware of the time each structures, the kind of strokes involved, the avoidance of decision making or problem solving, and the investment of time and energy in the past rather than the present.

Yes, But

The game of *Why Don't You? - Yes, But* is very likely one of the most common played between staff and line individuals. It's a way to put people down, quite frequently without their being fully aware of it. There is a special payoff if the game puts the "experts" down, or anyone else, such as a consultant, who takes a helpful or authoritative stance. *Yes, But* players only *appear* to be looking for helpful solutions to problems. In the end, any advice they receive is rejected. As a consequence, the person the game is played with ends up being defined as not-OK.

Almost everyone at some time or other has experienced a *Yes, But* game. In *Yes, But* the person who is "It" (the initiator of the game) lays out a problem. The problem is the hooker. The complementary hand is giving advice or possible solutions to a problem.

On the plausible Adult to Adult level the transaction appears to be, "I have this problem and I would like you to help me solve it." The response on the plausible Adult to Adult level might be, "Yes, I have some good ideas to help you solve your problem and here they are."

At the ulterior level the Child in the initiator of the game is actually saying, "I have this problem. You just *try* to help me solve it and I'll put you down!" If hooked, the responder may continue to give solutions for a long time in the effort to "help" the other person. *Yes, But* is diagrammed in the following way.

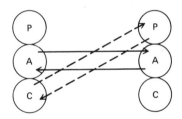

Yes, But players often structure time in a business meeting to play their game. The dialogue may go like this:

Mr. K:
I've called this meeting so that we can discuss the problem of morale in this department. Within the last ten months there seems to have been a rapid deterioration of good feelings and esprit de corps. Our turnover rate has increased. Four key people have asked for transfers to other departments. Absenteeism and tardiness have been on the upswing; and it is my belief that something is wrong that we need to work out.

First responder:
I think, Mr. K, that we need to reevaluate when people have to be at work. We've had a very rigid policy about people being here at a certain time whether it's essential to their job or not.

Mr. K:
It seems to me we are letting people get away with far too much already. It is part of a worker's discipline to be here on time. If I let one person come in late, just because it doesn't seem to be important that he is here at 8:30 in the morning, then I'm going to have everybody else on my neck.

Second responder:
How about sending out an anonymous questionnaire and seeing what people will say about how they feel about working in this department.

Mr. K:
It seems as if every time we have a problem you want to do some kind of study. The last time we did that we didn't come up with any data that helped us solve the problem, and I don't know why you think it would work this time.

Third responder:
Well I think we should call a general meeting of the whole department and just put these facts on the line and see what people say in response. Maybe we could open them up.

Mr. K:	Well, yes, that might give us some feedback. But on the other hand, we are the managers and the supervisors of the department. We certainly ought to be able to put our heads together and solve this problem without having to call in everybody that works in this department. What a waste of time.

Mr. K is likely to continue soliciting suggestions, advice, ideas, and solutions from the group members. He also is just as likely to continue rejecting them somehow. When everyone has given up on giving Mr. K any ideas, he has won the game. Underneath, the little kid in him may experience a sense of triumph that once more he has proven "parents can't tell me anything."

Yes, But can consume a great deal of an organization's time. Problems that need genuine solutions go unsolved. Again the energies are invested in playing the game (for the payoff of rejecting the advice and ideas of others) rather than in the solution of the problem.

Yes, But is not always played in meetings; it can be played in a hallway when one person stops the other with "say, you know there is something that is really bothering me" and then states the problem. The other person may be hooked into this interaction for forty minutes and go away with the feeling of "good grief — no matter what I say to that guy, it's not going to work."

Learning not to be hooked into a *Yes, But* game can save a great amount of company time. The classical antithesis is to refuse to offer advice or solutions. If a player starts a game, "I'm having the worst time trying to get those clerks motivated to take more training," a responder may withhold suggestions with, "That can be rough, Mabel. What are your plans?"

Ain't It Awful (About Them)

Ain't It Awful also illustrates how a game can inhibit problem solving in a very serious way. I attended a luncheon meeting where individuals from the Heart Association, March of Dimes, Mental Health, Planned Parenthood, etc. were gathered together to share their particular achievements, questions, and happenings. The day before this meeting was held, the vaccine for polio was announced. This was surely a time for celebration. On my way to the meeting I fantasied what kind of a celebration we might have. Throw away the usual peanut butter and bologna sandwiches and have champagne and cold cuts!

When I arrived at the meeting, the woman from the March of Dimes was not there. I was not the only one anticipating her entrance. Most of us expected something special, and an air of excitement filled the room.

The woman finally arrived. She entered the room visibly slumped. Assuming a downcast physical posture, she walked over to her place and tossed her sack lunch on the table. Plopping herself down in her chair, she look up dejectedly at the rest of us and complained, "It is certainly going to be hard to get people interested in another disease."

This woman had a reputation of being a dedicated, hard worker and a dynamic fund raiser who was able to get volunteers to work. On the surface she was doing a great job helping the unfortunate. Underneath, she had no intention of solving problems, no intention of *really* rescuing anybody. Her energies went into her game of *Ain't It Awful*.

SOME GAMES BLAME OTHERS FOR PROBLEMS

See What You Made Me Do

See What You Made Me Do is a common blaming game. The person who plays this game makes a mistake in the presence of another person and then blames that mistake on the other person. For example, a lab worker concentrates on a slide as the supervisor approaches. Just as the supervisor looks over his shoulder, the lab worker drops the slide and breaks it. Rather than taking responsibility for his own mistake, he turns angrily to his supervisor, saying, "See what you made me do!"

Once I was giving a workshop in an industrial setting and had just finished explaining this game. At that very moment a loud crash was heard in the hallway. Someone had dropped a tray of test tubes that went crashing, scattering down the hallway. In the midst of the noise and hubbub, a man hollered out, "See what you made me do!" I'm sure the workshop participants thought I had set this one up.

Another common version of the game is the typist who makes a typing mistake when the supervisor walks by. Then, instead of taking the responsibility for the mistake, turns angrily to the supervisor saying, "See what you made me do."

The individual that plays *See What You Made Me Do* is often a collector of angry feelings about others and inadequacy feelings about self. Sometimes, however, this person is collecting feelings of self-righteousness and purity. "Nothing is ever my fault, but it's yours." This is similar to the disclaimer for not-OK behavior, "The devil made me do it."

This kind of blaming game often leads the person to isolation. After enough encounters of being blamed, people tend to avoid the player. In a work situation such people may be more productive if they are semi-isolated and not subject to a great deal of supervision.

If It Weren't For You

If It Weren't For You is another blaming game. People who play it often feel inadequate themselves and cop out on their own achievement or development, blaming their inability to achieve on others. In one company this game went something like this:

> For two years T.C. complained that if it weren't for D.J., he would have long since been the manager of the department. In T.C.'s eyes, D.J. was unfair, uncommunicative, and seemed to take a special pleasure in holding people back. D.J. was then unexpectedly transferred to another plant in another state. The head of the department went to T.C. with the good news, "D.J.'s job is now yours. You've wanted this promotion for a long time." To the manager's surprise, T.C. became frustrated rather than joyful, and he eventually quit.

In the above case, T.C. had gotten satisfaction out of blaming someone else for the lack of promotions. When the chips were down and he was offered the job, he *backed off.*

In a similar situation, a woman manager complained that if it weren't for the size of her office, the productivity in her division would be higher. When the plant was eventually expended, her working area was given special attention, and it was considerably enlarged. After six weeks of working in the new surroundings, this manager asked for a transfer to another division. It was known that the division which she asked for was housed in very small quarters in another part of the state.

This game often baffles people in personnel. Someone complains "If It Weren't For Something or Someone," yet when they get their chance, they don't come through.

It is useful to watch for the words "If it weren't for. . ." as a clue to the possibility of a game involvement rather than an honest complaint. If a game involvement is suspected, a trial period in the new position may be enough to test it out. Otherwise the individual, rather than functioning better under the new circumstances, will be frustrated, ask for a transfer, or may even quit.

Another variation of this game occurs if blaming "company policy" or the "establishment" is used as a cop-out. For example, employees may complain, "If it weren't for such rigid company policy, we could be creative." They are playing a game if they are actually fearful of their own creative abilities. Unknowingly they seek, but complain about, oppressive management.

SOME GAMES ARE PERSECUTING AND ATTACKING

Let's You and Him Fight

This game involves at least three hands. One person goes to a second person in an attempt to engage the second and third person in an argument. It is not uncommon for a game to start as *Let's You and Him Fight* between W.J. and M.H. and end up as *Uproar* between M.H. and T.L. One worker, W.J., goes to another, M.H., saying in confidence, "It makes me feel terrible to tell you this, but I thought it over and think you need to know what T.L. is saying about you." And then the person proceeds to reveal, distort, or fabricate what T.L. is saying. It is likely that M.H. will soon engage in a conflict with T.L.

Illustration

Mary was unhappy and complaining very loudly to a co-worker about the inordinate amount of overtime she put in. She complained, "This is the third night in a row that I've stayed after work." A co-worker, George, listened for a while and then began to encourage Mary to go have it out with her boss, Tom. In fact, he prodded her with, "I know all the ropes around here and I'll help you. There is no reason for you to have to stay overtime night after night and get nothing out of it."

This kind of coercion and encouragement to confront the boss went on for about 20 minutes and finally George successfully riled up Mary. Together they went down the hall and knocked on the door of the boss. When they got inside, Mary began her complaint about all the extra work that she had done without any reward, and how she was fed up with it. George chimed in occasionally, "That's right," and, "We have committees to take care of this kind of problem. Employers have no right to exploit their employees, especially women."

The boss was puzzled by this confrontation. He seemed especially upset when he showed Mary a memorandum on his desk which stated that she had been considered for a promotion into a new position. There was a statement of appreciation for her dedication and hard work, sometimes even without additional pay.

At this time Mary turned back to George with a look on her face, "Why did you get me into such a mess? I was about to get my reward." George looked back with a quizzical look on his face and said, "Gee, Mary, I was only trying to help you."

In this particular instance the dynamics of two games were skillfully combined. It started out as *Let's You and Him Fight* in a three-handed manner, ending up with George being an *I'm Only Trying To Help You* player. Rather than sitting back and smirking at people acting like fools (which is what a typical *Let's You and Him Fight* player does), George was there to collect his kick for being a phoney Rescuer. Mary could have started the whole thing with her version of *See How Hard I Try*. As a consequence of this encounter, Mary's promotion was delayed.

Sometimes the home front gets in on this kind of game. For example, a spouse may encourage a mate to go back to the boss and fight.

Illustration

One man discovered that he played this game with his wife and her boss in the eventual hope that his wife would get fired. At this particular time, he opposed her working. Rather than talking it over with her straight and coming to some kind of resolution of their personal problem, he continued to set up hostile situations between his wife and her boss. For example, in one such situation his wife came home complaining that her boss had made a critical remark about a report that she turned in. The husband did not question her to check out if the criticism was justified or whether it was irrational or if the boss had perhaps had a bad day. Rather, he went into a long tirade, "You should not allow anyone to speak to you this way. If your boss gets away with it this time, he will only become more and more critical." He insisted that she go in the next day and confront him with his criticism and rudeness.

She took this bait, went to work the next day, and confronted her boss. A very unpleasant encounter ensued. It was then brought to her attention that what he had criticized was a piece of data that had been inaccurately reported. It was at this point that she began to recognize that this was only one of the many times she had been set up to pick fights with her boss.

After this particular encounter, the woman above decided there would be no more fights unless she had carefully gone over the available information and made her own decision that a confrontation was necessary in order to straighten out a problem. She and her husband were then able to begin to work more realistically about solving the problem of his attitudes about her employment. Games always inhibit rational problem solving to some degree. Time and energy go into playing the game rather than solving the problem.

Blemish

The *Blemish* player is the office nitpicker. The person who plays *Blemish* is looking for the little flaw or the Achilles' heel. A *Blemish* player may read through a ten-page report and call attention only to a comma or a semicolon or a word that is misspelled. This kind of game player tends to pay far more attention to tiny, inconsequential details than to full content.

An instructor playing *Blemish* while reading over a student's work is likely to whip out the red pencil and mark only those mistakes that don't make any difference anyway.

Blemish players seldom write comments such as, "this is really clear," "you said this well," or "this paragraph could be understood by anyone." Instead they tend not to see the whole picture or purpose of a project, but pick on only those items that are trivial mistakes. *Blemish* players occupy themselves with minutiae.

If a particular activity, such as programming the ascension of a missile, is worked over with a fine tooth comb eliminating all mistakes, this is not *Blemish*. The particular procedure is necessary for the functioning of the missile blastoff. Indeed, a colon instead of a period could cause a missile to blow up on the pad.

It is the inconsequential things, the unimportant things, the subordinate items that the *Blemish* player is drawn to.

One style of *Blemish* player almost gives a positive stroke but whips out a discount in the end. This was the style of a decorator who frequently said to a staff member something like, "That's beautiful the way you've arranged the colors. But don't you think an olive green would be better than the green you chose?"

Blemish players usually make it their business to pass out lots of anger stamps or inadequacy stamps to subordinates, co-workers, and sometimes even to supervisors. One man remarked, "My boss would be great if he didn't have that damn beard."

The people picked on can become resentful and angry and may eventually cash in. I have seen a *Blemish* player give away so many anger stamps to other people that in one particular case a co-worker had collected enough resentment to finally switch the game. She caught the *Blemish* player in a relatively important mistake and, at this point, nailed him, feeling, *Now I've Got You, You S.O.B.* This is an illustration of the classical switch in the roles of Victim, Persecutor, and Rescuer that occurs in the intermingling of games. [1]

In this particular instance one individual Persecuted the other, causing the other to feel Victimized. Eventually a switch occurred and the Victim became the Persecutor and the original Persecutor ended up the Victim. If a *Blemish* player laments, "I was only trying to help you make your report better," a switch from Persecutor to Rescuer occurs: "I was only telling you about these little commas so that your report would appear better to the boss. How can you attack me for being such a nice person? All that I am doing is trying to help you improve your work!" *Blemish* gives way to *I'm Only Trying To Help You.*

Now I've Got You, You S.O.B.

When this game is played within the organization, the player who is It lies in waiting or arranges a setup for someone to make a mistake. When the mistake occurs, the player pounces, venting wrath and cashing in anger stamps. A supervisor who gives incomplete instructions or unclear standards can be setting up such a game. This game can also be started if it's likely that the other person cannot come through on a contract.

Illustration

A premises analyst took the low bid on carpeting for three floors of a new building. The company submitting this low bid had a reputation for poor quality and an inability to stand behind its guarantees. The bid was let anyway. When the carpeting was put in, two of the three floors were filled with flaws. In fact, in several spots the carpeting appeared almost threadbare. Upon discovering this, the premises analyst went to the carpeting contractor and in her words, "really socked it to him." In addition, the legal department drew up papers, and then the analyst *really* had him. The carpeting contractor got his "kick" in a very serious way and the premises analyst had caught somebody in the act and relished punishing him.

This game interaction wasted a great deal of company time. It disrupted two floors of office space for a period of three months. Not only was there a diversion of the time and talents of the premises analyst but also many other people within the organization had their productivity lowered because of the upheaval in their working space.

This version of *Now I've Got You, You S.O.B.* is reminiscent of the father who left his money on his dresser, then pounced on his young son for being a thief.

Within organizations *Now I've Got You, You S.O.B.* sometimes ends up in court. Other times it simply ends with someone getting a bawling out, a dressing down. This was evidenced in a supervisor who bragged, "I really gave that guy a piece of my mind. I let him have it with both barrels, and he had it all coming." Underneath this dialogue lies the sense of justification that a person usually feels in playing this game.

If the complementary player plays *Kick Me,* these two may live unhappily ever after. Their games fit.

Illustration

A pediatrician played a variation of *Now I've Got You, You S.O.B.* with the mothers of the children he treated. Each time a mother brought her child in for shots, she was given a little sheet of paper noting the immunization. This was done instead of keeping a booklet that would present an orderly record of the child's immunizations. Few instructions were given the parent about immunizations — nothing was printed. If a child stepped on a nail, the mother might spend considerable time trying to read through slips of paper to give information over the phone as to when the last tetanus shot was given. Every time this occurred, the doctor pounced on "Stupid Women."

In addition, he combined this game with his variation of *Corner.* He scolded mothers for bringing a child in who was not "really sick," yet he also scolded them if they failed to bring in a child that appeared sick. This doctor got along very well with mothers who played *Kick Me* or *Stupid.*

Corner

A *Corner* player is likely to maneuver other people into a situation in which, no matter what they do, they never come out right. In one such situation worker G.S. complained, "If B.U. would just take more responsibility and be more aggressive about getting this data in on time, our whole department would run more smoothly." When B.U. attempted to get data in on time, G.S. always found something wrong with it. B.U. had not been able to analyze clearly what had been going wrong. He expressed to me, "No matter what I do I always come up wrong. If I am not aggressive about gathering the information and having my data in, then I'm wrong. If I forge ahead, then I've reported it in a wrong way or inaccurately by his standards. It seems as if literally, no matter what I do, I can't please him. There is no way to do it right. I feel like I'm damned if I do it and damned if I don't do it."

This particular feeling is typical of the individual who feels cornered. If this person is playing his or her part, then it is very likely that his being cornered is provoked by his not being responsible. This is not, however, the case in the situation mentioned above. B.U. solved this particular problem by going to G.S. and asking him who he would trust that could check out information. B.U. was given the name of a very competent woman that worked in this same division. The next time there was a deadline for the data sheet, B.U. met this deadline, had the data checked to see that it could not be contested, and presented it to G.S. At least with B.U., G.S.'s game was called. He no longer put B.U. in this situation of either not getting his reports done on time or not having them complete enough.

A woman secretary played a variation of *Corner* with her male boss. She began to complain more and more that she disliked the personal things that he asked her to do. Among these were buying presents for his wife, doing occasional shopping for his wife and daughters, and even buying him quite personal things such as underwear or socks. She pointed out that he often made these requests of her to do at lunch time or on her own time, and she became more and more verbal about her resentment. Her boss, hearing her complaint, apologized to her, "I didn't realize that this was so upsetting for you. I will manage some other way in the future."

Not too many days after that, he came to work after his own lunch hour with a watch that he purchased for his teenage daughter. He was rather proud of his new-found purchasing abilities and displayed this watch to his secretary, expecting a nice stroke. To his surprise her response was, "If you had asked me to get that watch for you, I could have saved you $5.00." At this point he was quite baffled and experienced what it feels like to be *Cornered*. His secretary appeared angry at him if he asked her to do personal shopping, and then she turned around and became angry because he had done his own personal shopping.

This particular situation was resolved by a leveling encounter in which he simply described to her the position he felt himself in. She later was able to realize that she had literally put him in an impossible position in which no matter what he did, he was wrong. Part of their new contract was that he could make shopping requests, and she could say "no" if she felt it inconvenienced her or was distasteful to her.

An organizational game of *Corner* that fits into many organizational scripts regarding sex role expectations is sometimes played with women. Aggression is described as a necessary quality for a good manager. Yet, the word *aggression* when applied to women is a negative. In such a case, a woman is in the position of being "damned" if she's aggressive and unacceptable for upward advancement if she's not.

Bear Trapper

Bear Trapper is played by baiting someone, then letting the trap fall.

The bait is often a false promise. Organizations can play *Bear Trapper* in their hiring practices. For example, some organizations in their zeal to attract the young college graduate student, paint an unrealistic, overglamorized portrait of the position they are offering.

The realization that the position has many nitty-gritties and is not all that glamorous comes eventually to the new job holders. At that time they may indeed feel trapped.

This particular game backfired for one organization. Consciously or unconsciously, the interviewers painted a superglamorous picture to specifically entice male candidates only. They gave women candidates all the details concerning the unpleasantries of the job with a minimum of information about the other side of the position.

As a result, many of the men chose to quit when the trap fell, but the women stayed. Most of the women were happy to discover that the position had a glamorous side too.

Another organization discovered that this game contributed to its unusually high turnover rate. To stop this practice, a series of short movies was arranged which described all important facets of available positions. Job candidates could select and view the movies which applied to their job aspirations. Such realistic data stopped the game and employee turnover diminished.

Uproar

Uproar is another common organizational game which fits into a hierarchy structure. *Uproar* usually starts with a discount, such as a critical remark. One person may stomp into the office of another, throw a report on the desk, and accuse angrily, "You've been in this division for four years and you haven't learned to write a decent report yet." The expectation for the complementary hand is defense,

> "Well, I'm sorry. I thought I had included everything that you wanted."

> "What do you mean you put into this everything I wanted? You ought to know better than. . . ."

This attack/defense dialogue might continue for several minutes until finally the defendant is worn out. The two people are likely to stomp away from each other in a physically angry posture.

Uproar is often a loud, shouting kind of game. However, it can also be played with a more subtle barb. Instead of an outright attack, the dialogue could have begun,

> "Now, this is a great improvement over your last report. However, it is still not good enough to convince top management."

The response:

> "But I thought I had included all those corrections that you had given me."

And then:

> "Well, yes, you have made several positive changes, but if you look this over now, there are some additional things that you should be able to see on your own."

The dialogue goes on with a more subtle attack and defense. The interaction may even be carried on with facial smiles and with an "I'm only trying to help you" attitude. But the dynamics continue attack/defense, attack/defense until the defendent is worn out and the people move away from each other frustrated and angry. In the last case the player uses *Yes, But* as one method of attack.

One man who played partner to this game learned to break it up by feeding back (reflective listening) to his attacker rather than defending himself.

When his boss attacked as usual,

> "You've messed this whole deal up, Harry!"

Harry, instead of his usual self-defense, looked straight at his boss and said,

> "You seem upset, Bill, by the way I handled the Anderson contract."

This unexpected response so frustrated the boss that he discontinued his attack. This approach would not work if the criticism were legitimately based on Adult data rather than the need to put someone else down. If it had been Adult, data would have been exchanged and a resolution made possible.

Some people counterattack and switch the hands in the game.

Illustration

A male supervisor called a woman in and confronted her with, "You've been spending too much time in the ladies' restroom."

Instead of the expected self-defense, the woman retorted, "Do you mean you spy on women in the restroom?"

At this unexpected counterattack, the supervisor blurted out a defensive response. The game was switched.

Rapo

In a work situation, the game *Rapo* can heighten the sense of hostility that in many cases already exists between men and women. Many women in their early childhood experiences learn not to trust men. Such mistrust grows from a range of experiences — from rejection or abandonment to rape and brutality. But for whatever reason, some young women have experiences that cause them to take the position that "men are not-OK."

If this is acted out in a work situation, a young woman often wears a costume that facilitates her game. She reveals parts of her body that are titillating to men. She moves in provocative ways. She tilts her chin downward and looks up at men through batting eyelashes.

In this particular game the woman — often without any awareness of it — sends sexy, seductive invitations to the men around her. (Her sweat shirt message is "I'm available.") Some men will merely feel threatened and avoid her, others will take the bait. It is the man that takes the bait whom she eventually slaps down.

This might be played out as a light game. One young woman who played *Rapo* came to worked dressed in very seductive clothes. They were tight, revealing, and short or low cut in the "right" places. If a man in her office whistled or gave any response to the way she groomed herself, she would walk off in a huff, saying, "You're nothing but a bunch of dirty, old men around here! You men have only one thing on your minds." The dynamics are the suckering in by laying the bait. Then, when the bait is taken, cutting the person down.

If there happens to be a male *Kick Me* player in the same department, he and the *Rapo* player are likely to have numerous encounters since their games fit. He wants to be kicked and she wants to kick men. They both are using company time to reinforce distorted self-images of their world and themselves, images of people and life as seen through the eyes of small children.

Men play *Rapo*, too. Little boys who are reared by a tyrannical woman who hates men, or who are abandoned or brutalized by a woman, can, in response, take the position, "women are not-OK." While a woman is likely to play this game by being physically provocative, a man is likely to act it out by sweet talk and lavish attention. At the end of his game, he may simply drop the woman like a hot potato (perhaps refocusing on another woman present) — a form of *Kiss Off*.

There is a variation of *Rapo* that ends with a very different kind of kick. The final hand is Rescuer rather than Persecutor. One man was very flirty with the women in his office. He had one young woman who was resisting physical contact with him, backed into a tight spot in the storeroom. Just as she began to give in to his advances, he switched his behavior. He took her by the shoulders, looked down at her with condescension, and said, "Aren't you a lucky girl that I'm the kind of fellow that I am." His phoney Rescue likely left her feeling Persecuted.

Another woman in the same office had gathered data about this man's behavior. One day she found herself in a situation with him. When he began to make an advance toward her, she stood up to him and said, "Don't pull any of that unless you really have something to offer." He never approached her again.

As women express themselves more fully and participate in upward mobility programs designed to advance them in organizations, this game can have a very destructive influence. [2] The organization that can foster the attitude that Men are OK and Women are OK is likely to utilize the full possibility of all its human resources regardless of sex. Effective use of all human resources is good management.

SOME GAMES REINFORCE SELF-NEGATION AND SELF-PITY

Poor Me Games

Many games are variations of *Poor Me*. The undercurrent of such games reflects positions like "I'm stupid," "I don't deserve to live," "I can't do anything right," "I'm handicapped," "I'm ugly and clumsy," "I can't help myself," "I'm no good," "I feel sorry for myself," "It's not my fault," etc. For example, *Why Does This Always Happen To Me?* and *Ain't It Awful About Me!* always reinforce some form of self-negation and self-pity.

Employees who do plenty of griping but never move to change their situation are likely to be acting out Atlas scripts — carrying the burdens of the world on their shoulders.

Many of the following games have some element of "Poor Me."

Kick Me

Kick Me players say things on the job like, "I could kick myself for doing that," "That was a terrible thing for me to have done," "I've been kicking myself all day for that," or "I really felt like kicking myself." If acting out the game, the player provokes a put-down. Such players invite, manipulate, provoke others to kick them. Being fired is one of the most common forms of acting out a hard game of *Kick Me* in organizations.

Illustration

One young man had a record of absenteeism and tardiness that was abnormally high. He promised several times to come to work on time, since his being there was essential to the functioning of the department. Counseling session after counseling session, he received his kick from his supervisor. Eventually he had accumulated so many kicks in his personnel file that the company felt justified in kicking him off the job.

Illustration

One training officer who arranged programs for his organization played a combination of *Let's Get Joey* and *Kick Me*. Here is only one example of the way he set up these games.

He conducted a morning session and let the class out for a lunch break 20 minutes earlier than scheduled. The afternoon speaker arrived on time only to find an angry class that had been sitting there 20 minutes waiting for her. Several "unkind" remarks were made toward the speaker, who was not aware of what had happened. Later, when she learned why the class was unhappy, she "kicked" the training officer for having changed the time without explanation or notification.

Kick Me players prefer people who will kick them. Withholding the negative stroke is one way to discourage people from playing this game with you. The player will go elsewhere for the negative strokes.

In one version of this game people do indeed kick themselves. An example is the "skull game" in which people kick themselves with destructive dialogue in their own heads. "Beating oneself up" is a common practice of a person who was manipulated with guilt as a child.

People who operate from an I'm not-OK and You're not-OK position may catch a worker in a mistake and make that person suffer (*Now I've Got You, You S.O.B.*). Then later, on reflection, they play a skull game of *Kick Me*, feeling great remorse, "How could I have spoken to Mr. Howell like that. I feel terrible about it." The roles switch from Persecutor to Victim.

Stupid

Stupid is a variation of *Kick Me*. The dynamics of *Stupid* are the same. There is provocation, manipulation, and/or an invitation to put the player down. However, the put-down involves putting down the person's brains or literally calling the player "stupid." *Stupid* players have learned to negate their own intelligence and to seek negative strokes from others.

Illustration

One woman who played a very hard game worked as receptionist and secretary. An instance of her stupid behavior occurred when her boss came in one day, very much in a hurry, saying, "This report has to be at the home office by the day after tomorrow. I want you to give it top priority. Stop whatever you are doing and see that this gets in the mail by four o'clock." The secretary became a little flustered but dutifully promised to put all other things aside and get this report on its way. Two weeks later there was a great deal of hubbub at the secretary's desk. She was fussing out loud about, "How could I have done this? What a stupid thing for me to do when this report was so important." Her boss, on entering the scene, got the picture that the secretary had found this important letter in her desk where it had been hidden away for two weeks. As the secretary had expected, she got a thorough scolding for her stupidity.

She acted out her game of *Stupid* in other ways — by filing things in the wrong places, putting letters on the wrong desks, coming in with coffee at the wrong time.

This young woman is very likely to play her game so hard that unless some therapeutic change occurs, she will be kicked off the job for being too stupid to handle the work, thus fulfilling her "loser" script compulsion.

Such behavior fits with *Now I've Got You*. In this case the boss makes no attempt to resolve any of the stupid behavior as it occurs but saves up anger stamps with each incident. After a certain number are collected, the boss feels justified in saying, "When she makes one more mistake, that's it. She's fired!"

Stupid might be played in the operating room if the wrong leg is amputated, in the courtroom if an important piece of evidence is overlooked, in the classroom if dumb questions are asked or the student appears on the wrong day to take the final examination.

Schlemiel

The game of *Schlemiel* is related to the games of *Kick Me* and *Stupid*, but the expected payoff is different. The payoff sometimes fulfills a secret wish of the player, "Somebody love me no matter what I do or how bad I am."

Illustration

One young man was transporting a new piece of equipment from one table top to another. In the process he dropped it. After he dropped it, he went into a long performance about how dumb it was of him to do such a thing. "Here is a new piece of equipment worth several hundred dollars. No one has had a chance even to use it, and I am so clumsy that I dropped it and broke some of the important parts on it. How could I do such a dumb thing. I don't know how people can stand to have me around here."

This young man's pitch was not to evoke a kick or a scolding. He was asking for something else. He was asking for forgiveness. His expectation was that if he put on a pitiful enough act, that if he could come on remorseful enough, someone's nurturing Parent would eventually say to him, "Don't worry about it, George, it is only a piece of machinery and no one was hurt." Next week he may spill the ink on the freshly mimeographed programs.

This is similar to the cigarette burn that the visiting sales representative puts on your desk and then successfully feels so bad about it that you say, "Oh, now forget it. Don't get upset. I'll take care of it."

If you work with someone who has learned to play this game, avoid giving the expected "forgiveness" stroke. For example, in the illustration above of the young man who dropped the machinery, a better response would be straight Adult, "It looks as if this part is broken. Please take it to the repair shop and have them contact me when it's fixed."

Anyone can make a mistake or have an accident. However, the *Kick Me* player, the *Stupid* player, and the *Schlemiel* player create an inordinate number of mistakes and accidents. This is a pattern, not something that happens rarely from which they learn and change.

The individual who is more of a winner makes mistakes but rarely makes the same mistake twice. One of the marks of a winner is to learn from experience. The game-playing loser, the person who is programmed to fail, does just the opposite. Mistakes are repeated over and over again. Clumsiness is repeated over and over again. Stupidity is repeated over and over again. Statements such as "Oh, I forgot," or "Well, I had such good intentions," or "Gee, I can't remember everything," or "How clumsy of me, I seem to be doing the wrong thing all the time" are often manipulative ploys. While the person is taking a Victim posture, the people around are literally being Persecuted. Avoiding the forgiveness stroke helps stop the game.

The Lunch Bag Game

Lunch Bag is a favorite game of executives who collect purity or self-righteous feelings about themselves — which we call white stamps. An executive who plays this game uses his self-righteous position to manipulate and control other people. He is literally likely to bring his lunch to his office in a brown paper bag, not a bag he purchased, but one that his wife saved for him from the supermarket or drugstore.

Rather than going out and having a pleasant lunch with co-workers, he sits in his office at lunch time eating out of his little grease-stained bag in which is tucked away last night's meatloaf or left-over sliced beef. With this ploy he is able to ward off the demands of other people. After all, how can you approach this humble man with a request for better carpeting or larger office quarters when the fellow sits in his office at noon eating his lunch out of a little brown bag?

With this maneuver he makes others feel too guilty, sometimes too fearful, to approach him with their requests and demands. Even his wife may not have anything frivolous. How could she ask for jewelry or a fancy coat from such a big, important man who humbles himself by eating last night's leftovers?

I observed a variation of *Lunch Bag* in a woman social worker whose run-over shoes and frayed dresses outdid those of the clients that came to her seeking help.

People working in this atmosphere must take responsibility for their own guilt feelings.

Harried Executive

Harried Executive is a common game among modern men and women, and the organization is a perfect setting in which to act it out. This is a particularly serious game. It can structure many decades of people's lives; and often, by the time the game is recognized, the players have worn out their bodies to the extent that irreparable damage has been done. Unfortunately, organizations are sometimes set up for *Harried*, and they stroke favorably this kind of behavior. One reason is that the *Harried* player comes on originally as Superman or Superwoman, able to keep all the balls in the air, able to say "yes" to all requests, and always "Johnny on the spot" to take on another responsibility.

Such players structure their life's time with work — sometimes "busy work." As long as they are working hard, they maintain their false sense of "OKness." There is very little play or leisure activity or just plain inactivity in the lives of typical *Harried Executives*. If *Harrieds* try to play for relaxation, they tend to work hard at it. As *Harried* players move ahead on the job, they take on more and more work and responsibility. They are likely to bring work home at night and even on weekends. There is always one more project that can be taken on. Such a load may be carried successfully for 15 to 30 years. The player may come on competent and confident, successfully covering up an "I'm not-OK" feeling by appearing super-OK.

I remember one man after 23 years of hard work bragging, "I haven't spent a vacation with my family for 16 years." He expressed a proudness in the amount of time he had devoted to his work, yet there was a pathetic, regretful ring to his voice.

Illustration

One woman executive discovered that by playing *Harried* she was using her work to destroy her health. She displayed a portion of her shoulder which was covered with sores that her doctor had diagnosed as "nerves."

This woman decided on the following program: complete health checkup and health plan; time out for "doing nothing"; more work delegated; saying "no" to more requests; and helping staff members to develop more independence (*Harried Executives* often keep staff members dependent).

At our last meeting she had made a good start on her plan. She remarked, "I've always been critical of people who are killing themselves with alcohol. I don't drink; but I've been digging my grave right here in my office."

Eventually there comes a day in the life of *Harried* when he or she can no longer come through. At this point the deterioration of the *Harried Executive* begins to manifest itself. The individual may call in with symptoms, appear disheveled, be unable to come to work, and eventually be unable to perform any more. By the end of the game, the person who tries hard to be everything to everybody collects enough justification to have a total collapse. Depression is a common payoff of the game. Other payoffs may be severe physical ailments and even heart attacks.

Illustration

One executive played *Harried* for 27 years, using his organization as the setting. He died falling face forward into an unfinished report. He was writing this report at home on a Saturday night — a classic ending to his script.

Not all *Harried* players are business executives. There are *Harried Telephone Operators, Harried Desk Clerks, Harried Waiters, Harried Teachers, Harried Housekeepers, Harried Farmers*, etc.

No matter where or how it is acted out, the game of *Harried* is of such a serious nature that people caught up in it need to stop as soon as possible. Bringing balance into one's life means having time for oneself — time for other people, for pleasures, for resting and relaxation, as well as for work. The person stopping *Harried Executive* often has to learn how to say "No," how to judge when an adequate day's work is done, and how to structure time in new ways — particularly in ways that will be personally fulfilling and psychically healthful.

One useful exercise in working with *Harried* players is to have them take a fantasy trip. For example, in a training session I ask the participants to close their eyes and imagine themselves as white haired and very aged, approaching 100 years. They are to visualize themselves in a place, such as on a bed or a chair. After they have fixed themselves at this age and place, I ask them to imagine that they know this is their last day. Their whole life now begins to pass before them. I allow time for each participant to flash back and walk through his life again. At the end of the experiment I ask the people to come back into the present, to come back to now. [3]

At this time we share some of the things that we thought about. One of the most common responses that I hear from *Harried* players is that they regret having neglected their families and friends. It is quite common, for example, for *Harried Executives* to lament that they never really had time for their children. This exercise is one way for people to gain perspective as to where they are heading in life and what the real priorities are.

Another useful tool in working with *Harried* players is simply to ask them to think for a moment about "Where will I end up if I keep doing what I'm doing now?" *Harried* players can become aware that they are using their work to depress or kill themselves.

Illustration

One department manager quit the organization after reevaluating the direction of his life and career. He decided he had been unhappy in his work for years, had not honestly done well by his company, but had stuck it out because it seemed the "right thing to do."

A Phoney Game of Harried

Some organizations *require* employees to play *Harried*. Unless employees look busy, overworked, and haggard, they are looked down upon somehow as not being loyal to the organization. Such a case was exposed when a man who had play-acted to the hilt to show how busy he was, how overworked he was, and how much work he took home evenings and weekends was stopped by a security officer when leaving the building. The security officer had his orders mixed up. He had been ordered to check briefcases, purses, and any bags carried into the building. But somehow on his first day, he confused the directions and was examining briefcases, etc., as people *left* the building. When this particular executive was forced to open his briefcase, it was found to be filled with *Playboy* magazines. Rather than doing homework, he had a little bag full of goodies which he fantasied with on the commuter bus.

In a similar situation the individual's briefcase was filled with toilet tissue that had been taken from the organization's rest rooms. In a sense this was getting something back for having to put on such a ridiculous act. The payoff was in toilet tissue. It would seem that his Little Professor outsmarted the organization. He had little intention of killing himself with work and made the maneuver to overcome the indignity that such a job requirement placed on him.

A variation of *Phoney Harried* is a game I've come to call *Don't Give It to Me to Do*. One woman caseworker played this game by stacking many, many files on her desk until they were piled high. This gave the appearance that she was frantically busy and had far too much to do. However, it was discovered that mainly these were completed cases that she simply pulled out and put on her desk. The purpose that it served for her was to avoid work, to avoid a load of things to do. People would walk up to her desk with a case file in their hands, see that she had more than she could possibly handle, and walk away without saying anything. The message that this *Harried*-appearing desk gave to other people was "Don't give it to me to do. See how much I'm doing already!"

These games are called phoney because they are not motivated by a childhood decision but are a response to the work situation. Players are usually aware of what they are doing.

Wooden Leg

Wooden Leg is a cop-out game played to avoid accomplishment or work. The person who plays *Wooden Leg* uses a physical or social handicap (which in itself may be real enough) as an excuse for lack of performance. The attitude is, "What can you expect from a poor person with a wooden leg."

As an example, one worker said, "If I work too long under these lights, I get a terrible headache." This person used a susceptibility to headaches to manipulate other people to finish up the work. Another person who was having a hard time holding down a job would lament when counseled, "What can you expect of me, I came from a broken home." With this ploy the expectation was that the supervisor should feel pity and should not expect good job performance.

One woman did this quite literally. She broke her leg on a skiing trip and after a stay at home returned to work. She was perfectly able to move around, but she did need the assistance of a cane. However, she

used this disability to manipulate the people around her into doing
things for her. She sat behind her desk with her cane hanging off the
front of the desk in full view of the other workers. Looking up
woefully when someone went by, she would say in a rather pitiful tone,
"While you are up. . ." Then she would ask the person to run an errand,
to get her a file or to put something back, or to bring her something.
Needless to say, her fellow workers collected feelings of anger and
resentment against her. These feelings were cashed in on her when an
office birthday was celebrated in another part of the building. She was
not invited because (as she discovered later) "it was too far for her to
walk."

People who come from deprived backgrounds may learn to play
this game well. They use their early life experiences an an excuse to
underachieve, sometimes refusing or quitting training opportunities.
Using *Wooden Leg* in this manner accounts also for a high number of
job losers — "What can you expect of someone from such a poor
background?"

Psychiatry

It's not uncommon for participants just introduced to TA to be
tempted to play *Psychiatry*. This happens if people use the newfound
language of TA to "psych" out friends, relatives, and working
associates, giving pain to others rather than improving relationships.

One new participant gleamed, "I've underlined all the things in the
first three chapters (of *Born to Win*) that fit my wife!" Another
exclaimed, "So that's what my boss has been doing all these years. Just
wait until I get back to my desk!"

TA, like any theory or philosophy, can be used to help people or
to hurt people. It is my hope that it will be used to help people. People
who are winners go after what they want out of life but not at the
expense of other people.

Illustration

Dan was in personnel in a large hospital. He was adept at the use of
TA but never used it's jargon to put anyone down that didn't
know what he knew. For example, one young woman complained
that the men were always making passes at her. As she sat in Dan's
office with her skirt pulled high, one arm stretched over the back
of the chair, head tilted with a pouting expression on her lips, she
said, "I don't know why the men always pick on me. Heaven
knows I don't ask for it." Dan asked her to look closely at her own
posture and dress. "You may not be aware of it, but the way you
sit and the way you dress send messages to men." Dan refrained

from saying, "You are playing *Rapo*. You bait men with your dress and gestures, then complain about them making passes." Instead, he put the meaning of TA into everyday language that could be understood and thought about. He did not accuse or threaten the young woman, but he did ask her to evaluate her own behavior. He worked on the problem, using his knowledge, but he avoided playing *Psychiatry*.

Psychiatry hurts. Don't play it.

SUMMARY

Games focus energy on the past. The interchange emphasizes something that happened to the person in childhood that resulted (1) in a negative self concept and/or negative attitudes about others, (2) in seeking and giving negative strokes, and (3) in structuring time in ways that are ulterior and devious rather than straightforward and honest. Eric Berne writes:

During early infancy the child is straight, starting off in the first position, I'm O.K. — You're O.K. But corruption quickly sets in, and he discovers that his O.K. is not a completely undisputed, automatic birthright, but depends to some extent on his behavior, and more particularly on his responses to his mother. . . By the time he enters school, he has probably learned a few soft games, or perhaps two or three hard ones, or in the worst cases he may already be game-ridden. It depends on how smart and tough his parents are. The more they "play it smart," the crookeder he will be; and the tougher they are, the harder he will have to play in order to survive. [4]

Organizational scripts often encourage game playing. Established patterns can encourage self-negation, play-acting versus authenticity, undercutting others, and uncooperativeness.

The goal of understanding games is to free people's psychic and physical energies so that they can become more aware of what is happening *now*. This allows them to invest their human potential in solving real problems that exist in the present. For many people this newfound connection with the present gives them a sense of exhilaration. For organizations, it gives new life.

When games are given up within organizations, it paves the way for more open, honest, and authentic encounter among workers. In addition to saving time and money, the lessening of organizational games helps people.

FOOTNOTES AND REFERENCES

1. cf. Stephen B. Karpman, "Fairy Tales and Script Drama Analysis," *Transactional Analysis Bulletin*, 7, No. 26 (April 1968): 39-43.

2. Dorothy Jongeward and Dru Scott, *Affirmative Action for Women: A Practical Guide* (Reading, Massachusetts: Addison-Wesley). In press.

3. cf. Muriel James and Dorothy Jongeward, *Born to Win: Transactional Analysis with Gestalt Experiments* (Reading, Massachusetts: Addison-Wesley, 1971), p. 252.

4. Eric Berne, *What Do You Say After You Say Hello?* (New York: Grove Press, 1972), pp. 156–157. Reprinted by permission of Grove Press, Inc. Copyright © 1972 City National Bank, Beverly Hills, California; Robin Way; Janice Way Farlinger.

3

GAMES CAN BE
STOPPED MANY WAYS

*A first line supervisor remarks, "Every
time I have a counseling session with H.D., I
come out feeling two inches high."*

*A retailer muses, "I swear I'm not going to
buy from that man again. Yet he always
manages to trick me into it."*

*An editor ponders, "I try not to, but
it seems that B.T. always does something I
end up scolding her for."*

Without information, most of us play our games in a completely
unaware way. When a game is over, however, we often have some
awareness that the "same old thing" has happened one more time.

The repetitive nature of games is one way to begin to recognize
them. It is not unusual for us to find ourselves repeating almost the
same series of transactions again and again, perhaps with the same
person.

Games structure differing amounts of time. Games such as *Kick Me*
or *Blemish* may be over in a few minutes while *Alcoholic, Debtor,* or
Harried may fill up a lifetime.

Adult input about games helps us become aware of them, recognize
them, and consider options. Usually the first step is hindsight. "Good
grief, I just did it again." The next step is likely to be middlesight.
"There I was right in the middle of it and suddenly I knew what was
going on!"

With persistence, the third step is foresight, "I really felt compelled
to give her solutions and advice, but I managed not to." With enough
foresight, games can be stopped before they start, hopefully in favor of
a more authentic means of encounter.

GAMES ARE TWO-WAY TRANSACTIONS

Games can be broken up on either side. However, if we effectively
thwart someone else's game, it is unrealistic to assume that the person is

61

cured of game playing. That person is only "cured" of playing this game with us in the work situation. A therapeutic change is often necessary for permanent change. There is a high probability that the game will continue to be played elsewhere. However, a knowledge of transactional analysis gives us far more effective control over hurtful or wasteful interpersonal relationships on the job.

In addition to helping us control what other people do to or with us, the application of TA helps us know ourselves. In fact, the most useful aspect of studying games in organizations is to give us more insight and control over our *own* games — those games we play in response to the people we work with and those encouraged by the organizational scripts. It isn't what we can do with or to the other person that always counts the most. It is what we learn about and are able to do about ourselves.

It is not uncommon for participants to discover within a training session that they themselves play some games. People who become aware of game playing can either stop it, cut down the amount of time invested in it, or play at a less intense level.

AVOID THE COMPLEMENTARY HAND

The classic way to thwart a game, of course, is not to play the expected complementary hand. Do something unexpected. Avoid giving or taking the negative payoff. For example, if a *Yes, But* player has you cornered, refuse to give advice or solutions to the stated problem. One method is to throw the problem back to the initiator of the game. Say perhaps, "It is a pretty rough problem, Harry. What are you going to do about it?"

It may be doubly hard to stop a *Yes, But* player if you play *I'm Only Trying to Help You*. These two games often fit, wasting considerable company time. In fact, anyone prone to collecting "kicks" may be easily suckered into *Yes, But*. Knowing the games we play helps us figure out what games of others we fall into most easily. For example, *I'm Only Trying to Help You* needs to be examined by anyone working for rescuing agencies or in the helping professions. If clients are not being cured, if illnesses are not being conquered, if social problems are not being alleviated, time is likely being invested in *I'm Only Trying to Help You* and/or *Ain't It Awful About Them* rather than solving problems.

STOP ACTING PHONEY ROLES

One way to stop playing our own games is to stop playing the classical roles involved in games. Through an understanding of script, people may realize that they play a particular role more frequently than others. For example, some people gain insight into the fact that they often playact at being a Victim. They use words, gestures, postures, and other behaviors to invite people to either Persecute or Rescue them. To stop games, stop playacting at being a Victim. Stop playacting at being a Persecutor. Stop playacting at being a Rescuer.

Illustration

J.B. discovered in a training session that he played the Victim role every time he went to see his manager. Usually he acted defensive about his work, frustrated the boss, and got kicked. He also saw his manager as a Persecutor like his father had been. J.B. took responsibility for triggering the kicks. However, he needed some way to work on the false authority he attributed to his boss. We therefore worked out an imaginary exercise in which he imagined his boss nude and standing in his socks. This imagery switched his feeling level from Adapted Child to Natural Child. Instead of feeling defensive when he confronted his boss, he giggled to himself. Since he was not experiencing not-OK feelings, he talked straight more easily than he thought he could. To his surprise his manager also came on straight and their relationship continued to improve.

STOP DISCOUNTING OTHERS

Games always involve someone being discounted — either one's self or someone else. One way to gain better control over one's own games is to become aware of, and refrain from, putting down and discounting others. Stop emphasizing other peoples shortcomings. In a game of *Blemish*, for example, part of the ploy is to initiate feelings of guilt or inadequacy in the other person. This discounts others, even though it is usually a projection of the player's own sense of inadequacy.

The point of discounting in a game may lie in different places within the game. For example, the game of *Uproar* starts with a discount — usually a critical remark or gesture. In contrast, the game of *Rapo* usually ends with a discount. Refraining from putting people down or defining them as insignificant avoids the discount and helps to stop games.

As is suggested by McGregor's Theory X, some managers operate from a You're not-OK position. Consequently, they may tend to inhibit the growth of the people they manage. They are likely to play from the Persecutor role, act out games that put others down, and distribute negative stamps. This can be changed.

Illustration

One vice president in a very large organization attended a four-day TA training program. At the end of the first day he exclaimed, "My God, it's never occurred to me that I come on Parent almost all the time. I even come on too Parent with my own kids."

In the next session (a week later) he reported that he had played ball with his son and "rather enjoyed it." He had not allowed himself to do this before. This was his first breakthrough in his problem which he had defined as Constant Parent. [1]

When he came on Parent, which he did frequently, he came on primarily from the prejudicial, punitive behavior of his Parent. The kinds of strokes he gave were most often critical or punishing. He had seen this as a way of managing people — "simply tell people what they are doing wrong and they improve." When he was asked what he might do to change this pattern in the work situation, one of the things he suggested was that he needed to say more positive things to his staff.

In the third session this same man reported that he also realized he was not much fun to be around. He was rarely playful or humorous with the people in his department. He decided that a few key people had left his department because the atmosphere was austere. There were few pleasurable strokes. He managed from a contamination that said "work and pleasure don't mix; if you're really working, it can't possibly be enjoyable."

Now he claimed that he found it much easier to laugh, be playful, and take a moment for a joke or smile with his fellow workers. He admitted, "It really isn't that hard. I've just never thought about it before." At this point he stated that developing his sense of humor was a long-term goal; however, he felt he was immediately able to listen to other people better, and to smile and laugh when things were funny. He also discovered that when things became tight and people had to stay overtime, or when they were under a great deal of pressure to get a job done, a laugh or a joke facilitated the process more than his previous pattern of scolding and demanding.

Even though this executive had attended only three sessions in transactional analysis, he was already able to apply the information in very significant ways, both in his home life and in his job performance.

STOP DISCOUNTING YOURSELF

Negative feelings are either collected or distributed in all games. One way to help relieve the game playing is to refrain from collecting negative feelings about yourself — feelings of inadequacy, fear, stupidity, anger, guilt, self-contempt, hurt and/or depression. Stop exaggerating personal shortcomings and practice accepting gold stamps.

Illustration

D.S. discovered that every time someone tried to compliment her work, she warded off the compliment. Standard phrases she used were, "I would have been better if I'd had more time," "Gee, it wasn't anything," "Well, it could have been worse." Sometimes she would not only refuse to accept a gold stamp but would send back a gray stamp in return. For example, when she was complimented by her immediate supervisor for a report she had presented to management, she retorted, "You of all people ought to know that it could have been much better!"

In a TA training session she became very aware of her pattern and its affect on other people. Her parting shot in class was, "A simple 'thank you' is a lot easier than the antics I usually go through!"

LEARN TO ACCEPT POSITIVE STROKES AND GIVE POSITIVE STROKES

People who have learned to get most of their strokes by playing games will suffer feelings of stroke deprivation when they give up games. The task becomes one of getting positive strokes through alternative ways of structuring time. This often takes continuous practice, lengthening the time span between game encounters.

Some people will need to increase the number of strokes they give and get through simple rituals. Even though rituals are superficial ways of structuring time, nonetheless, they supply people with maintenance strokes.

In addition, learning how to carry on a pastime with another person — simply talking about some innocuous subject — is an improvement over the hurtful interchange that a game involves. For any one person this means learning the facility of making small talk with other people. Such small talk might be centered around weather, travels, hobbies, schools once attended, favorite places to eat, etc. Too much time devoted to pastimes on the job can be inappropriate. However, a few pastimes are likely to be less destructive to the organization than games. The person must decide with the Adult what's OK.

Rituals and pastimes provide low-intensity strokes which do not equal the intensity of game strokes. However, the quality of strokes through activities can be high if the job is enriched with intrinsic strokes. Therefore, more time needs to be invested in activities centered around getting the job done — productivity. Productivity feels good if it is tapping actual human potentials. People who learn to get and enjoy positive strokes by experiencing their unique potential through their work are winners.

People who learn to give more effective strokes to others are also winners. Negative patterns can be changed.

Illustration

One man in charge of the international division of his company gained insight from TA training into his stroking patterns. After viewing the film *Second Chance* and participating in a discussion on strokes, he reported (in the second session), "I went home and looked at my 11-year-old son watching TV and thought to myself, 'I haven't touched that kid in years'. I walked up behind him and put my hands on his shoulders and just rubbed him a little. He looked back at me, first in surprise, and then broke into a broad grin. It felt good to both of us."

Later, this man realized that he failed to give many warm strokes that would be appropriate in the work setting. He smiled when he said, "I'm starting at the ground floor and working up. This morning I stopped and chatted with the security officer. I've never even looked at him before."

This man structured a moment's time in experiencing intimacy with his son. The strokes we receive from intimacy are so intense that we "feel" them for a long time. You probably have experienced going back in your memories and reliving a special encounter with another person. If so, you may also have experienced the good feelings again.

The above cases illustrate that a not-OK position towards others can be modified at home as well as at work. These changes would probably not have occurred so rapidly in seriously disturbed persons.

In addition, these people were beginning to experience many more of their possibilities as whole people. Self-actualizing people are those who are doing just that: being more and more of their possible selves.

SOMETIMES IT'S BEST TO LEVEL

Risking authenticity is sometimes difficult. However, leveling with another person about what you think is happening between you can sometimes clear the air. This is especially useful if you both know TA language. In any case, using the "I" message approach and avoiding accusations raises the probability of being heard.*

---

*   See leveling procedure, Chapter 5.

Illustration

J.J. felt that his boss played *Yes, But*. He had been called in several times in the guise "getting your feel for the problem." No matter what his response, his boss reached for a reason why it wouldn't work — often not even hearing him out.

Finally, J.J. went to his boss and explained what seemed to be happening from his point of view. "From the way I experience these sessions, I feel that my ideas aren't going to be considered anyway. I feel discouraged about giving suggestions or solutions. It appears to me that before I can lay my plans on the table, they are rejected. If there's anything you think we can do to improve these sessions, I'd appreciate it."

This approach was a surprise to the boss. However, he asked for time to think it over.

They talked about it another time and decided that all ideas should be laid out before any acceptance or rejection was given.

J.J. reported that the incidence of *Yes, But* diminished considerably.

Illustration

In another situation R.W. would call in the staff she supervised for their suggestions on a new procedure. If the new procedure didn't work, she blamed her staff, "See what they (staff) made me do!"

A staff member finally learned to ask, "If this plan doesn't work, whose fault will it be?

Authenticity does not always mean being honest, open, and straightforward. Sometimes it involves the release of feelings of tenderness and affection — intimacy. People who are working together on a tough project and are supportive of each other, attuned to each other, oftentimes develop caring feelings towards one another. The moment when the whole project comes to fruition, or perhaps collapses, can be a moment of genuine feelings of tenderness and understanding.

Moments of authentic intimacy can occur in the work environment. Unfortunately the word *intimacy* is often misused to mean sexual relations. Sexual relations can and often do occur without intimacy and intimacy can occur without sex.

The essence of intimacy is its game-free nature. Intimate moments are free of ulterior transactions and are often experienced as a release of affection and tender concern.

MANAGEMENT CAN HELP STOP GAME PLAYING

There are many ways in which management can diminish the time invested in games. This can be encouraged by reducing boredom on the job; by enriching the work environment with positive strokes; by allowing people to express and develop their own potentials (self-actualizing) so that they receive intrinsic strokes from their work by identifying personal goals and integrating them with organizational goals; by constantly examining the appropriateness of organizational scripts and facilitating necessary change.

YOU CAN'T WIN THEM ALL

Even with sufficient input about games, it's not always possible to bring about the kinds of changes we desire.

Often the best we can do is to control our own games better and to refrain as much as possible from giving others their expected negative payoff. Managers are not therapists, and they may experience a sense of inadequacy if they try to be. They can only be expected to do their best with the data available in the reality of the setting.

If you have faced this problem, learn to give yourself a stroke for doing the right thing. For example, if you successfully withhold giving a *Kick Me* player a kick, that's worth giving yourself a stroke.

Illustration

S.K. supervised a man who made it a practice to come in daily 1 1/2 hours late, bring his newspaper to read at work, and take extra-long coffee breaks. This employee often bragged that he couldn't be fired anyway, which was close to the truth. His previous supervisor, unlike S.K., had invested considerable time each day scolding, making demands, and making threats about the tardiness and low productivity.

S.K., though frustrated, decided he would not give this employee the kicks he vigorously asked for. Instead, he was patient, tried to discuss the problem rationally, and sought mutual problem solving.

He experienced several sleepless nights and many frustrating days worrying about his inability to change the other person. It took him awhile to learn that he was doing the right thing by withholding the kicks. In the meantime the subordinate, no longer getting the negative strokes he evidently wanted, quit his job.

This manager had set as his goal the changing of an employee who played a hard game of *Kick Me*, rather than having a more realistic goal of withholding the kicks. As a consequence, he was unable to feel good, not only about their relationship, but also about his behavior in relation to it. When he understood what had happened, in terms of strokes, he was able to stop kicking himself and appreciate the fact that he had successfully withheld negative strokes. It was the subordinate's decision to respond by quitting rather than changing.

Managers who set unrealistic goals may never feel OK about what they've accomplished. In fact, they may not even realize *what* they've accomplished. It's important, sometimes, to accept the fact that you can't win them all.

SUMMARY

We structure our life's time six various ways: by withdrawal, rituals, pastimes, games, activities, and intimacy. Structuring time with games provides us with negative strokes. Although games keep our spinal columns from shriveling up, they also maintain and reinforce a distorted perception of self and others, a collection of bad feelings, and a furthering of the negative aspects of our scripts.

We can give up games if we

1. refuse to play the complementary hand.
2. stop playing roles and are ourselves.
3. stop discounting others.
4. stop discounting ourselves.
5. learn to give and accept positive strokes in favor of negative strokes.
6. invest more of our life's time in activities and intimacy.
7. learn to level.

Some of us have not stopped to think about how we are actually spending the moments of our life experience. In addition, many of us invest a great deal of our time within the structure of an organization. Time examined from this point of view may help us figure out what changes we want to make. Such an investigation paves the way for a higher risk toward authenticity and openness, toward creativity and productivity.

Organizations benefit if employees are free to channel their physical and psychic energies into solving current problems, making decisions, and developing their talents and potentials. Happy, productive people contribute to profits. Everybody wins.

REFERENCE

1. Muriel James and Dorothy Jongeward, *Born to Win: Transactional Analysis with Gestalt Experiments* (Reading, Massachusetts: Addison-Wesley, 1971), p. 219.

4

TA CAN HELP DEVELOP
EFFECTIVE MANAGEMENT STYLES

Men work to meet their basic, <u>animal</u>
needs. When they do, money is the medium. But
money is not enough to satisfy <u>human</u>
needs — to achieve and to grow psychologically.
If he cannot do so in the job he now holds, he
will go elsewhere if possible; in any case, the
maintenance items will be much the same
wherever he goes. If he feels he cannot leave,
he will tend to become a ward of the company
with the company as his custodian until
retirement or death does them part. The
bargain is an uneasy one for both. [1]

Our economy has moved from the agrarian to the industrial age. We now stand on the verge of a postindustrial age in which there will be less labor and more professionalism involved in what we now call *work*.

In the past, employees were often undereducated and underdeveloped. As a consequence, a Parent-Child relationship frequently existed between employer and employee. Such a relationship may have worked well in the past when citizens themselves often assumed a childlike posture. Many could not read and most had little training. However, such a relationship in modern times is significantly less appropriate. Employees, congregations, and students are better educated than ever before in our history. Many seek their own autonomy, their own control over their life destiny, and their own individuality.

We find a clear example of a former Parent-Child relationship in an organizational structure within organized religion. Historically, the administrators and those administered to within organized religion have had a Parent-Child relationship. These administrators often had life or death control over congregations — sometimes over nations of people. If a congregation could not read and the minister or rabbi could read, the two were set apart — on one side the role of authority, and on the other side the role of follower, the flock.

In current times, congregations are often unwilling to sit as unquestioning children expected only to obey. Members of congregations read and study and can now become experts in theology just as easily as the leader. Such a dramatic change demands a more effective Adult-to-Adult basic relationship with Parent-Child transactions occurring only when they are appropriate to a specific situation, such as illness or a death in the family. Many religious groups are finding that their previous organizational structure is crumbling and they are unable to meet the needs of a changed congregation.

More persons are attempting to actualize their own uniqueness and their own potential within the structure of organizations. Organizations that fail to see and meet this changing human need are likely to be organizations that will themselves fail, being rejected by the new life that is necessary to keep any organization alive.

If we look at Maslow's hierarchy of self-actualization, we can readily see that there are many more Americans who have met their basic needs for survival than ever before. Once people's need for food and water are met, they experience another need. They seek a shelter from the elements and want creature comforts. Safe and tucked away in this shelter, they begin to experience an emotional need for other people. This need may be met in the family group or in some kind of social group structure. The expression of affection and love towards other people is all part of fulfilling the needs of this level of human existence.

But growing people are not satisfied with remaining at this level either. Out of the needs being met at this level, there develops another urge — the search for development of high self-esteem. People move out and embrace the group, but not at the expense of their own growth and competence. The individual who has a high level of self-esteem has attained a level of competence and is ready to actualize. Maslow sees self-actualization as the epitome of the pyramid of human motivation. [2,3]

Our society has a potential for more people to become self-actualizing than ever before.

The need for self-actualization affects organizations. People may no longer be grateful for "jobs." Simply taking a paycheck home may satisfy some — it would be unrealistic to think otherwise — but this is less and less true of an educated, inner-motivated citizenry. Young people more and more want to give, want to be, and want to devote their lives to something that is satisfying and fulfilling in terms of themselves and their social conscience.

Sometimes people doing personnel interviewing are programmed with Parent tapes, such as "people looking for work *should* be grateful for any job offered to them; they *should* be highly motivated by the promise of a steady paycheck, good medical benefits, and a good retirement plan."

For many people today this no longer holds true. Their jobs are not visualized as providing a place where they earn money so they can *live* someplace else, but rather, as a setting in which they look forward to going, to being, to working, to developing, to exploring, and to fulfilling their own possibilities. This will tend to make many young men and women appear dissatisfied and ungrateful, but what we may not be aware of is that they are simply asking for something new to many of us, that is, for another level of human existence.* In its truest sense this opens the way for the integration of personal goals with organizational goals.

THE TIMES AND PEOPLE ARE CHANGING

Half of the people who have ever walked the surface of this earth are alive today. [4] In addition to these vast population problems, we live in a time when change is something to be expected. This is a recent phenomenon in human history. For most of the history of mankind, change has occurred painfully slowly, often taking many generations to bring about even a slight social or political evolution. Most of the change that has occurred has come within the last few centuries. We are now living in a time when we must cope not only with change, but also with rapid acceleration of change.

For generations it was traditional that young people might figure out what they would do in life by looking around at what other people were doing. Sometimes a particular occupation could be passed on from generation to generation to generation.

This is no longer true. We are at a stage in social and economic development that accelerates so fast that ten years from now it may be difficult to predict what work will be available to do.

Human beings are faced with an accelerated rate of change that is almost unbelievable and which can be destructive to individual personalities. Many people are not adaptable enough to meet ever changing and new situations. Neither are many organizations.

For example, people who play psychological games, who reinforce and act out their early childhood decisions and positions, are essentially maintaining their own status quos. These kinds of behavior will become more destructive as the ability to change becomes more essential for survival. In terms of personality this has many implications. For instance, Adult input that was sufficient five years ago may be obsolete now.

The strain on the Adult is to keep current with input so that the individual is operating on the most recent data within the context of

---

*   It has been my observation that many young people born into the "lap of plenty" (born into the third level of existence) want to experience the survival and safety levels. Many have taken to the woods with knapsacks, attempting to live off the land. This may be a natural urge to reorder their own level sequence of development. Some "executive dropouts" seem to be doing the same thing.

the "here and now" to maintain or improve productivity. Although methods and approaches become obsolete, human beings do not have to become "obsolete."

People who function from rigid patterns in their Parent-Child ego states and who are unable to allow the psychic energy to flow between ego states are likely to be unable to keep up with society.

As the social and economic structure changes, individuals may experience more of the phenomena of their scripts literally running out. Or they may find the settings formerly available to act out scripts now gone. This is currently true of men who retire and women who were scripted to rear children but find themselves living many years after the children are grown. [5]

In order to combat this human problem even partly, people more than ever need to come in touch with and actualize their own uniqueness. People who are self-actualizing are constantly in a state of flux. They are ever growing, changing, developing, adapting, and becoming. People who are actualizing rather than manipulating are using their psychic energies to continue to enhance and experience themselves and their own possibilities.

In contrast are the individuals who are locked into being the manipulators. These people will pass life's time reinforcing old patterns, using their manipulative techniques over and over again, techniques that worked when they were three years old. Yet such patterns may cause people to lose jobs when they are thirty-five. Those who remain manipulators become actors. They are playing parts in life rather than being or becoming more of themselves everyday.

The individual who can survive the future shock [6] of accelerated change learns to explore and understand all parts of his personality and learns not to be fearful of moving in a stream of life that is constantly in flux.

In addition to the problem of individuals falling by the wayside, organizations whose basic premises are contrary to environmental needs and to human growth can themselves fall by the wayside. To survive, organizations must be able to make the flexible adaptations necessary to meet the changes that lie just around the corner.

Organizations that cannot see or meet this need may go down rumbling "ain't it awful about the young people today," not realizing that they have a possibility for highly motivated and productive employees, people who are better educated, have more Adult information, and are more humanly motivated than perhaps ever before in our history.

People at the developmental level who are experiencing a need to actualize their own humanness need organizations that are also actualizing, changing, growing, and developing in flux, with which they can associate themselves. Organizations can become senile too soon, just like people.

ORGANIZATIONS CAN CHANGE

The traditional method of structure of an organization on a hierarchy scale is giving way. The more modular, loose structuring of group models, in which the leadership fluctuates and changes as the group reforms to perform another task, is on the increase. Horizontal or lateral forms of organizational structure emerge.

Transactional analysis offers an excellent model for this kind of structure. What is occurring in TA terms is that the traditional Parent-Child relationship is giving way to a basic Adult-Adult relationship. More people are trusted in leadership roles as the leadership fluctuates.

Such an organizational model often requires team-building techniques within the organization. New organizational scripts must be formed and practiced. In addition, the success or failure of this kind of model can depend a great deal on what tool the organization uses for the interpersonal problems among its team members. Often differences are seen as threatening rather than facilitating.

Team building depends upon a good integration of the *unique* talents of each person. A basic Adult-Adult relationship does not mean the members always function from their Adults. It means that the unique talents of each person are appreciated and utilized. Some people will be better at gathering data, while others may be better at uncensored thinking — not having limits (using the Little Professor in a creative way to assist problem solving). These two kinds of people functioning as part of a team can facilitate and enhance one another by bringing their own individuality into the problem-solving procedure. While some people have their heads in the clouds, others have their feet on the ground.

A comprehension of transactional analysis can help team members understand and appreciate what each person is most capable of giving. By integrating their talents they can successfully form a whole that adds up to more than the sum of the parts involved. [7] In addition, when interpersonal transactions get in the way of doing the job, TA may be used to help solve the problem.

Many large organizations are recognizing that the traditional hierarchy structure built in the organizational script spells disaster for the continuing health of the organization. Such a hierarchy often limits decision making to a chosen few, today often isolated geographically, who sit at the top of an organization.

If a large organization decentralizes its authority, the decision making may be spread across the entire nation. Sometimes, however, decisions are simply spread to the various departments housed within one building.

Here again, the Parent-Child relationship gives way to a more egalitarian relatedness. It is saying I'm OK as the president of the company and so are you OK as the manager of your department. It is saying we can rely on your decisions; we can trust your competence; you can run your department and call many of the shots; you no longer need a corporate Parent to tell you what to do and when to do it. Decentralization of authority is essential for many organizations in breaking their old script patterns. Many employees can take the responsibility of decision making if they have the opportunity to take such responsibility.

When people within an organization are doing their best to increase the number of I'm OK — You're OK transactions, decentralization of authority is facilitated. Organizational scripts can change. Earl Nightingale recently reported:

Professor Douglas MacGregor of MIT adapts Dr. Abraham Maslow's Third Force theory to business management in his book, "The Human Side of Paradise." MacGregor's concept, called Theory "Y" management and more recently "participative management," is based on Maslow's hierarchy of human needs. This advanced theory of leadership advocates giving workers greater freedom, greater responsibility, and giving more consideration to their non-financial needs.

Andrew Kay, President of Non-Linear Systems, decided to test the ideas of Maslow and MacGregor in his own company, which manufactures digital voltmeters, a highly competitive field. He threw out his assembly line approach and divided production workers into teams of three to nine people. Each team had full responsibility for assembling, calibrating and testing complete instruments. They were given considerable freedom in how they accomplished this task. Kay said, "We regard management as basically an affair of teaching and training, not one of directing and controlling. We control the process, not the people."

Arthur Kurioff, Non-Linear Vice President said, "Gregariousness, affiliation, belonging — all these human needs are served in the group."

Time clocks and regular coffee breaks were abandoned — workers took a break when it was convenient. Salesmen were no longer required to submit detailed expense reports. Instead, they were given a reasonable allowance which they could use or not as they saw fit and pocket the difference. They were only accountable for the results they produced. Within three years productivity per worker had increased thirty per cent and company sales by 100 per cent, employee turnover dropped to one-fourth the national average and customer complaints went down more than seventy per cent. An unexpected bonus was increased corporate flexibility. New models that had taken eight or ten weeks to develop were now developed in two or three.

Vance Packard, describing Non-Linear in the Reader's Digest, said, "Andrew F. Kay has staked his company's future on the belief that ordinary people have great potentiality for growth and will perform far better if they are trusted with important responsibilities." [8]

TA CAN ASSIST MANAGERS IN UNDERSTANDING VARIOUS FORMS OF AUTHORITY

Anyone who manages other people develops a management style. There are four basic approaches which are likely to be used. [9] Some people lead and manage others out of competence. In other words, they have authority that is an *authority of competence*. Their sheer knowledge and skills are so highly developed that others accept them as an authority.

Other people possess an authority that is the *authority of integrity*. These people are solid in their ethical structure and fair in their dealings with others. Subordinates may be motivated to work for this kind of individual, attributing authority to him or her out of a deep feeling of trust and respect.

Still a third method of authority with others is the *authority of personality*. Such managers are likely to be open. They are reachable. People can get to them. They are likely to have the skill of being good listeners. They do not alienate others by cross transacting, by domineering, or by preaching.

A fourth kind of authority with others is the *authority of position*. These people have power over others because of the title they hold within the organization. The title may be connected to other status symbols, such as an office on a higher floor, carpeting, more space, a window, etc. This individual is likely to have people do what he wants done because he says so, and because he believes he has the position behind him to back him up.

It is interesting to look at the ego state involvement in these particular forms of authority. People who have power with others because of competency are likely to have highly programmed and well-developed Adult ego states. These individuals have often acquired a great deal of data. They know their material. Knowing their own field well gives them a relationship with others that commands authority.

Individuals who have a high degree of integrity are very likely to have had parents that are well programmed with high ethical standards.

To these individuals, how they are thought of, their fairness, and their ability to be trusted by others are primary. This, of course, does not exclude their functioning Adult and Child ego states. However, it does mean that they have Parent ego states that are useful and the Child in them can be trusted. They do not alienate other people but exhibit an integrity that commands respect.

Individuals who rely on their personalities to gain power of authority are likely to use all three ego states equally with their subordinates. The open individuals — the individuals that will listen — often have Parents within their heads who are good listeners. They care about people and they refrain from critical or punitive behaviors with people. The Adult has sufficient input so that the individuals are able to deal with the data necessary for the particular line of work. The individuals are likely to be pleasant to be with, which often means that they have a happy, OK-feeling Child and that being around them "feels good." This kind of individual is likely to have the degree of autonomy that allows a great deal of spontaneity so that psychic energies flow rapidly from ego state to ego state. These individuals are able to trust a great deal of their past programming, or perhaps they have changed previous negative patterns.

Authority of position often comes out critical, prejudical, or punitive Parent. The individual with this kind of authority may wield his power over others in the sense that, "I am bigger and stronger than you and if you don't do what I want, I have the power to punish you." I see this in the long run as the most ineffectual method of managing and leading people. It is often very efficient in the short run. Things may be done rapidly because the "old man" gets angry if they're not done his way and on time. However, in the long run intelligent workers resent this kind of management; and, even though they may not be aware of it, they tend to collect feelings of hostility and anger that someday, in some way are likely to be "cashed in."

It is my belief that many of the sabotaging slowdowns within divisions and departments are a result of this kind of management. When managers come on from the prejudicial, punitive side of their personalities, they are very likely to activate the not-OK feelings or the rebellious impulses in the Child ego states of their subordinates. While there may be no overt resistance or revolution against the manager's authority, there is likely to be sulking, subtle slowdowns, outside talk about the departments or organizations that are degrading to the organizations, and the many other techniques of "getting even" employed by subordinates. This very much parallels a child's ability to outsmart a critical parent.

While there may still be some organizations in which an immediate obedience is primary for functioning, unless there is the urgency of immediacy, this particular method of authority may in the long run lead to low productivity.

The type of management style that is Parent oriented was more appropriate when employees lacked education and looked for leadership that told them what to do. It would be unrealistic to think that this no longer exists. Many people who seek jobs today have difficulty reading and lack salable skills. As a result, managers may be put in a position to manage from a firm Parent position. Employees may expect strong direction. Just as good parents are those that are working themselves out of their jobs, good managers of overly dependent people can assist in motivating personal development.

The firm, fair, accepting, encouraging Parent sometimes helps workers to grow. Managers faced with this problem are more effective if they get strokes out of seeing people develop and move on toward independence.

In contrast, the punitive, arbitrary type of Parent manager may keep workers dependent. This kind of relationship tends to be "locked in." One stays rigidly in the Parent. The other is kept in the Child.

JOB ENRICHMENT IS RELATED TO STROKES

Managers can enrich jobs by increasing the number and quality of positive strokes people get from their work.

Imagine a little boy experiencing an ice cream cone for the first time. He may run it across his forehead, let it drip in his hair, or suck the ice cream from the bottom of the cone while it slides down his fingers and hand. He is enjoying himself and his sensations thoroughly. He is getting his strokes from the activity in which he's engaged.

Now imagine Mother entering the scene. She scolds him for his sloppy behavior and instructs him on the proper way to lick ice cream cones.

The next time little Johnny experiences an ice cream cone, he is likely to look over his shoulder to get his strokes. Rather than getting strokes from the activity he's involved in, he now gets them from outside approval. His expression says, "See how good I'm doing, Mom." His stroke motivations have been adapted from intrinsic to extrinsic.

Job enrichment means increasing the number of intrinsic strokes gained from the work activity. In Ford's studies at AT&T's Treasury Department, [10] he found positive results were gained both for the people and the organization by enriching each person's job as much as possible. It is Ford's premise that, in general, organizations motivate few people to live up to their full capacity. Enriching the job helps tap people's unique capacities. Motivations for work were discovered to be the actual achievements of the individual employee, the recognition the employee got for these achievements, the increased responsibility because of the quality of performance, the opportunities given to grow in both knowledge and capabilities at performing the tasks, and the opportunities for advancement.

For example, one of the tasks changed was dropping the verification of correspondence sent out by a group of women employees. The usual procedure had been that each piece of correspondence had to be OK'd by a supervisor or a verifier before it could be sent out. In the new setting, correspondents signed their own names to letters and were held responsible for these letters, instead of having the responsibility shifted to a supervisor. In TA terms, this was giving the employee Adult responsibility rather than forcing the employee to seek Parental approval of her correspondence. The Adult ego state of employees was stroked. In addition to this particular aspect, the correspondents were also encouraged to become more personal in the way they wrote their letters. They were to avoid a form-letter approach. Here again, rather than following the previous corporate Parent policies, correspondents were encouraged to interject their own personalities into their letters.

Job improvement assumes that the job probably does not have to be done as it is done now and that it can be made more challenging. Some ideas for consideration in the vertical loading of jobs are shown in the listing that follows.

Method of Loading	*Motivator Involved*
Removing some controls without removing accountability.	*Responsibility and personal achievement.*
Increasing the accountability of individuals for their own work.	*Responsibility and recognition.*
Giving a person a whole natural unit of work (module, exchange, district, division, area, and so on).	*Responsibility, achievement, and recognition.*
Job freedom; that is, giving additional authority to do or decide.	*Responsibility, achievement, and recognition.*
Making periodic reports directly available to the worker himself rather than to the supervisor.	*Internal recognition.*

Introducing new and more difficult tasks not previously handled.	*Growth and learning.*
Assigning specific or specialized tasks to individuals, helping them to become experts.	*Responsibility, growth, and advancement.* [11]

There are many ways in which a person can increase intrinsic strokes. The following are a few.

- People who are part of setting the goals get more strokes from reaching those goals.
- People who take responsibility for decision making have more strokes invested in the outcome.
- People who perform job tasks that are related to their inborn potentials get more strokes from performing these tasks.
- People who see the results of their own planning get more strokes from these results.
- People involved in creativity get more strokes from what is created.

It appears from these observations that whenever we invest ourselves in any way in a project, that project serves as a source of intrinsic strokes.

Strokes are of differing intensities. Rituals and pastimes offer us superficial, survival strokes that are soon forgotten. Games offer powerful strokes that may be remembered and felt for a long time. If the activities of work can be enriched so that the resulting positive strokes are potent and long remembered, there will be less need to play games. Nervous systems are kept healthy and vital through the pleasure and challenge of more meaningful productivity. What secretary can help but feel good if a carefully composed letter solves a problem? What scientist can forget the moment of discovery?

Managers can improve their *own* capacity to understand the kinds of strokes that employees need to enrich their job experience. In addition, managers can learn how to be more effective in giving themselves more positive strokes. For example, time managing can often be an unrewarding chore, but it doesn't necessarily have to be. What kind of strokes do you glean from your time-managing process? Dru Scott, who has been one of the leaders in the field of relating transactional analysis to time management, has contributed the next section of this chapter.

TA HELPS PEOPLE MANAGE THEIR TIME

by Dru Scott*

But Time Management Feels Rotten!

This complaint diagnoses what is wrong with traditional books and seminars on personal time management. Here is just one example of how this problem shows up. As a trainer, I frequently talk with managers and employees about their personal time management problems. Comments like the following constantly come up.

> "How can I ever get anything done?"
> "I'm busy all the time!"
> "Is there something that will help?"

I frequently answer something like this:

> "Do you know the value of a daily 'must do' list? It's a list of four or five vital projects you're determined to finish that day. The list helps you focus on the key projects that are most important, rather than diffusing all your energy on things that may not be as important."

And I may receive an answer like this:

> "Yes, I know daily planning can work. And I have made lists. I know I should plan every day. After all, a stitch in time saves nine. But most days I just don't feel like it. So I stopped."

And here we have Adult data and Parent messages taking a back seat to Child feelings.

A systematic method of planning time is fine. A list of proven techniques is helpful. Internal messages about "not wasting time" and "getting things done" help. But if an individual is to use time management techniques effectively in the long term, there must be something in it for the Child. Something for the Child may consist of using a shiny, gadgety dictating machine; taking off tight shoes and working with toes rubbing the carpet; or sucking on some hard candy while deep in thought. Something for the Child may be the way someone scratches off a completed item from the "must do" list. Scratching through the item once is Adult, but scratching through the finished chore the second, third, and fourth time with a wide, red felt tip marker is likely to be for the Child.

---

*   See Dru Scott's biography at the beginning of Chapter 8.

Just What is Time Management?

Managing time means investing your time to get what you decide you want out of life, including what you want out of work. This definition implies goal-oriented action. It assumes that you know where you want to go in life. This concept of managing time also assumes that you have clearly focused values about your work, your family, your social activities, your possessions, and, most of all, yourself and other people.

Why Does the Problem of Time Management Persist?

The two general reasons I found why people spend their time ineffectively are

1. a lack of information and
2. a lack of motivation.

People may lack information on the importance of setting goals, having clearly focused values based on current reality, concentrating on one thing at a time, and finishing completely. They may not know how to save time by using dictating machines, daily planners, advance agenda for meetings, or delegation techniques. These people don't manage time because they don't have the facts.

But there are still many other people who can recite the facts without any hesitation and yet do not manage their time. Many of these people frequently and loudly say how much they wish they could manage their time better. They don't manage their time because they lack motivation.

Although the symptoms are the same, the diseases are quite different. Lack of information can be cured with a healthy dosage of principles and techniques. Reading a book on time management techniques may be all the person needs. Or attending a seminar on personal effectiveness may cure the problem.

Lack of motivation, though, requires a far different cure. Reading a book or attending a training seminar on time management will not solve the problem. In fact, a person with this trouble may comment after reading a book on time management,

"Oh, I knew those techniques all along."

The problem is much deeper than a lack of information. If the information is not consistent with the person's psychological position, script, and games, it won't even be heard. The response to an attempt to "help" someone else manage his time may frequently be a game of *Yes, But, Harried,* or *If It Weren't For. . .*

"Study some time management techniques! Why, I don't even have time to take a vacation." And "Those techniques are okay for people who don't have a lot to do. Our department is just too rushed for any of those fancy ideas on planning."

"Managing my time?" "Why, I could manage my time if it weren't for this organization. They keep changing priorities. And the people around here! No one can get anything done with them."

And so these games keep a person from managing his time well. The games make sure he does not truly hear the information that could solve the problem.

Powerful internal messages from the Parent and Child block out Adult time management information.

TA Can Make Time Management Feel Better

It can help people understand why they're having time management problems, why these problems persist, and why not managing time makes sense to some people. TA not only gives the "why" for the problem, but it gives a practical "how." The how is more than a list of techniques.

Incorporating TA in the treatment can make sure the person who has the information but lacks motivation can build in rewards to keep him managing time the next day and the next and the next.

Get Your Parent and Child on Your Time-Management Team

Usually the Adult is already an active team member. The problem is getting the Parent and Child to be fully functioning team members. Just as in any team project, getting the most from your time depends on all team members working toward a mutual goal, all team members getting what they need from the work, and all team members contributing what they do best.

How are you taking care of your team? As an experiment, think through this example. You have five items on a list of daily goals. It's now 2:30 in the afternoon and you've finished three of the items. You have just looked down at your list. What thought goes through your mind? Is it any of these?

"If you hadn't gone to lunch, you'd be through with all five things."
"You should have everything done by now."
"Oh, I'll never be able to get everything done."

Or, is your comment likely to be something like this?

"I'm glad I've got all three of those projects done."
"Wow, is it good to get those things out of the way!"

You can choose to give yourself a carrot or a stick, a positive stroke or a negative stroke, a warm furry or a cold prickly. Your Adult can decide which stroke for your Child will get your Child on your production team.

The chances of continuing to get the job done is much greater if there is a reward built into the process. If your Child feels its going to get a stick after you accomplish a goal, you're going to have resistance on your time management team. If your Child feels there is going to be a carrot after you accomplish your goal, the team will run much more smoothly. Adult effectiveness can be crippled by Parent or Child disruptions.

It's useful to figure out what messages may be going on between your Parent and Child that may be bringing team progress to a grinding halt.

Here are some Child reactions that may be causing problems.

"If I just look helpless long enough, someone will come and take care of me."

"Since I'm always getting hurt around here, I'll just hide."

"Push! Push! Push! No matter how much work we do, we never have enough time for fun around here."

"Always it's you can have fun only after you get all the chores done."

Polite procrastination with "In a minute, Mother."

Some Parent messages encourage overplanning and overcaution.

"Don't swim in unknown waters."

"Don't make any mistakes."

"Always do it the right way."

A person who learns messages like these won't venture into a new job until every possible contingency is accounted for. This person may spend so long planning just *the perfect way* to finish a job that he doesn't have enough time left to do the job.

Other messages may discourage people from doing any planning.

"All things come to those who wait."

"Good things are always unexpected."

"Take care of today and let tomorrow take care of itself."

The following Parent messages can discourage good time management by overstressing motion and activity.

"Don't waste any time."

"Don't just sit there, do something."

"Idle hands are the devil's workshop."

"Always work hard."

Most messages that people learn about time emphasize efficiency rather than effectiveness. Peter Drucker defines efficiency as getting anything done right. He defines effectiveness as getting the right things done. Effectiveness means being efficient on the high-payoff parts of the job. There are plenty of instructions on *how to do things* and *how to get there*, but few on *where to go*. It's like telling someone to go to an airline ticket counter and say, "I need to buy a ticket in a hurry," without knowing what city he wants to land in.

While a stitch in time may save nine, obviously if the stitch is in the wrong place, it's not going to contribute to an effective use of time. The supervisor who spends time trying to be prepared for every situation may have his time completely filled. And yet he may not be prepared to meet the few situations that are of vital importance.

You may want to check out the messages you learned. Do they encourage only efficiency and not effectiveness? Do they encourage being overly cautious or not planning at all? And how do the decisions your Child has made affect the way you manage time today?

A Dirty Four-Letter Word is Contaminating Time

The four-letter word that is doing more to corrupt American industry than any other word in the English language is B-U-S-Y. Strokes for looking busy and not necessarily getting the right things done are so easy to get that some people have made a career of only looking busy. Such a person creates a great deal of activity and movement around his desk. Papers never seem to settle on the desk. His greatest delight is when someone says, "My, you look busy!" Or he may tell other people, "Oh my, I've been so busy." In spite of all this busyness no work goes into the outbasket. He's too busy looking busy to get the job done.

On the other hand, the person who produces but does not look busy may end up getting more work to do. For example, when a rush assignment comes into the office, here's what might happen: "Well, we can't give the assignment to Bill, he's already so busy. Let's give it to Paul. He doesn't look as if he had much work to do." Or, "Let's give this assignment to Sally. Her desk looks cleared off." The person who produces but doesn't look busy may end up getting an unfair share of the work. (This continues until the person learns to look busy or finds another job.)

What You Stroke is What You Get

People produce what they get strokes for. It may be for getting the job done or for only looking busy. People need strokes to survive. In the era of large and often impersonal organizations, the need for strokes is more acute than ever before. Although positive strokes are the most desirable, negative strokes are better than none at all. The field representative who always turns in his reports on time may not receive any strokes. He is just doing the job everyone expects him to do. But what about the field representative who turns his reports in one day late every time? He gets strokes. Granted they are negative ones, but negative strokes are better than no strokes at all.

In your organization, what and who gets the strokes and how are the strokes given?

Many times strokes are given for action contrary to the organization's stated objectives. The strokes may actually be given for not meeting the objective or for doing something completely opposite. Or the strokes may be given for accomplishing the objectives of the organization. In looking at these situations, see if the behavior that is stroked conflicts with the objectives of the organization.

Who gets the most strokes?

- The supervisor who rushes in and solves each subordinate's crisis again and again?

    Or the supervisor who trains subordinates to avoid crises?

- The noncommission salesman who stays in the office most of the time rather than being out calling on customers? He keeps up on all the news and the latest activities in the office. He's in the office when there are interesting people to take out to lunch, and when there are rush, prestige assignments to take care of.

    Or the noncommission salesman who is out of the office and on the road selling?

- The bookkeeper who complains loudly and often about the work load?

    Or the bookkeeper who works steadily without complaining?

- The stenographer who looks "busy" but transcribes few letters?

    Or the stenographer that types a number of reports and still "looks unrushed"?

- The staff specialist who makes few decisions of any kind, even the decisions that need to be made?

    Or the staff specialist who makes the needed decisions and sometimes makes a wrong decision?

- The shipping clerk who can explain in great detail why a problem isn't solved?

    Or the shipping clerk who solves the problem and says nothing?

In each of these cases, it's most common for the person who is doing things contrary to the organization's long-term goals to get the most strokes. No matter how much time is spent telling people, "You should plan well," time will be poorly invested if strokes are not delivered for planning well.

The organization that pays its fire-fighting-crisis-stopper more strokes than it pays its skillful planners will get more fires. The same organization may protest loudly and frequently, "Why don't people plan better?" The answer is simple. The stroke salary is higher for fire-fighters than for planners.

The long-term, effective use of time depends on using all three ego states. There must be something in the time management program for each part of a person's personality. The technique must not only make sense, but it must feel good. If it doesn't feel good, there must be a reward coming quickly after a small goal accomplishment.

People work to get strokes. If there are more strokes, either positive or negative, for *not* getting the job done than there are for getting the job done, there will be less work completed. If the people who stomp out emergency fires get more strokes than the effective planners who avoid constant crises, you can expect more fires.

Just one way in which TA helps people manage their time is showing them that "what you stroke is what you get."

SUMMARY

The rapid acceleration of change has provoked many people in management to examine and alter their management styles in order to become more effective in today's organization. Transactional analysis can give a framework both for the examination process and for pointing the way to effective changes.

New generations of people are no longer able to look around their neighborhood and see what kind of "work" there is to do. Discovering, selecting, and preparing for work in today's organizations has become an increasingly complex problem.

It is important for today's people to strengthen their Adults in order to survive emotionally and maintain a necessary adaptability and spontaneity. It is just as important for organizations to increase their Adult to Adult transactions, as horizontal methods of management grow.

New management styles emerge as more and more employees become educated and willing to accept a share of corporate responsibility. There is no one set managerial style that serves as a perfect model for every possible manager. People can manage effectively using divergent managerial approaches. Some will manage effectively through competence in their field; others, through a personal integrity. Still others will be respected as people of authority because of their reachable, open personalities. Managing from a position of status is perhaps the most archaic method. However, there are still prospective employees who are undereducated, dependent, and ill prepared for the job market. In such cases a Parental approach that often goes with managing from position may still be used effectively. This will be especially true if the approach is firm, nurturing, caring, and supportive rather than punitive, and if the aim is to develop autonomy in the employee.

Many people are confronted with a boredom that repetitious, monotonous jobs engulf them in. Jobs can be enriched by rotating tasks and by using flexible time scheduling, but most importantly by adding new responsibilities. One of the most effective ways to enrich a person's job is to raise the intrinsic positive stroke level. Such a move helps a person get strokes from the activity of doing the job itself. The Adult ego state is endorsed. The Parent may be pleased and the Child feels good.

Intrinsic strokes spark self-motivation. These strokes increase as people are more participative and take more personal responsibility in the work setting. Intrinsic strokes will always be more intense if the individual is doing something that is truly plugged in to his or her own unique potential.

People can also learn to manage their time so that all ego states are pleased. If only the Adult is in on the planning, the good feelings of the Child may be left out and motivation lags.

By fostering healthy patterns of stroking in a work environment which are both positive and intense, everybody wins. Such a work climate allows people to be and become much more of their possible selves — winners.

FOOTNOTES AND REFERENCES

1. Robert Ford, *Motivation Through the Work Itself* (New York: American Management Association, 1969), p. 26. Reprinted by permission.

2. Abraham Maslow, *Motivation and Personality* (New York: Harper & Row, 1954).

3. cf. Clare W. Graves, "Theory of Levels of Human Existence and Suggested Managerial Systems for Each Level" (Management Center, University of Virginia, 1971).

4. *Oakland Tribune*, Oakland, California, 13 February 1970, p. 10.

5. Dorothy Jongeward, "What Do You Do When Your Script Runs Out?" *Transactional Analysis Journal*, 2:(April 1972):2.

6. Alvin Toffler, *Future Shock* (New York: Random House, 1970).

7. Douglas McGregor, *The Professional Manager* (New York: McGraw-Hill, 1967), pp. 29, 30.

8. Earl Nightingale, *Publication No. 2803 – Freedom Works Wonders* (Chicago: Nightingale-Conant Corp., November, 1972). Reprinted by permission.

9. William Oncken, "The Authority to Manage", Circular No. 36 (California Institute of Technology, Industrial Relations Center Pasadena, 1970).

10. Ford, *op. cit.*, p. 26.

11. *Ibid,*, p. 29.

5

TA CAN IMPROVE INTERPERSONAL EFFECTIVENESS (Bank of America Study)

Motivation is an emotional force. Moreover,
the evidence grows that intellectual
creativity (as well as artistic creativity)
is a process involving emotional factors.
Clearly, management does not desire to
eliminate these characteristics of human
nature from its own or its employees'
behavior. In fact, if a human being existed
who was completely unemotional, objective,
and logical, he would by definition have no
interest in the success of any organization
He would not be motivated.

The real desire of the manager is that human
beings (particularly those with whom he must
interact) should express certain emotions and
suppress others. He would like to eliminate
such emotional characteristics as antagonism,
hostility, resistance, defiance, uncooperative
attitudes, and unrealistic points of view. He
would like to eliminate emotional forces that
are associated in his mind with bad, selfish,
immature, and unreasonable behavior. [1]

TA offers people a way to sort out "where they're coming from" and make decisions about which behaviors to suppress and which behaviors to express more fully.

TA IN INTERPERSONAL RELATIONS AND COMMUNICATION

The four-session model discussed here is similar to the model that I have been using at the Bank of America World Headquarters in San Francisco since 1969. If you are not interested in an interpersonal relations model, you may wish to skip to page 109. Each session meets from 9:00 A.M. to 4:00 P.M. If at all possible, we space the four sessions a week apart so that participants (there are usually 15 to 30) can integrate, practice, and read between sessions. I have found this a most effective learning design.

The goal of these sessions is to make participants more aware of the function of personality in communications and to give participants a tool for improving interpersonal relationships. Awareness gives them new options in behaviors.

The method is transactional analysis. The text used is *Born To Win: Transactional Analysis With Gestalt Experiments*, which is sent to the participants three weeks before the first session. Other materials are a small notebook, large paper for note taking, pencil, copies of printouts entitled: "Ego State Reaction Quiz" [2], "Exercise in Psychological Positions" [3], "Win-A-Thing Memo" [4], "Games People Play Sheet" (Appendix C), projector, the film *Second Chance* [5], chalk board, and chalk.

Day One, A.M.

At the first session, write on the board a list of those subjects which will be covered during the four days. Put this outline where it can stay for most of the day.

> Script
> Psychological positions
> Psychological hungers
> > Strokes
> > Time structuring
> Structural analysis
> Transactional analysis
> Games people play in organizations

At the beginning of the first session, a short discussion of the goals of the course is held, plus an introduction to the method. Explain briefly that transactional analysis is concerned with analyzing the scripts that people and organizations may live by, the structure of personality, the transactions that occur between people, and the games people play.

The emphasis in this kind of class is on transactional analysis as a communications tool. Its purpose in this setting is to give people insight and awareness that will increase their effectiveness in their relationships with other people. The focus is on awareness and options.

It is sometimes useful to discuss with the participants how they thought and felt when they first came into the room. Participants will often experience an anxiety or an excitement or a fear that is related to early childhood experiences. This begins to make the Child ego state real. In the same way, each participant may have a unique expectation from the leader. Some have experienced at least a moment's Parent-Child relationship between me and themselves. This is useful to deal with, since we can begin to relate the theory of transactional analysis to their present feelings and behaviors.

Participants are given permission to get drinks, take walks down the hall, take a stretch break, etc. There are also structured break times. However, it is useful to give people permission to take care of their own needs in a learning situation. It is stressed that misery is optional.

Participants are instructed that the small notebook is a "thinking and feeling diary" for ideas or flashbacks of feelings that occur to them during the course. I find that it is important for many to have something separate in which to record such experiences. Some people are reluctant to write personal comments in their class notes. In addition, an old memory triggered in a participant may divert that person's attention from what is going on in the learning situation. By writing down a word or phrase, the experience is not lost. The participant is able to come back to the experience at a more appropriate time. At the end of the course, I ask the participants to glance over their thinking and feeling diary. Often the fragments begin to fit together and many people gain useful information about themselves.

The first concept that I deal with is *script*. We define script, seek examples of script from everyday life, particularly in organizations, and use exercises from *Winning With People: Group Experiments in Transactional Analysis* and the Instructor's Manual of *Born to Win*. In brief, we base the script concept on messages received around specific subjects. For example, I write a list on the board such as:

Education	Appearance
Work	Femininity
Religion	Worth as a person
Masculinity	Intelligence

Participants work in groups discussing messages received around these subjects. Do the messages in any way affect behavior now? Following this, I raise these questions. Did anyone ever tell you where you are going to end up? Did anyone ever tell you who you were going to be like? If you keep doing what you are doing now, where will you end up? [6] We allow time for thought and discussion.

Out of this brief discussion of script, participants begin to relate the interaction they had with significant authority figures to the dramatic program in their own life script. They are not expected to do a thorough self-analysis. They simply begin to relate script theory to themselves.

The next concept is *psychological positions*. After discussing the four basic life positions, we do an exercise on positions, which appears in *Winning With People* (Exercise 4, page 12). The emphasis, however, is placed on managing people. For example, if an individual manages someone else from the I'm OK and You're not-OK position, how might that person act on terms of (1) trusting self, trusting others, (2) handling conflict, (3) kind of strokes given to other people, and, (4) kind of strokes received from other people.

This exercise generally takes about 45 minutes with participants working in small groups taking each position in turn and relating it to specific behavioral traits. If time is short, it is useful to give the group the first two columns of the exercise and then discuss briefly as a total group the possibilities for the next two columns. It is important, however, to conclude with a comparison of behaviors from the I'm OK – You're OK position. From these discussions many recognize some of their own traits.

Integrated with the discussion on psychological positions is the concept of strokes. After briefly discussing the importance of strokes for survival and for a sense of well-being, the film *Second Chance* is shown. This film is clinical in its approach. However, I have found that it helps participants understand the reality of the necessity of strokes for survival. Many people in business and government have had little information on human development. Immediately following the film, the participants discuss the relationship of strokes to the work environment: positive strokes and enriched environment, strokes as motivation, negative strokes and personnel problems.

Since psychological trading stamps are related to the kind of stroke that an individual learns to get and to give, trading stamps are brought in at this time.* A chart may be developed on the board from the point of view of positions. For example, if the person operates from the I'm not-OK – You're OK position, what kinds of strokes may that person go after? What kinds of feelings does that person collect and give out? Of the roles of Victim, Rescuer, and Persecuter, which is the predominant role acted out? The chart may come out looking something like this:

Position	Feelings	Stamps	Role	Games
I'm not-OK- You're OK	Inadequacy Stupidity Depression Inferiority	Grey Blue	Victim, yet persecute others with martyrdom	*Poor Me* *Why Does This* *Always Happen To* *Me* *See How Hard I Try* *Ain't It Awful About* *Me*

---

*   I prefer to use the term gray stamps rather than brown stamps for negative feelings since all that is brown is not feces. Such a relationship is an affront to many people of color. People who know color are familiar with the reality that when primary colors are mixed, gray is the result. It is likely that a person who has not sorted out his or her reality learns to feel gray.

The classical roles of Victim, Rescuer, and Persecuter can be discussed in relationship to life positions. Participants select a work-related situation and role-play to illustrate each of the life positions and the switch that occurs in roles.

Day One, P.M.

The afternoon is devoted to ego states, contamination, and exclusion.

I use the following exercise to help the participants begin to get in touch with their own Parent and Child ego states.

The process is to begin to evaluate the Parent and Child with the Adult.* The purpose is to attempt to increase the probability that (1) negative Parent and Child behaviors will be filtered through the Adult more frequently and rejected, and (2) positive Parent and Child behaviors will be used more often when appropriate. It is a first step toward such awareness. You may wish to try this exercise now. See what you discover. Be aware of your feelings.

Ego State Exercise

Picture in your mind your most significant Parent figure. Try to go back as far as you can in your memory of when you were a child. When you have this imagery firmly in mind, begin the exercise. Allow enough time to work each section completely.

1. List three things you really liked about this person.

How would these traits make a child feel?

---

* It is also important to remember that different cultures and subcultures have unique kinds of programming. For example, people programmed for ancestor worship may have considerable difficulty identifying negative Parent behaviors and negative adaptations. Such differences need consideration from trainers who may be operating from their own cultural sets. A useful approach is to allow the group to give the illustrations and, if appropriate, make some cultural comparisons. This need was very evident to me when working with a group of stewardesses and pursers from all parts of the world.

2. List three things you did not like about this person.

How would these traits make a child feel?

3. Which of the above lists was the most difficult for you to make? (Try to figure out if messages sent by Parent figures influenced the ease or discomfort you experienced while doing this. You may have experienced how your own Parent ego state influences your behavior. For example, a Parent tape like "be grateful for what parents have done for you" may make it difficult to evaluate negative Parent behaviors.)

Did you have any particular feelings while doing this, i.e., guilt, anger, affection?

4. Recall a time in your childhood when you were ill. How did this person treat you?

How would this treatment make a child feel and behave?

5. Recall a time in your childhood when you were naughty or broke a rule. How did this person treat you?

How would this treatment make a child feel and behave?

6. Describe the essence of this person in three adjectives.

How would the person you described affect a child?

7. List two or three messages — either verbal or nonverbal — this person sent you.

What might a child do in response to these messages?

8. Now ask yourself, Would any of these things fit me? Would anyone describe me in these terms?

Now ask yourself, Do any of these feelings describe me as a child?

Do I ever feel this way now?

If so, in what circumstances?

Do I ever behave this way now?

If so, in what circumstances?

9. Now look at the messages
   that were sent you (7).
   How would these messages
   affect the way you manage
   other people for better
   or for worse? (If
   appropriate, discuss the
   effect of these messages
   in a group.)

How might these feelings and
behaviors effect how you feel
and behave on the job today?
(If appropriate, discuss
these in a group.)

If you followed through on the above exercise, you know what
might be experienced by participants in a TA training session. Knowing
oneself a bit better is a key to improving communication patterns. What
are you like when you deal with other workers from your Parent ego
state? What are you like when you deal with other workers from your
Child ego state?

After this exercise is completed, we discuss the possibility that it is
the Adult ego state in the participant that is gathering information and
beginning to evaluate the Parent and the Child. Also, the importance of
all ego states is discussed and defined in specific behaviors within the
organization.

After the participants are able to identify their own ego states, it is
fun to conduct a PAC meeting. These role-playing meetings often
reflect the kinds of ego state transactions which happen at actual
business meetings.

To start the meeting, I usually role-play the person that has called
the meeting to order and lay out a problem. For example: "Our
department seems to be suffering from a problem of low morale. We
have a high turnover rate. Several complaints have been filed with the

department head. People come in late, and some leave early without explanation. Our time invested in counseling sessions has increased. It appears that something needs to be done toward solving this problem." (The same problem can be used to role-play *Yes, But* as illustrated in Chapter 2.)

The class is grouped and each group of participants can react from only one ego state. At this time I pass out cards which assign an ego state to each particular table. Our agreement is that each group replies from only one ego state: Parent ego state-sounding responses or Child ego state-sounding responses or Adult ego state-sounding responses. Note: The method of ego state grouping depends on the number of participants and on the room arrangement. For example, it is often useful in a large group to have participants working together in smaller groups (five or six persons) around tables. If this is the case, it is usually easier simply to assign each table with one specific ego state.

The participants have a few minutes to discuss with one another what might be typical responses to the problem presented from their assigned ego state. The meeting is then called to order. The chair person lays out the problem. The group begins to function, tackling the problem from the assigned ego states. This exercise is usually fun. Inevitably, someone coming on Child says "Let's forget this and have a party!" (Compare this to a similar exercise in Kathy O'Brien's article in Part II.)

An alternative exercise to the PAC meeting is to divide the group into small groups of three or four persons. Have each group design a typical problem in supervision. After each group has defined a specific problem, the groups role-play with one another, "solving" this problem from each ego state. For example, if only the Parent ego state is engaged, how would the conversation sound in relation to this particular supervisory problem? How would the Adult ego state sound? How would the Child ego state sound? If time allows, have the group role-play the situation in which the responder comes on with the Adult in charge, but uses appropriate reactions from all ego states.

The phenomena of *exclusion* is discussed in the context of Constant Parent, Constant Adult, and Constant Child. [7] The assumption is that a person operates more frequently from one ego state than the other two. The participants do an exercise in which they work together in small groups dealing with the question, What kinds of occupations would a person who exhibited each of these problems be drawn to? Three lists are drawn up by each group and then shared. They then pursue the positions within their organization that might attract similar people.

The phenomena of *contamination* is defined. An exercise is done in which the participants are asked to make a list of ten adjectives or phrases which complete the following phrase written on the board.

Women are _____ . The participants work in small groups, developing a list of ten adjectives or phrases that might be commonly heard by a small child growing up in our culture. After this exercise, the participants do the same thing completing the sentence: Men are _____ . Again, the only criterion is to select words or phrases that would commonly be heard by little boys and girls in our culture. This exercise is usually fun for men and women working together. They often have a good laugh at some of the stereotypes under which they've been brought up.

After both lists are completed, the participants are asked to take each list and develop an ego state portrait, using various sizes to represent the various ego states which relate to the words in their lists. For example, if they had selected five adjectives such as weak, fragile, emotional, irrational, and dumb, they are likely to draw a portrait with a very large Child. On the other hand, if they had a preponderance of words such as rational, trustworthy, strong, decisive, and leader, they may draw an ego state portrait with a very large Adult and a very small Child and Parent. These portraits can help the participants visualize the effects of contamination on many male-female relationships within organizations.

After this exercise, the group discusses how this particular Parent contamination of the Adult affects organizations and effective management practices.

Homework: For the third or fourth day, participants are to bring in a problem relevant to their work situation — either a piece of writing or a case situation or dialogue in which they were recently involved. Participants are responsible for duplicating copies for the rest of the group.

Day Two

At the beginning of the second session, there usually is a feedback time in which the participants share and relate situations that illustrate their new insights into behavior. This is a valuable part of the class because it enhances the internalization of the concepts. It is not uncommon for participants who live in a family relationship to relate this information first to their family situation.

Internal dialogue is discussed and also its effect on performance. Participants are made aware of possible inner conflicts that may interfere with their own performance. We sometimes have a Gestalt illustration of inner conflict, using the empty-chair technique, to develop a dialogue between the Parent and Child.*

Participants do an exercise to reinforce the concept of stamp collecting. This exercise is fully explained in *Winning With People*,

---

* This should not be attempted without training in Gestalt techniques.

pages 66-71. However, basically, participants role-play a typical situation in which feelings may be associated, a situation such as going over a person's performance report, a supervisor telling a stewardess that she is overweight, or discussing tardiness with a clerk.

Two participants select the roles that they're going to act out. Each participant is given a pile of gold stamps and a pile of gray stamps. If either feels that he is *giving* a gold stamp or a gray stamp to the other person, he moves that color forward. If either feels that he is *receiving* a gold stamp, he moves a stamp toward himself.

After one or two stamp role-plays, the people who participated discuss with the group what was happening to them, in terms of feelings, while the exercise was going on. Often members of the group will have questions or will have experienced the situation at a different feeling level from those who acted out the situation. From this exercise the participants can begin to draw parallels in their work situation in which they collect feelings that eventually result in enough resentment for them to "cash in" on themselves or somebody else.

On some occasions, *if it is appropriate to the group*, the Gestalt method of role-playing is discussed and demonstrated. An individual who is collecting negative feelings towards another sits in one chair and faces an empty chair. On the empty chair is projected the person toward whom resentment is held. Participants are taught how to unload feelings and do their exploding toward an empty chair rather than toward another person.

Occasionally a collection of bad feelings is a motivating force for confrontation or a leveling session with another person. If this occurs, it is useful for the participant to learn how to use this unique role-playing method to unload negative feelings. In other words, the person learns to say whatever he or she wants to say toward the empty chair with no censorship. Often this allows the person to deal with the problem at the emotional level first before he or she actually faces the person to be leveled with. As a result, the probability is raised that the individual will be able to level Adult to Adult, without interfering emotions.

Day Three, A.M.

At the beginning of the third day the Ego State Reaction Quiz is passed out. Participants will first work alone, checking out their responses from a new point of view. This is followed by a brief group experience in which they compare, check out, and justify their individual responses to the group of five or six participants. It is now useful to have a midpoint checkout in terms of understanding TA theory, so questions can be discussed that participants may have raised from the previous sessions.

The Win-A-Thing Memo can be used to illustrate the relationship of TA principles to writing. Working in small groups, the participants evaluate the memo, diagnose the ego state problems occurring in the writer and the reader, and then rewrite sections from a point of view that would be more effective. We spend parts of the third and fourth days dealing with the homework brought in and applying TA to other organizational problems.

Depending on group size, each person in turn usually discusses with the group his own particular problem and the way he has been able to relate TA to this problem. The rest of the group gives feedback as to how it sees the situation and perhaps offers further suggestions. Sometimes role-playing is useful.

As an example, one man brought in a letter that was typical of the kind of letter he was writing to his client who lived in another part of the world. He described the situation, "This client is angry with me most of the time." He felt the client was close to asking for another person to supervise the account. The class analyzed the last letter sent out by our participant. The opening sentence in the letter began, "As I told you in my last letter . . ." On the first page were 12 "shoulds." It did not take the class long to decide that this person was coming on far too Parent in his written transactions with this client.

Another participant turned in the following analysis of a problem which had bothered him for some time.

> Each morning the Boss would come into work looking very sober and generally out of sorts. He would acknowledge no one as he passed to his own office. One of the women would always make it a point to speak to him (Adult ego state) regardless of his seemingly unfriendly mood. The rest of us wanted to speak to him but felt it was his duty, as our leader, to speak first (Child ego state) or at least come to work in a friendlier mood.

> He would go into his office and read the newspaper for 20 or 30 minutes, then come out and approach the desk of the assistant. They would exchange greetings and other pleasantries (Adult ego states).

> This ritual always upset me because he seemed to go out of his way to ignore some of us (discounting). I didn't realize that the Boss was collecting stamps until time for my performance review. At that review I received a very high overall rating (Adult ego state). Then the Boss "cashed in" by criticizing me as being very unfriendly toward him and my co-workers (Parent ego state). When I asked what he meant (Adult ego state), he informed me that I usually did not speak to him in the mornings and on one occasion had declined to have lunch with one of the other officers (Parent ego state). (This latter was a personal matter which should not have

come to his attention.) When I attempted to defend my position (Child ego state), I was quickly put down (Parent ego state).

I left the session with mixed emotions. However, each morning thereafter I made a special effort to greet the boss. In so doing, and to my surprise, it invariably changed his mood and made for a better day for all of us. What a relief!

This is an interesting part of the class since each person often contributes something unique.

Next is introduced the concept of listening with the Adult. Contrasts are drawn among listening from the Parent or the Adult or the Child. Emphasis is placed on listening from the Adult to the Child in the other person. This kind of listening transaction is most useful if a worker is exhibiting unusual behavior or if someone seems unduly emotional, angry, or upset. The basic assumption is made that the Adult in the listener is listening to the Child in the sender in this particular feedback transaction. [8] Ground rules are laid, such as don't interrupt, don't add new information, don't take the subject off in another direction, don't rehearse in your own head, don't interrogate, don't teach, and don't give advice. The task of the listener is simply to reflect back to the sender what the listener is observing and how the listener calculates what the sender is feeling. The group then decides on one or two situations in which this transaction would be appropriate. Two participants then role-play the situation, one acting the part of the listener and one acting the part of the sender. The observers interfere if the listener stops listening. Reflective listening is one way to stop games. This use is illustrated in Chapter 3.

Sometimes the feedback transaction gets at a *hidden* cause for agitation or unhappiness in an employee. The individual who is able to listen is often able to get past the *presented* difficulty to the *real* difficulty.

Illustration

A woman who had been a secretary to one person was moved into a pool of secretarial services. She became crabby, lost her cheerfulness, and complained to her supervisor that she really hated working with all those "other women." The supervisor, who was in the transactional analysis workshop, simply listened to this distraught woman. As the secretary continued to express her feelings, she finally said, "Well, that's not what's really bothering me. What's really bothering me is that I don't get any attention anymore. When I worked for one person, my birthday was remembered, I had somebody to talk to, and I felt better. Now the work is left in a pile. Several people leave work, and it really seems like nobody cares."

The supervisor understood that this woman was suffering from a stroke deprivation after having been moved from a high-stroke situation to a work situation that provided very few strokes. This problem was relieved by better understanding. The supervisor requested all people who brought work to the secretarial pool to give feedback to the people who did the work for them. Follow-ups were made on this project until the pattern was established.

Listening simply to know what is going on with another person, and not trying to solve problems immediately or give advice, seems to be one of the most difficult transactions for people to learn. The appropriate time for reflective listening needs to be explored.

Day Three, P.M.

Discuss the six ways of structuring time: withdrawal, rituals, pastimes, games, activities, and intimacy. (This can also be done on Day One, relating the way we structure our time to the script messages we've received or to the organizational script.) Have the participants reflect back on the last staff meeting attended. Analyze it in terms of: What methods of structuring time were used? How effective were these methods? Do any of these methods need to be used more? used less? stopped?

The participants then raise any questions they have about games and how games are played. This is time for a checkout on whether people understand the principles of positions, stamps, the classical roles, and games.

Questions about games are handled and the Games People Play Sheet is distributed to help facilitate the understanding of psychological games. Now is the time to answer questions that participants may have about game theory. Often simple input on particular games is useful, making a clear diagram of one game in particular. The game of *Yes, But* is a good one to diagram because everyone has been involved in it one way or another and participants understand it easily. A brief discussion follows on the adaptation of games to the organizational situation. Different groups and different levels of employment may be prone to playing games in different styles.

At this time participants break into small groups. First they spend time simply chatting about the way they see games being played within their segment of the organization. This sharing of information and insight is very important and needs to be given sufficient time —

approximately 20 minutes. The groups also discuss the games that are encouraged by the organizational script.

Out of this discussion the participants select one or two games that they will eventually role-play. Each group then has about 15 minutes to develop dialogue and arrange the scene in the context of the game they are going to act out. Groups make their own decision as to whether only two people or the entire group will be involved in the role-play demonstration. After the group has had time to select the games, to decide on the parts to be role-played and the scene and the props needed to act out the drama, each group presents its games to the rest of the class. The audience then analyzes which games have been demonstrated. A discussion follows about alternatives to playing the game or ways of breaking up the games. After role-playing games, participants deal with the following questions.

- What are the consequences to you and to your organization if these games are continued?
- What could be done as an alternative to game playing?
- In what more effective ways can time be structured?
- How could negative strokes be exchanged for positive ones?
- What real problem was left unsolved?

Sometimes the role-plays spill over into the fourth day.

Day Four

On the fourth day the participants role-play "straight talk" and practice a leveling procedure.

The outline for the discussion of straight talk is as follows:

1. Be relevant — listen, receive, respond.
2. Be free from ulterior motives.
3. Avoid monologue. Do not rehearse, rehash, detour, play old tapes, etc. in the head while others are sending a message.
4. Be free from discounting. No one is put down, although someone may be confronted.
5. Attempt to preserve the dignity of both people.
6. Use transactions which define self and others as both significant.
7. Confront the problem rather than use passive aggression.

In the leveling process the procedure is outlined as follows:

1. Give the other person "a set" that a serious talk is coming up. This is "making an appointment," but the appointment needs to occur

as soon as possible so that undue anxiety is not experienced by the person being confronted.

2. Level physically. Face the person you're talking to and make eye contact. If possible, remove physical barriers. For example, if sitting behind a desk, simply move a chair to the side of the desk and turn your chair around. If you stand looking down at the person you are supposedly leveling with, or if you are sitting behind a desk that is laden with symbols of authority, this is not leveling. It sets up a basic Parent-Child transaction.

3. Get to the problem. A short chat to pass time may help ease into the situation, but too long a "pass time" is uncomfortable for a person who has been set for a serious talk. If appropriate, send "I" messages rather than "you" messages. For example, "I need to have this problem straightened out between us, so that I don't feel that I'm the one who must come in early each time and set up the training room. I always have the expectation that you and I are going to do this together, and yet it is very rare that I am not the one that comes early and sets things up."

Contrast this with, "You always come in late. You never take any responsibility for seeing that the room is set up in time before the participants arrive." The second message is likely to activate the Defensive Child in the other person, and the probability of solving the problem goes down. The goal is to activate the Adult in the other person by giving him data as to how his behavior is affecting you or the situation. This raises the probability that problem solving can be initiated.

4. The discussion can go in many directions after this, depending on the skill with which responsibility is shifted to the person being leveled with. It is sometimes useful to endorse the intelligence of the other person and verbalize a feeling of basic trust that the problem can be worked out. For example, "This problem has been bothering me and I've been keeping it to myself. I'm sure that if we talk it over, there is something we can do to keep our working relationship a good one." At this point it may also be appropriate to use the listening transaction. Perhaps there has been a misunderstanding or resentment held on the other side. Using a listening transaction would depend completely on the nature of the problem and the direction that the leveling session takes.

5. Don't hit below the belt. It is too easy to throw in all past misbehaviors. This is not relevant to solving the problem that exists at the moment. If hitting below the belt begins to occur and such words are used as "and furthermore" or "and it's not only that,

but last year you . . .," it is likely that the session is a cashing-in one rather than a leveling one.

6. The goal of a leveling session is to confront the problem honestly and to resolve that problem, hopefully in such a manner that *nobody loses*. If a leveling session has gone well, and an answer to the problem is mutually negotiated, both people will end up winners.

7. It is sometimes useful after a leveling session to firm the new contract with a ritualistic body contact, for example, "As I understand how we've agreed to work this out, we will alternate coming in early to set up the training rooms. You've said that this is agreeable to you and seems fair to you. From my point of view, I feel much better about that too." While the new contract is being stated, it is appropriate to shake hands and reaffirm the agreement.

Occasionally a participant takes the time to give feedback. The following letter resulted from the leveling process.

Dear Dorothy:

. . . The jobs of the people who work for me demand unusual technical ability, close attention to detail, and a special insight into logical processes. One of my employees seemed to be quite intelligent and possessed admirable personal traits, but just did not possess the peculiar aptitude necessary for the work. His immediate supervisor shared my perception and had tried to discuss the matter with the employee. Their discussions had not been productive and, in fact, had resulted in the immediate supervisor becoming very upset about the situation.

I had avoided having conversations with the employee myself, principally because I didn't feel I'd be any more successful than the immediate supervisor. Your description of the "leveling" interview gave me new insight, so I decided to give it a try. I began by describing to the employee the problems that I have in comparing the performance of employees working for me, in making appropriate job assignments, and in administering a fair promotion policy.

As I went on, I described the kinds of perceptions and measurements that I use as a manager. After a few minutes of providing background of that kind, I described the particular difficulty that I was having in relating his performance favorably to that of his peers, then asked him how things looked from his viewpoint.

The employee's response rather startled me: he had been going through a similar comparative process and had concluded that he does not possess as strong an aptitude for his job as he perceived in his co-workers. He had even made some inquiries about programs in oceanography, a subject in which he has great interest. At the conclusion of our meeting he mentioned that he was going to pursue his interest in oceanography more actively.

Had I approached the subject differently, I think I would have aroused the same kind of defensive reactions which the employee expressed in his interview with his immediate supervisor. He might well have felt that he had to continue with the organization to defend his self-dignity. I feel that both the organization and the employee gained from the interview as it actually developed.

The employee's performance was not poor enough to warrant his being discharged. Were he to continue his employment, he would continue requiring a great deal of direct supervision with only marginal productivity. The organization can now use his salary to hire someone else with the required aptitude who will be more productive. The employee was assisted in his objective evaluation of his present situation and reached a conclusion which will get him into a more satisfying career in a short time.

I was pleased as a manager for _____ at the favorable outcome of the interview. I was even happier as a human being to feel that I had acted as a catalyst for another human being to make a rational evaluation of a subject which has a great deal of emotional content . . .

Best regards,

T.C.
Assistant Chief Analyst

After role-playing the leveling process, time is spent on discussing organizational scripts in relationship to the person. The group may answer some of the questions related to its department or team that appear in the chapter on organizational scripts.

The session continues with a discussion of the remainder of the "homework" brought in by participants.

In the last hour of class, participants do an exercise in which they give feedback to others and receive feedback from others. This can be done in small groups or by dividing the group, depending on its size. Each person is given a stack of 3×5 cards and assigned a number. Later, these cards are collected by number and given back to the participants.

On the cards participants jot down their impressions of each person. For example, if Helen Smith (who is number 1) were an *animal*, what animal would she be? Five or six other people write their impressions of Helen. Words on the board are:

Animal	Season of the year
Color	Room in a house
Food	Piece of furniture
Part of nature	Country

Many other items can be used. Select about six, or it takes too long. This is usually a fun exercise, yet it most always conveys a message to the persons receiving the feedback. Sometimes it gets to their sweatshirt messages — those invisible messages we send to others through posture, gestures, tone of voice, etc.

As a last exercise, it usually leaves the Child having fun and the Adult with some new input.

Sometimes it is appropriate at the end of a session to check with participants what changes they may have decided to make as a result of having been through this kind of training. This can be done through the use of a commitment sheet. Participants state anonymously what it is they are going to work on. Some groups prefer to talk about it.

Making a commitment fits into management by objectives. A person sets goals for change — making a contract — and makes plans for bringing about the change. Participants can also pair off and arrange with at least one other person in the class to make a future contract. At that time they exchange what is happening in terms of their commitment. Having follow-up adds force to the commitment.

The last 15 minutes are for wrapping up, doing evaluations, and saying the goodbyes.

The validity of the value of such sessions is difficult to establish. Changes in behavior are often difficult to measure objectively. In an attempt to gain some feedback as to the long-term effect on the participants of such a training session, 143 questionnaires (random sample) were sent out to former middle-management participants at the Bank of America World Headquarters. These participants went back as far as 1969. Out of this sample, 68 returned the questionnaire. The following is a resumé of their responses.

BANK OF AMERICA'S INTERPERSONAL RELATIONS
AND COMMUNICATIONS RESEARCH QUESTIONNAIRE RESULTS
(September 2, 1972)

1. Did the course material give you more Adult control in your interpersonal relationships?

   Yes it did   100%

2. Has it helped you to more effectively handle an overly dependent person?

Yes it did	71%
No opportunity	22%
No it did not	3½%
No comment	3½%

3. Has it helped you to more effectively handle an authoritarian, bossy person?

Yes it did	71%
No opportunity	19%
No it did not	6½%
No comment	3½%

4. Has the information been useful to you on the job, at home, or both?

Both	79%
On the job only	10%
At home only	9%
No it did not	2%

5. What was your toughest interpersonal problem before this class. (These responses are ranked in order of frequency of appearance.)

Relationships with others
Difficulty communicating
Feeling I'm not-OK
Playing games
Seeing a problem and solving it
14% made no comment

5.a) Did this course in any way help you to manage this problem better?

Yes it did	86%
No comment	12%
No it did not	2%

6. Please give three brief examples of using transactional analysis successfully at work and/or in your personal life. (These are the ones most frequently mentioned.)

Giving strokes
Understanding others' behavior
Communicating better
Improving interpersonal relationships
Improving confrontations

Handling negative behavior in others
Discontinuing games
Self-awareness
No comment   10%

7. As you recall, how did you rate this course when you took it?

Excellent   79%
Very Good   19%
Satisfactory   2%
Poor   0

THERE ARE PROBLEMS TO WATCH FOR WHEN TEACHING TA

A problem that sometimes occurs in teaching PAC in organizations concerns the Parent. Even though each person has a unique Parent ego state, the Parent is often stereotyped as the critical, oppressive part of the personality which should be avoided. This often needs special understanding. It is true that some Parent behaviors are not worth transmitting. However, most parents transmit useful and nurturing behavior of some kind. Indeed, the human race would be in trouble if Parent behaviors were not transmitted generation to generation. In addition, many Parent behaviors are useful or essential to the work environment.

Illustration

Mr. B managed a department that functioned much like a stock exchange. For two hours after opening, the place was in a frenzy. Phones rang constantly. Much hollering occurred between the people on the phones and the people checking current price changes. The noise level was high, and the pace pushed on relentlessly.

Mr. B seemed to be the perfect manager for this department. His gentle, calm ways soothed other people. He gave warm strokes, including pats on the back as he moved about the room. His attitude was accepting, supportive, and very nurturing — just what people moving fast and furiously, dealing with millions of dollars and making quick decisions that had to be their best, needed. He operated like a caring and concerned Parent.

In a like manner, a stewardess faced with a scared passenger is dealing with the frightened Child in this person. It is likely to be more useful to respond sympathetically, for example, "Now don't worry. You're in good hands. Let me bring you something warm to drink," than with Adult data, "We haven't had an accident in three years; and then only 30 people were killed."

A knowledge of ego states encourages people to examine alternative ways of responding both to themselves and to others. Emphasize the positive uses of all ego states in the organizational setting.

TA TRAINING SESSIONS ARE NOT THERAPY

In many instances people in organizations are "invited" or sent to training sessions. Many are there without having made an Adult decision that they want to change their behavior. *In such a setting, it is inappropriate for the leader to act as a therapist.*

For example, one of the skills every good therapist learns is to make a proper and powerful intervention with a client. Clients who are thumping their hands or kicking their feet or who whine or speak to others in a punitive manner are sending messages that a trained therapist challenges. Such an intervention would be inappropriate in a group setting within an organization *since usually there is no contract between the participants and the leader.* Contracts that are forced are equally inappropriate.

TA is basically a contractual method when used in psychotherapy. If used as a therapy tool, the client makes a contract with the counselor as to what it is the client wants to change. Clients thus assume a responsible role in their own treatment. The contract's function is to define and clarify what the client is after. It eventually serves to let both the client and counselor know clearly when the contract has been met. However, in an organizational setting where there is no contract for personal therapy, many therapy techniques are not appropriate to use.

An example of inappropriate training is forced encounter and self-disclosure. If a person has a contract for treatment, a therapist may provoke encounter and encourage a high level of self-disclosure as part of long-run treatment. This is not appropriate for a weekend from the office.

On some occasions, when encounter or self-disclosure is forced, a person becomes unstrung and the available leadership is unable to reintegrate those painful areas that have been opened up. The process is much like taking a fine clock apart and leaving it that way. Most often there is no long-term treatment provided for those who may need it. If such an approach is used, long term care needs to be provided.

It is my opinion that some attempts at breakthroughs in interpersonal relationships in organizations fail because coercion for change occurs without a genuine commitment from the people who are supposed to change.

TA IS A SUPERIOR INTERPERSONAL RELATIONSHIPS MODEL

TA is usually nonthreatening to participants. Its approach relies on their intelligence to make choices on the basis of new data. People are not forced to encounter each other with gut-level feelings. This is not its purpose.

When using transactional analysis within an organizational setting, the emphasis is on its use as a communications tool, as a method of analyzing organizational scripts, and as a blueprint for change. It is not used to "cure" anyone but to facilitate things for them.* It employs people's intelligence and opens up options to them. And, in addition, its rational approach to people problems seldom fails to capture a workshop participant's interest.

Still another advantage of TA is its *lasting* value in personal and corporate life. It is far more than a temporary "high." Those who choose to use it have a skill which can grow and develop over the years. Lay people who have studied the basic ideas of TA can form groups, share common work experiences, and strengthen their knowledge and application of TA.

For these reasons transactional analysis is a nonthreatening interpersonal-relationships model appropriate for organizations. TA can indeed give people a lasting tool for change.

SUMMARY

Small groups, spaced sessions, and group participation and involvement all contribute to an effective workshop on TA applied to communication skills.

TA provides an excellent model for organizations because it is easy to learn, is nonthreatening to participants, and gives a lasting model for evaluation and change.

TA applied to organizations is neither sensitivity training nor psychotherapy. Only in those instances where participants volunteer and are provided long-term treatment, if necessary, should a therapy approach be used. It is not up to the leader to form contracts for participants.

---

* People who are self- or other-destructive, who are depressed or unhappy enough to have daily functioning interfered with, usually need professional treatment. This is not the function of a TA training session.

Most participants enjoy learning about and applying TA. It's all right for learning and changing to be fun.

FOOTNOTES AND REFERENCES

1. Douglas McGregor, *The Professional Manager* (New York, McGraw-Hill, 1967), p. 23. Reprinted by permission.

2. Dorothy Jongeward and Muriel James, *Winning With People: Group Exercises in Transactional Analysis* (Reading, Massachusetts: Addison-Wesley, 1973), p. 3.

3. *Ibid.*, p. 12.

4. *Ibid.*, p. 37.

5. The film *Second Chance* can be obtained from Association-Sterling Films, 25358 Cypress, Hayward, California.

6. Eric Berne, *What Do You Say After You Say Hello?* (New York: Grove Press, 1972).

7. Muriel James and Dorothy Jongeward, *Born to Win: Transactional Analysis with Gestalt Experiments* (Reading, Massachusetts: Addison-Wesley, 1971), pp. 219, 220.

8. *Ibid.*, p. 49.

6

TA APPLIES TO MANY ASPECTS OF ORGANIZATIONS

*The model of the successful manager in our culture
is a masculine one. The good manager is aggressive,
competitive, firm, just. He is not feminine; he is
not soft or yielding or dependent or intuitive in
the womanly sense. The very expression of emotion
is widely viewed as a feminine weakness that would
interfere with effective business processes. Yet the
fact is that all these emotions are part of the human
nature of men and women alike. Cultural forces
have shaped not their existence but their accepta-
bility; they are repressed, but this does not render
them inactive. They continue to influence attitudes,
opinions, and decisions.* [1]

One of the most difficult script patterns to break within organizations
is the expected role of women. Even within the federal government,
which has been the leader in upward mobility programs for women,
76.9% of women employees are at the very lowest G.S. (General
Schedule of pay scale) levels. Only 1.6% are G.S. 16-18. Two-thirds of
all working women are either heads of households or living with men
who earn less than $7,000.

Even with concerted effort these patterns have been difficult to
change. Not only are the organizational scripts fixed and inflexible, but
also there is the problem of the individual scripts of women. Many
women are scripted towards career failure or at least are not motivated
towards finding their success within organizations.

Research indicates that typical scripts of girls often dictate that
they equate success with loss of femininity. As women, they may feel
guilty if they use their intelligence and tend as a result to belittle their
own successes. [2]

TA FACILITATES EFFECTIVE AFFIRMATIVE ACTION

Under new regulations from the federal government, organizations are
now compelled to examine their organizational scripts which perpet-
uate discrimination against women. The following program takes a day

115

and a half. It is designed for middle management and is open to both men and women. The classes function better if they can be kept small, under 20, so that discussion is free flowing. What follows is only part of a total program for effective Affirmative Action. The outline and comments here are intentionally brief since Dru Scott has detailed a more extensive Career Woman's Seminar in Part II.*

SEMINAR ABOUT CAREER WOMEN

The following announcement on the seminar about career women is sent to participants before they come to class.

Seminar:
: A one-and-a-half day workshop for management concerning the problems of career women in the organization.

  First day: 9 A.M. - 4 P.M.
  Second day: 9 A.M. - 12 Noon

Goals:
: To give management insight and information to help them

  • better understand the psychology and motivations of working women.

  • better understand their own attitudes about women.

  • recognize potential in women employees.

  • develop and improve counseling skills with women.

  • deal more effectively with women.

  • develop a positive role in relation to facilitating working with women.

Methods:
: The framework of transactional analysis is used as a basis for understanding the history and psychology of women. Movies, lectures, and class discussions are the approach.

Participants:
: Limited to 20 participants.

Materials:
: Movie: "51%"

  Text: *American Women: The President's Commission on the Status of Women.* Also, read Chapter II in *Born to Win.*

  Handouts: Prepared by the instructor.

---

* For more information on women's programs, see Dorothy Jongeward and Dru Scott, *Affirmative Action for Women: A Practical Guide*, (Reading, Massachusetts: Addison-Wesley. In press.)

Instructor: Ms. Dorothy Jongeward, Consultant to the Bank of
America since 1968.

Schedule of Seminar

Day One (1)

I. Case study

This case study is used as the class opening.

You're at lunch with George Smith, a colleague from another
department. He is just relating:

"I'll sure hate to lose my secretary. She's such a bright, capable
girl. She hasn't said anything yet, but I know her husband has
just gotten out of the Army, so she'll probably quit. I'll have her
a few months or maybe a year and then she'll quit to stay home
and have a baby. That's the way it always is. And you know,
she's happy in her job and she makes good money for a woman."

Go ahead and respond to George.

A. Participants in small groups discuss how the conversation
might continue.

B. Analysis of attitudes and assumptions

II. How women are scripted

A. Define script.

B. What messages are little girls likely to receive about their

Brains	Appearance
Vocation	Masculine behaviors
Education	Feminine behaviors
Marriage	Life goals

How would these messages affect their performance in
organizations?

III. Typical scripts of women

A. Cinderella (delusion of rescue from work)

B. Sleeping Beauty (script runs out; returns to work)

C. Beauty and the Beast (personal life disrupted; affects
performance)

D. Lady Atlas (chronic complainer; will not change things)

E. (See Appendix D.)

IV. Ego states (define)

(P) A. Which ego states are "stroked" in many women?

(A)

(C) B. What is the Parent programming likely to be about male/female roles?

C. What are the feelings in the Child regarding femininity?

D. What is the influence of the mass media?

V. Contamination exercise. List ten commonly heard adjectives. (See Chapter 5 and Dru Scott's contribution for models.)

(P) Women are _____.

(A)

(C) Men are _____ .

VI. Games women are encouraged to play

A. *If It Weren't For You*

B. *See What You Made Me Do?*

C. *Rapo*

VII. Games the organization plays with women

A. *Corner*

B. *Blemish*

C. *If It Weren't For Their Families*

VIII. View film "51%"

A. Discuss cases in film.

B. Relate to opening case study.

Day Two (1/2 day)

Participants decide which areas they want to discuss and often make suggestions about their own concerns.

I. Examine recruiting practices.

A. Where?

B. Who?

C. Studies: Why do women quit?

II. Interviewing practices

A. Don't ask about family life directly.

B. Avoid use of words "girls," "gals."

C. Don't judge women by own wife.

D. Middle management most complained about.

III. Three types of women

    A. 9 - 5ers (many Cinderellas, some Sleeping Beauties). Most women here.

    B. Professionals: one-slot jobs, i.e. (typical of professional women) executive secretary, systems analyst, teacher, nurse

    C. Career managers. Fewest women here. Also fewest men.

IV. Particular problems of women

    A. Lack of training opportunities

    B. Grievance line

    C. Lack of mentors, models

V. Picking out career women

    A. Review transcript, check out life goals.

    B. Note personality qualities.

    C. Uses all three ego states.

    D. Collect data from women, don't assume.

        1. More Adult-Adult transactions

        2. Fewer Parent-Child transactions

        3. What are the traits looked for in men?

        4. What are the job requirements?

        5. What requirements are legitimately sex based?

        6. What are the educational, experiential requirements?

        7. Which of these are sex based?

        8. Is there any objective reason a woman couldn't hold the job?

        9. Redefining jobs.

VI. Three ways to change

    A. From top down by directive

    B. Setting about change with no directives

    C. Combination

VII. Special problems of black women

VIII. An historical perspective (optional)

The most important function of these sessions is the process of decontamination that often takes place. Consciousness raising always involves decontaminating the Adult ego state so that hopefully the participants' Adults are freed to think more clearly about women's place in the organization.

For example, in our discussion of the Cinderella script, which is one of the most pervasive in organizations, we reveal the delusion that many young women have that causes them to seek low-level positions and then wait for someone to rescue them. The typical Cinderella is likely to do her low-level job well, but not really be satisfied with either her work or her supervisors. She sees her job not as a place to express her own unique possibilities, but simply as a place to mark time until Prince Charming, perhaps in the disguise of a visiting salesman carrying his briefcase, comes along and rescues her from the terrible world of work.

The delusion of rescue can be so strong that even in the face of many facts it goes unexamined. One vice president who was participating in this class went back to his desk at lunch break and spent a few moments talking with his secretary. He discussed with her a few of the things we had been talking about in the seminar about career women. Before he had much time to explain the class content, she looked up at him and said with strong determination, "Well I know that I for one would leave this job tomorrow if I could get married." This woman had served as his secretary for 15 years and was 45 years old. Even though the facts seemed to be against her rescue, she remained in this job still clinging to the delusion.

Cinderellas are likely to be apathetic about upward mobility programs for women. Even though they may complain about having to do "other people's dirty work," they tend not to participate in any activity that would change things. A Cinderella may sit behind her typewriter for 15 years waiting for someone to come along. It may never occur to her that no one is coming. She is likely not to have planned in the first place to have devoted 15 years of her life to the organization. It is also likely that her own scripting towards work was either as something to pass time until a better deal came along or as an "insurance policy" just in case.

The facts are that nine out of ten women will work. Those who marry devote an average of 25 years to paid employment. Those who remain single, 45 years.

Insight into their own attitudes, and insight into typical script patterns for women can often help managers understand why so many women are not motivated to achieve or to fulfill their potential within the structure of the organization. Increased insight also helps management make some decisions about what might be done to motivate

Cinderellas who will likely contribute over 25 years of their lives to the organization. For example, simply asking a Cinderella where she expects to be in the organization within the next five years is one way to motivate her to think about her life goals. More detailed information about the Sleeping Beauty script can be found in Appendix D.

The input on personality development, scripts, and contamination is probably one of the most painless ways for men and women to deal with their attitudes about women in organizations. If top management is supportive of equal opportunities for women, it facilitates the program to give this kind of training to men and women in middle management. The primary goal of these sessions is to encourage the intelligent use of the skills and potentials of women in effective management.

TA IMPROVES CUSTOMER CONTACTS

In addition to its application to organizational development, effective interpersonal relationships, and Affirmative Action, TA is a natural for consumer contact problems. It is a way to figure out what is going on in those most difficult customer situations. Its application can enhance the trust and credibility felt toward an organization which are essential for good customer relations. Let's look at an interview with Susan Sinclair*, Manager, Flight Services Field Training, Pan American World Airways.

INTERVIEW WITH SUSAN SINCLAIR

Q.   Susan, of what value is TA to a large corporation such as Pan Am?

A.   From my experience as a stewardess, Dorothy, I can remember instances when the anxiety and aggressiveness of passengers would in turn bring out rudeness, anger, or even tears from employees. On one of my first flights I remember serving a drink to two people in the economy section of the aircraft when suddenly I received a

---

*   Susan Sinclair is Manager, Flight Services Field Training, Pan American World Airways, Training and Development Center, Miami, Florida. She is responsible for the development of advanced course material for on-line flight service personnel, and she has administrative and budgetary responsibility for training in Houston, London, Miami, and Washington, D.C. Most recent projects: special program for F/S personnel with three or more years' seniority, and a company-wide human relations program involving the theory of transactional analysis.

Susan has held many positions with Pan Am, starting as a stewardess in 1964. She raises and shows standard poodles, enjoys interior decorating, painting, collecting U.S. fractional currency, casting metal jewelry with lost wax method, doing metal sculpture, and designing and making clothes.

resounding swat on the bottom from an older lady seated on the other side of the aisle. When I recovered both my balance and my composure, I turned to discover that all she wanted was a scotch and water. TA can be an effective tool that employees can use to handle themselves in any situation and to provide an awareness of self so they can better deal with others.

Q.   What methods do you use to teach TA?

A.   Two of our major criteria in putting the program together were having as much student participation as possible and making the concepts relevant to both job and home. The program was made up of a combination of lecture, visual aid presentations, and discussion. Our basic technique is to talk about a concept, to show or listen to some sort of audiovisual aid, and then to involve the participants in an activity or discussion that will reinforce what they have learned about the concept. For example, after presenting the concept of ego states, the students are divided into three groups and assigned an ego state: Parent, Adult, or Child. They are then instructed to devise two or three appropriate responses to a specific situation according to their group-assigned ego state. These four pictures are taken from our slides and illustrate typical situations. [3]

One of my favorite examples is derived from the situation in which a passenger says, "I'm not hungry right now. May I eat later?" Responses from the program participants in their assigned ego state will vary widely but each will lend perspective and will help the employee discover more effective ways of responding in any given situation.

Some sample responses from stewardesses to the question have been the following:

Nurturing Parent: That's all right. I'll keep it warm and bring it back later.

Critical Parent: You'll eat now or you won't get any dinner!

Adult: We will be landing in approximately an hour. Perhaps you would prefer a cup of coffee and dessert instead?

Child: What am I going to do with this tray? (whiny tone)

Q.   Are there special problems or concerns which make TA more valuable to an airline than to some other business?

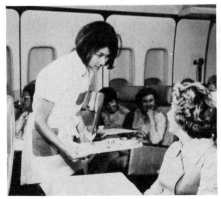

Passenger: I'm not hungry right
now. May I eat later?

Stewardess:

Scheduling Representative: Miss
Redford, I've called to advise
you of a change in your schedule.

Stewardess:

Supervisor 1: (to Associate Supervisor) Those dum-dums you got
working for you fouled up again.

Supervisor 2:

Passenger: Miss, this has been the
worst service I've ever had on a
flight . . . and I fly over . . .

Purser:

A. Definitely. The unnaturalness, if you want to call it that, of man's flying builds in a lot of challenging factors which sometimes make it more difficult for human beings to give warm, gracious service to others. Consider the usual rush and excitement in packing for a journey, a possible traffic jam in getting to the airport, a natural nervousness of the unknown, the fact of millions of other people hurrying to get somewhere on the day you decide to travel, and the personal problems most people cannot leave behind. Each passenger has a different set of needs to be met, and his or her own set of problems. It is an enormous challenge for a stewardess just to keep sight of all that and respond under stress.

Q. What was Pan Am's motivation in exposing its employees to TA?

A. Basically, Dorothy, it was a desire to improve customer service at all levels. There were two goals set for the program initially, one personal and one corporate, but they have now nearly merged into one. The feeling was that if one were happy outside of work, he or she would tend to carry that feeling over to the job. We sought to offer a communications tool that would be helpful at home, at work, or anywhere that one transacts with people.

Q. How was the program set up?

A. A working committee of eight was appointed by the heads of departments most closely in contact with the public: airport services, flight service, marketing, consumer action, and organization development. Of the eight representatives, half had training backgrounds while the other four had current line experience. A steering committee, which performed both a check and a guidance function, was formed from among department heads and a few other interested parties.

The first assignment was to determine if training of any type was needed to assist our employees in the performance of their duties when dealing with the public. Further, because of favorable reports from other businesses using TA, we in the work group were requested to consider whether transactional analysis could prove useful to our personnel.

One of the first steps was to conduct Needs Analysis Surveys to test whether we, in effect, needed to go any further. Random-sample surveys were taken in the airport services, flight service, and marketing departments to find out from the employees what they felt they needed in order to perform their jobs more effectively. Many items that were a problem to one department simply were not a problem in another. However, an extremely high percentage of employees in every department indicated an interest in improving communication techniques and further developing their human relations skills on the job. Interestingly enough, most of the survey results also correlated with Pan Am's 1970 Employee Opinion Survey, Pan Am's Consumer Action Reports, and the C.A.B. (Civil Aeronautics Board) Consumer Report.

Almost simultaneously with the surveys, the work team began learning as much as it could about TA and researching the applicability of TA to a business environment. Throughout the project the working committee set up target dates and checkpoints with the steering committee. When all the facts were in, we presented our findings. Based on the information we had gathered, the steering committee agreed that a knowledge of TA might be a very useful tool on the job and gave its approval for the working committee to develop a TA program.

December and January were established as the months in which we would test our program with a control group before proceeding with any larger group. The first half of December we were to offer phase one, which was to run a full day, and in January we would follow up with another half-day session for the same group of people who had attended phase one.

During the next month and a half the working committee helped the selected consultants in putting the final program together, finishing a week before Thanksgiving. By this time we had named the program "Pan Am Cares" which seemed a natural because of the initials and because of the company's motivation behind the program. In that week before Thanksgiving we held a three-day seminar for the more than twenty potential instructors of the program, and by December 1 we had run our first class.

Q.   Who attended this first program, Susan?

A.   December is a very busy month for us, Dorothy, especially close to the holidays. We felt that by exposing people to TA the first two weeks of the month, just before our busiest period, we would be able to get a more accurate estimate of what the value of a knowledge of TA would be for our employees in stress situations.

Personnel in the airport services, flight service, and marketing departments in New York were chosen for the control group. Passenger service agents who work at Pan Am's terminal building at John F. Kennedy International Airport and their direct supervisors were selected from the airport services department. As our Caribbean flights seem to be the fullest during the Christmas and

New Year holidays, flight service decided to expose whole crews whose schedules took them mainly to the Caribbean area during the month of December. And, finally, the marketing department decided on its Vanderbilt ticket office and the office located at 80 E. 42nd Street in Manhattan. Their classes included ticket counter agents, supervisors, and managers.

Q. How did they say they were able to use it?

A. It's interesting, Dorothy, that the majority in every department said it was able to use it at home first. Several of the men commented that they had been able to use TA very effectively with their children. One of our stewardesses said that over the holidays she had been able to assist in smoothing out some very strong marital differences between her parents. She attributed this ability to some of the things she had learned in December and had talked to her parents about. Quite a few of our married employees brought out that they were using TA at home with their spouses.

On the job the employees' ability to use TA varied from department to department. It seemed to be most effective in the airport services and marketing departments where people worked together on a daily basis and knew each other fairly well. In flight service, on the other hand, crews who were flying together in December had attended, but by January they had bid new schedules and were flying with entirely different people, most of whom knew nothing of TA. In that situation it became more difficult to apply what was learned.

Quite a number of employees, though, said that with their understanding of the ego states and how the ego states can be most effectively used, they thought a lot more about what they said and how they said it. A lot of little things that seemed to go wrong during busy periods on the counter or on the aircraft were not as burdensome as before. Several stated that they had a much deeper appreciation for the customers' and other employees' problems. For example, a stewardess heard a man grumbling about the fact that he could not get a window seat. She responded, "I'm sorry you didn't get one this time, but you can move about the cabin more freely than if you were at the window." Often there are times when the Child ego state can be used quite effectively in handling difficult situations, but good discretion must be exercised in each case. In one instance when it was quite effective, a passenger shouted at the stewardess, "Make me a scotch and soda!" The stewardess replied with a magical gesture, "Okay, Poof, you're a scotch and soda." The man laughed and a tense situation was avoided.

Finally, there were some employees who said that they were able to use little or nothing at all of what they had learned. Most of these people pointed out that they were already aware of the principles, although they did not call them by the same names, and that they were already practicing them.

Q. Are you satisfied with the program?

A. Anytime you are dealing with human behavior, "success" is difficult to measure. However, I personally am quite pleased with the results of the program. That's only one lady's opinion, and, of course, I'm prejudiced. Statistics can be dry, but perhaps they will illustrate how effective the participants felt the program to be.

In airport services, of the 225 who participated in the pilot program, 78% rated the overall program as excellent, 20% as satisfactory, and 2% as unsatisfactory. Almost every participant remarked that he felt he could use the principles he had learned both at work and at home. Based on 145 commentaries, 40% of the flight service participants rated the program as excellent, 48% as satisfactory, 10% as unsatisfactory, and 2% were without comment.

The ninety marketing department students almost all rated the PAC program as excellent. They appreciated the value of the program but, like some members of the flight service department, they expressed a fear that it might become "just another program that would die a natural death."

The PAC program has not died, though. Based on the results of the student commentaries and the recommendations of the members of the work group, the program has continued on a limited basis. All three departments have continued the program for specific groups throughout the company.

As of this moment, it appears too early to tell, with any degree of accuracy, the effects the program has had on our business as a whole. For one thing, too few people, when you consider our total number of employees, have been exposed. However, during the coming months the number of letters of complaint versus commendation should be a strong indicator. With these letters it will be possible to determine with greater accuracy the impact that the program had on those who participated. Up to this point, the trend has been that the number of letters of commendation has continued to rise. It is difficult to prove whether or not this comes as a result of some of our employee's exposure to TA. Other indicators will be the C.A.B. Consumer Report and Pan Am's Consumer Action Reports.

Q. Susan, many organizations have employed human relations methods and programs that have not worked well. Why do you personally think transactional analysis is more helpful in a business environment?

A. One of TA's most attractive features, I feel, is its simplicity. It is an easy and practical approach to communication which helps individuals sort out and categorize things they already know or have suspected. It helps to establish a point of reference for people so that they can act and respond more appropriately in any given situation. Unlike some other programs to which I have been exposed, transactional analysis seems to provide a nonthreatening, positive approach to communications quite useful in transactions between customers and employees and amongst co-workers. So far, Dorothy, it has been the most effective and beneficial human relations tool that I have used either personally or professionally.

I cannot end our interview without giving credit to the other seven people on the working committee, for without their dedication, loyalty, and hard work there never would have been a PAC program. They are: Burt Batson and Bob Flanagan from airport services, John Blackwood from flight service, Gene Mariner and Sylvia Sawyer from marketing, Gail Selton from consumer action, and Ron Miller from organization development.

Thank you, Susan.

The programs mentioned here and in the previous chapter are only a few of the possible applications of TA to organizations. The following sections in this book will open up further possibilities of applying TA to organizational problems. Again I wish to thank those people and organizations that have contributed their programs, time and energy, and ideas and analyses in the use of TA to help solve the people problems in organizations. These programs range from turning losers into winners to changing organizational scripts. They represent only a few of the successful applications of TA to organizations.

FOOTNOTES AND REFERENCES

1. Douglas McGregor, *The Professional Manager* (New York: McGraw-Hill, 1967), p. 23. Reprinted by permission.
2. Natina Horner, "Woman's Will to Fail," *Psychology Today*, 3, No. 6 (November, 1969), 36 ff.
3. Photographs are reprinted by permission of Pan American World Airways.

Part II

TA PROGRAMS APPLIED TO ORGANIZATIONS

7

RED, WHITE, AND BLUE TA
AT 600 MPH

by Lyman K. Randall

*Formerly Corporate Director Training and
Development for American Airlines, Lyman is
currently Director of Flight Service. In this
capacity he has both line and staff responsibility for American's nearly 5,000 stewardesses and stewards. In both his former and
current jobs, he has been responsible for
innovating applications of transactional
analysis to business problems. As an experienced OD practitioner, he has also worked
with Blake's Grid, Likert's System IV, laboratory training, survey-feedback, and job
enrichment. He has published in such business
journals as Harvard Business Review, California
Management Review, Personnel Administration,
ASTD Journal, American Management Association,
and Journal of Applied Behavioral Science. He
also enjoys writing poetry and hopes to pub-
lish a book of his poems.*

INTRODUCTION

Several years ago I was filling my time and earning my living by being
an "OD practitioner." In those days the label applied to anyone who
was doing organization development. One of my biggest frustrations
was trying to describe to someone else what "organization development" was. There were nearly as many definitions as there were
practitioners.

On a brilliantly clear and sunny spring morning in May, 1967, I was
flying between New York and Boston to attend a meeting of OD
practitioners. En route, I puzzled the OD definition riddle in free verse
form.

MUTTERINGS OF AN OD MAN

A doctor?
— perhaps —
Helping older children
Through the pain
Of being born
  again.

A pastor?
— perhaps —
Struggling
Through the quagmire
Of monotonous days
To help myself
  through others
Find our resurrection
  in the discovered
  eternity
  of here and now.

A shaman?
— secretly, perhaps —
Learning to be
A finite god
Finding miracles
  in the shadows
  of ourselves.

A human physicist?
— that seems to fit —
Exploring the possibilities
For splitting the collective atoms
Of the human spirit
  into the damndest
  positive chain reaction
    you and I
      ever dreamed of! [1]

A few months later I again wrestled with the definition ambiguities of organization development and once again in free verse form.

OF COURSE I BELIEVE

Trust you?
Sure I trust you!
(I wonder what he's after now.)

Be open with you?
Of course, I'm open with you!
(I'm as open as I can be with a guy like you.)

Level with you?
You know I level with you!
(I'd like to more, but you can't take it.)

Accept you?
Naturally I accept you — just like you do me.
(And when you learn to accept me, I might accept you more.)

Self-direction?
I've always believed in self-direction!
And someday this company may let us use some.

What's the hang-up?
Not a damn thing!
What could ever hang-up
  Two self-directing,
  Open, trusting,
  Leveling and accepting
  Guys like us? [2]

Although many businessmen responded positively and enthusiastically to the poems, they did not accept them as satisfactory answers to their question: "What is organization development?" So once again I tried to define what I was doing, trying to do, or hoped to do as an OD practitioner — this time in more traditional narrative.

Organization Development is a reorientation of man's thinking and behavior toward his work organizations. It applies the scientific method and its underlying values of open investigation and experimentation to individual and work group behaviors as they are directed toward the solution to work problems. It views both man and change optimistically. It applies a humanistic value system to work behaviors. It assumes people have the capability and motivation to grow through learning how to improve their own work climate, work processes, and their resulting products. It accepts as inevitable the conflicts among the needs of individuals, work groups, and the organization, but advocates openly confronting these conflicts using problem-solving strategies. Its goal is to maximize the use of organization resources in solving work problems through the optional use of human potential. [3]

This definition was more comprehensive, and it seemed to satisfy most businessmen who still cared enough to ask about OD. But it didn't satisfy me. Instead, I was becoming increasingly disenchanted. I was looking for a conceptional system that would more fully and accurately describe what occurred as people in large organizations attempted to accomplish work — a system that both I and Mr. Average Businessman could understand and discuss. I was ripe for my first introduction to transactional analysis.

In the spring of 1969 a small group of us OD practitioners in the New York City area attended a one-day transactional analysis workshop led by two members of our own group, Ms. Billie Alban and Mr. Robert Sanders. At the workshop, one of the participants recommended a book on transactional analysis that he had found in a bookstore one week earlier. He said it appeared much more layman oriented and comprehensive than Eric Berne's book, *Games People Play*, which most of us in attendance had read. The book he was recommending was, *I'm OK — You're OK*, by Dr. Thomas A. Harris. I bought a copy the following day. The workshop participation and my reading of Harris' book were catalytic experiences. I now had the beginnings of some new conceptional tools with which to work through my OD frustrations.

Several months later I was asked to give my reactions to an article entitled "OD — Fad or Fundamental?"[4] My reflections accurately summarized both my frustrations with the state of the art in organization development and the role transactional analysis was beginning to play in my dealing with these frustrations.

> The situation at the ASTD* Miami Conference described by Bob Blake and Jane Mouton is a familiar one: "In one OD division meeting participants pleaded with the moderator for a definition of OD, but the moderator thought it would be unproductive to try to agree to one. Great interest in 'something' with acknowledged experts unable or unwilling to define that 'something' is disturbing." I have experienced this many times myself. It is indeed disturbing.
>
> Sometimes when I am talking with others about OD, I am reminded of the children's story, "The Emperor's New Clothes." Many of us seem too anxious to point to the new "OD clothes" that we are weaving for our organizations so that it becomes difficult to

---

*   American Society of Training and Development

point out the nakedness of our situation. This is closely related to the fadism which Blake and Mouton point out.

I have no disagreement with the broad aims of OD as stated by the authors: helping organizations escape red-tape rigidities, aiding them to set high performance objectives, helping management become more diagnostic, improving conflict resolution skills, releasing untapped reservoirs of energy, changing the culture, etc. These may serve as an ego ideal for the organization in much the same way that Theory Y and the 9,9 management style represents ideals for individuals and groups. But I must add that in my own experience I have not found such aims very functional. Most managers respond in one of two ways: (1) "Of course I believe in these aims. Doesn't everyone?" or (2) "These aims are all very nice, but our organization just doesn't work that way." (The latter reaction is usually the more honest one.) If OD is defined using the aims listed above, it becomes a general goal analogous to love, peace, or democracy which most people will agree is desirable but will stumble on how to achieve it.

OD, as I have used the term and have heard others use it, too easily dichotomizes OD and the management process. Part of this is caused, I believe, by the manner in which we insiders and the outside consultants have sold OD as "something new" which all organizations should use and do. This is reinforced by the educative efforts that are usually a part of an OD effort. OD becomes associated in the minds of managers as something "you go off-site to do." Managers often have expressed concerns to me about whether they were "really doing OD" or were just managing similarly to the way they've managed before.

Most managers I know are results oriented, and they are anxious to see results from the time and energy they invest in activities we have labeled OD. In nearly every case in my own experience, tangible on-the-job results that are unequivocally related to the OD activities are impossible to point to. This leads to the disillusionment of managers, outside consultants and inside OD practitioners. Perhaps the hidden lesson is to learn from the work of Davis, Dunlap, et al., at TRW Systems not to get hung-up on the label "OD." If my recollection is correct, they described their efforts as "career development."

Their focus was to bridge the gap between individual needs and goals and those of the organization. This appears to me to be a more specific and achievable goal than OD.

I am troubled by several things that I sense are occurring in OD:

I am troubled by our almost exclusive reliance on variations of group dynamics, theory and techniques as our treatment tool. Our president, Mr. George Spater, has been quoted recently as saying: "Business is still in the stone age when it comes to applying the behavioral sciences." Although I initially flinched when I read the comment, I must also conclude that he was pointing to the nakedness of the emperor in his new clothes. Dr. Harry Levinson recently commented that OD today is in a position similar to the field of medicine 300 years ago when it used leaches as the single treatment for nearly all ailments. I agree with his observations.

Abraham Maslow once wrote, "When the only tool you have is a hammer, you tend to treat everything like a nail." Although group dynamics is an important force in organizations, in my opinion, it is not the only important force that we must be skilled in coping with. We need to have a theory of *individual* motivation and behavior.

Groups are, after all, comprised of individuals and their behaviors. We need to have a more useful theory of organizational power and of how individuals cope with authority. We need a more useful conception of individual leadership which often gets pushed into the background in group dynamics. The work that Levinson is doing at Harvard is encouraging to me since it focuses on these areas.

I am particularly enthusiastic about the potential which transactional analysis theory has for helping managers understand their own behavior and the behaviors of others with whom they work. Dr. Tom Harris' book, *I'm OK – You're OK*, is a translation of transactional analysis which most managers have found very readable and useful.

I am troubled by the tendency we seem to have for creating diagnostic labels that have strong positive and negative connotations and then, by example and by intent, teach managers to label others (Theory X and Y, 9,9 and 9,1 etc.). Too often labeling becomes another game that works against the stated goals of OD.[5]

With my new enthusiasm for TA, I immediately did two things that summer. I bought several copies of *I'm OK – You're OK* to circulate among members of my staff, and I enrolled in an introductory course in TA scheduled the following August. The reaction of my staff members to Harris' book and to TA was consistently positive and enthusiastic; and my TA course, taught by Drs. David Kupter and Claude Steiner, further kindled my excitement about the possibilities of applying transactional analysis to the problems of business organizations.

A month later I produced a simple set of slides which I used to introduce and discuss TA with members of my own staff as well as other interested corporate staff members. These same slides were also used, beginning several months later, to introduce transactional analysis to company line managers and supervisors attending one-week management seminars. At the end of these seminars participants were asked to identify the most valuable experiences they had had during the week. The transactional analysis session was usually top-rated. My confidence in transactional analysis as a tool that could link the businessman with a conceptual theory that he could effectively use to problem-solve was continuing to grow.

THE TACT PROGRAM

Coincidental to my growing interest in transactional analysis, a problem within the ground customer service employee group began attracting increased attention among the headquarters staff.

Six passenger surveys are conducted each year by the company. Each survey asks the customer to rate many aspects of the service he receives. He is given four choices for each item rated: Excellent, Good, Fair, Poor. These survey results have indicated a declining trend among the "Excellent" ratings received by the ground service employees who have face to face contact with passengers. The survey item which exhibited the downward trend was "courtesy and treatment" received by the passenger. Some form of corrective management action was clearly indicated. But what?

Some staff members suggested a campaign aimed at stressing the "do's and don'ts" of courtesy. Others favored some form of company-wide training program. Another group believed some type of incentive program might be the answer.

At this point I saw an opportunity to apply transactional analysis theory and training to an important and painful company problem. I suggested to two of my Training and Development staff colleagues a TA approach to resolving the problem. Both agreed the ideas were interesting, and one of them, Jim Thorpe, said he'd like to work on the project.

In my initial suggestion, I had used TA concepts to describe the kinds of behavior results we might achieve from a transactional analysis-oriented approach aimed at improving passenger ratings of our customer service. Since the concept of "courtesy" often lends itself to Parent kinds of definitions and strategies, I attempted to define "courtesy" within a TA framework. As work on the program progressed, Jim and I added to these initial objectives until they evolved into the following final form.

Public contact personnel should be able to

1. operate in the Adult and OK Child ego states the maximum amount of time.

2. avoid transacting with customers while using Critical Parent and not-OK Child ego states.

3. recognize, in most cases, with which ego state the customer is transacting, and, where Parent or Child ego states are counter-productive to rendering courteous and efficient service, to enlist the customer's Adult and OK Child.

4. identify crossed transactions which have redirected customer contacts adversely, and to realign conversational lines into healthy and productive communication (I'm OK — You're OK transactions).

5. identify parallel transactions which are unproductive or detrimental to good corporate or individual relationships and to redirect them into healthy Adult-Adult transactions (I'm OK — You're OK transactions). For example, if a passenger begins a transaction from his Critical Parent aimed at the employee's Child, the employee should not make the transaction parallel by responding with her Child.

6. recognize potentially destructive pastimes and games and therefore avoid participating in them even though encouraged to do so by the customer.

7. apply the concept of stroking (recognition) to accepted standards of courtesy so as to enrich good manners with empathy, e.g.,

- use of the customer's name is a particularly effective means of recognition.

- minimizing customer waiting time at ticket counters helps prevent his not-OK Child from being activated by the time he faces the salesman or agent.

8. analyze their own ego states toward building a strong Adult with which to deal effectively and healthily with customers, associates, and supervisors.

Supervisory personnel should be able to

1. meet all objectives cited above for public-contact personnel, and, additionally,

2. apply the concepts of transactional analysis to such responsibilities as customer impact observations, monthly performance reviews, merit-rating discussions, counseling, and coaching.

3. apply the concepts of transactional analysis so as to facilitate healthy and productive communications between himself and his associates, manager, staff personnel, and others with whom he transacts.

We soon reached agreement with key members of the passenger services staff regarding the objectives and the use of TA for the program. But what form would it take?

Over the next several months, Jim gradually shaped the program. He also created its name, TACT, which stood for Transactional Analysis in Customer Treatment. With this title, we could also call it Transactional Analysis in Courtesy and Treatment for anyone who insisted on directly relating our customer service "courtesy ratings" with the program.

In its final form the TACT script consisted of two sections, with each one requiring approximately two hours to complete. The TACT trainer, a line manager or supervisor, was to work with groups of 4 to 8 employees.

The TA content of TACT was to be presented in color slides accompanied by narration and music on a tape. The program opened with a prologue presenting a day in the life of Everyman. The prologue contained no narrative. Participants were to be left alone to infer the dehumanizing aspects of life in a technological society. Contemporary music was also to be used in the sound track to convey the message of alienation and human need.

The remainder of TACT was to utilize slides and tape to present the TA concepts outlined in the objectives. Many work examples were planned to illustrate how the TA concepts apply to customer service jobs. Group discussions were planned to follow the slides and were designed to clarify TA learnings and to apply them to the experiences of individual participants.

Jim, and George Comin, a professional photographer on our staff, now began to produce the audiovisual materials to support the script. As sections of the program were completed in rough form, we immediately tested them on both line and staff employees. And we often went back to the design board because of employees' comments.

We planned to give TACT training to all employees who dealt directly with our customers in ticket offices and at airports, and we knew that the supervisors and managers of these employees also had to participate, if any learning was to be reinforced.

Since this total group to be trained numbered approximately 2,200 employees, we concluded that our limited staff could not act as TACT trainers for the entire program. We therefore elected to train specially picked members of passenger services line management from each of our cities. These individuals would then, in turn, train all appropriate employees and management at their location. In most cases, these line management trainees were selected because of their previous participation in and reaction to the one-week management seminars in which transactional analysis concepts had been used.

Between March and July, 1971, approximately 2,500 ground customer service employees participated in TACT training. A slightly modified version of the original TACT Program was being developed during the spring and summer of 1971 by Bill Werst, another Training and Development staff associate. It was given to approximately 4,000 In-Flight Service employees (stewardesses and stewards) and members of management during August and September. Within seven months, therefore, between 6,000 and 7,000 company employees were trained to apply transactional analysis concepts to work problems.

Naturally, the question in many minds that remained to be answered was: "How do we determine if TACT produces any measurable results?" We decided on three different approaches.

1. We administered a questionnaire based on the TACT objectives to a large sample of participants 60 to 90 days after they completed the program. We also asked this same group to describe incidents in which using TA concepts had helped them work through job-related situations.

2. We implemented an experimental versus control group design involving management members in two pairs of matched cities. In the two experimental cities we administered pre-test Likert and How-Supervise questionnaires followed by TACT training followed by post-test versions of the same questionnaires. In the two control cities we administered the same pre-test and post-test questionnaires but delayed TACT training until the research data had been collected. Our hypothesis was that TACT training would cause improvement on post-test scores in the experimental cities.

3. We carefully watched the "courtesy ratings" given by passengers to both our ground customer service employees and our stewardesses. We were betting that the program would cause these ratings to go up again.

TACT was both a success and a failure. The courtesy ratings did not show any improvement. In fact, they continued their gradual decline in most cases. The controlled experiment with two paired cities did not demonstrate any statistically significant difference in pre- and post-test questionnaire results. The follow-up questionnaire we gave to over 600 TACT participants several months after they had completed the program did, however, yield very positive results. In the employees' eyes TACT had been an overwhelming success. Ninety-six percent reported they frequently or sometimes used TACT in dealing with difficult customer situations. Ninety-nine percent described the TACT Program as either very, or moderately, informative and interesting. (See the appendix at the end of this chapter for questionnaire results.)

Several employees reported that TACT "had changed their lives." Many volunteered that TACT had helped them greatly to communicate more effectively with spouses or with teenage children. In fact, 73% returning the questionnaire said they would invite their family or friends if special guest presentations of TACT were locally arranged; and 83% stated they frequently or sometimes used TACT concepts in dealing with family and friends.

TACT apparently changed perceptions people had of themselves and others, for 66% reported they saw themselves either somewhat or very differently than they had before completing TACT, and 72% stated they saw others either somewhat or very differently since completing the program.

Many individuals reported interesting anecdotes in which TACT had played an important part. One supervisor commented that after TACT training, his employees called on him less often to handle difficult passenger situations. He speculated that they felt more confident in handling crossed transactions themselves.

A stewardess shared the following experience.

I remember one flight between Toronto and Chicago that took three hours because of a snow storm at Chicago. The passengers were mostly business men with connections to make and meetings to attend. My first inclination was to grumble along with them as to how awful the situation was, but then I thought: "Is this the way to make a fun trip?" So, I smiled, and smiled, and smiled. I made it a point to chat with each passenger, feeding their Child with the attention it needed and answering their Adult questions. Pretty soon everyone in the first-class cabin was chatting with each other. By trying to be happy myself, it brushed off on others who, in turn, infected the whole cabin: A ballooning "I'm OK – You're OK" feeling. No one had a chance to cash in dirty stamps.[6] As a good stroke for me, the passengers voted to overfly Chicago and go to San Francisco to have a party at my house. The captain vetoed that quickly though! I'm pleased to say, everyone got off knowing he was "OK."

Another employee described how it had helped her in her marriage.

TA has not only helped me on and off the job, but it has also helped me to better understand my own feelings and responses to those around me. It has also brought a little humor and enlightenment to my many moods and reactions. For example, whenever I'm with my husband and I become rather stern, scolding, or critical, he merely tells me, "turn off your Parent." In this type of joking manner he can make me aware of my own behavior, whereas, before we were familiar with TA, we might have gotten upset with one another without really knowing how to get out of our present ego states into new ones.

One stewardess reported a unique incident involving stroking:

Mr. Smith flies with us regularly between San Francisco and Phoenix. I give him lots of good strokes by always calling him by name, asking about his wife, and how business is doing. I try to remember how he drinks his scotch, when he likes his dinner served, and that he drinks black Sanka instead of coffee. One day I found out that it was Mr. Smith's birthday, so I put matches in his dessert, lit them, and sang Happy Birthday to him. His Child was so elated. Little strokes mean so much. Traveling becomes boring very quickly to our seasoned traveler. By the way, Mr. Smith was 81 that day.

A supervisor told how she had used TACT to improve her relationship with one of her stewardesses.

I began supervising Josie with too much of my Parent being hooked. The former supervisor of my group advised, "Now with Josie you're going to have to get after her right away, keep reminding her not to wear that awful green nail polish or those hoop earrings. I've told her for at least a year to change her watchband. If I were you, I'd tell her a few more times; then if she continues, discipline her for insubordination." Being as green as Josie's nail polish, and expecting to obtain some good advice from a supervisor of a few years, I suppose there was no thinking done on my part of a more positive approach. So my negativity began . . .

On all of my meetings with Josie, from August through December, I was seeing things to correct in her and did so by frequent reminders. By my being the Parent, I hooked Josie's Child.

It was not until an observation ride in January that I saw the light. Josie showed her professional Adult; consequently, my reaction was also Adult. On this occasion, we discussed how we had both reacted unfavorably. Since then, we have been Adult — Adult and have established a good relationship. TACT helped us figure out our difficulty.

A ticket agent reported a personal experience involving an irate passenger.

There have been numerous times when I felt TACT helped me maintain a high standard as an American Airlines ticket lift agent and still feel intact as an individual. One such occasion was a morning working on a 747 departure to Los Angeles. The flight was full, and checking in the passengers was time consuming. One passenger, after waiting about 15 minutes, finally reached me and began shouting, throwing his ticket at me, and condemning American Airlines for its poor service. We were hampered by snow and ice conditions. The night before, all but three outbound flights were cancelled. Only three planes landed in Boston. We had an equipment shortage. All of this combined to add to the frustrations of the passengers. Although the passenger yelled and screamed at me, I was able to take his verbal abuse without being personally offended. After he had finished, I calmly asked his seat preference and assured him that we would get underway as soon as weather conditions improved. I was able to take a little extra time to give him all the information regarding his flight that he wanted. Because I did this, using what I had learned in TACT, the passenger realized that we were really doing all that was possible to give him a safe and comfortable flight. The things I had explained, but more importantly the way in which I did it, made him calm down a bit.

I attribute the good outcome of that situation to my TACT training. For a few minutes he and I held the attention of the entire gate. Later my conduct was praised by other passengers looking on.

Another good example of a TACT on-the-job application involved two stewardesses' successful handling of a hijacking attempt. A passenger later wrote:

As you know, there was an attempted hijacking which disrupted the flight and forced a landing at Salt Lake City. Because the disturbance took place within a few feet of where we were sitting, we were in an excellent position to observe and commend the outstanding efficiency of the captain and his entire crew. In particular, we noted the calm efficiency and psychological skill of the two stewardesses.

While we obviously would prefer never to have another experience like the one last evening, we certainly recognize that, despite its best efforts, the airline industry is unable to completely eliminate such problems. We want you to know that whatever preparation had been made for such contingencies was more than adequate and that you have reason to be very proud of those who served on the flight.

With all of this personal employee testimony regarding the effectiveness of the TACT Program, why did the program fail to have a measurable impact on the problem it was designed to resolve or minimize? What conclusions could reasonably be drawn from the TACT Program experience? There are at least three.

1. *Individual learning is not enough.* The TACT experience appears to have demonstrated once again what behavioral science research has indicated many times before, namely, that a brief training program emphasizing individual learning with minimal follow-up will probably not cause major or lasting organization change.

2. *Individual learning which is not reinforced will probably not be applied.* Even though two, and sometimes three, levels of management above the customer service employee received TACT training, the managers apparently did very little to reinforce TA applications to service and related organizational problems. For example, in the follow-up survey we found that 26% of the supervisors had not even discussed performance with their employees in the three to four months between TACT and the questionnaire. We found that 17% of the supervisors seldom or never used TACT concepts in later performance discussions with their employees, and that 34% of the supervisors only occasionally used TACT in employee discussions. This left 23% who frequently used TA in reviewing performance with their customer service subordinates. Why did this result occur? Probably because higher levels of management were placing pressure and attention on specific "problems of the moment" and ignoring the use of TACT concepts in analyzing and resolving them.

3. *Perhaps TACT could provide a basis for more extensive efforts toward organizational change.* It was evident that many employees, both at customer contact levels and in management, were turned on by, and continued to use, TA concepts. Therefore, there was a strong positive conclusion that the TACT Program was an effective instrument for teaching large numbers of employees (approximately 7,000) a few concepts used in TA structural analysis, the analysis of transactions between people, and some elements of game analysis. The potential application of TA to large-scale organizational change strategies still appears both promising and exciting.

TRANSACTIONAL ANALYSIS AND ORGANIZATION DEVELOPMENT

I have already described my early attempts to define organization development. Transactional analysis provided me with ideas and tools to describe OD in still different terms. I initially paraphrased one of Eric Berne's comments to apply to OD: "The major goal of organization development is to fight the past in the present in order to choose freely the future." I hasten to add, however, this description did not inspire many line managers.

I also developed a more behavior-specific definition of OD which has received positive responses from supervisors and managers who have already participated in the TACT Program.

> Organization development is an evolving set of specific activities designed and implemented to achieve the following: (a) To maximize Adult-Adult transactions between individuals. (b) To give an OK to the Natural Child in individuals to participate in transactions with others. (c) To identify and untangle quickly crossed transactions between people. (d) To minimize destructive game playing among people and between work groups. (e) To maximize authentic encounters (intimacy) between individuals. (f) To develop administrative systems, policies, and work climate that support the preceding objectives.

Before discussing the above OD objectives in greater detail, I want to establish an organization focal point map which has proved helpful

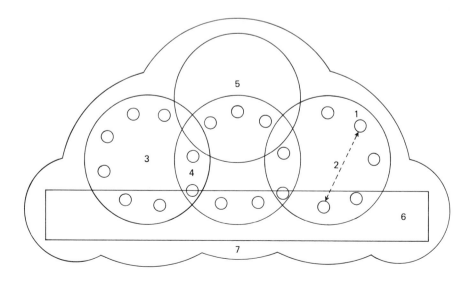

in doing OD work with line managers. When looking at what goes on inside organizations, at least seven focal points should be considered (see figure): (1) What goes on inside an individual? (2) What goes on between two individuals? (3) What goes on among several individuals comprising a family work group? (4) What goes on between two or more separate family work groups? (5) What goes on between hierarchy levels? (6) What kinds of administrative systems, tools, and procedures exist for people to use in getting things done? (7) What values, traditions, and other factors exist in the total organizational climate which encompass the six other focal points and exert psychological influences on employees?

The Goals of TA and OD

Hopefully, the following discussion will make apparent the relationships between the six TA activities in OD and the seven organization focal points highlighted above. (The numbers in parentheses refer to the focal points.)

To Maximize Adult-Adult Transactions

This requires concentration on several organization focal points. Individuals need to be able to sort themselves out reasonably well in order to manage their own behavior and keep in the Adult when appropriate (1). They also must be able to recognize what is going on between themselves and others so they can resist getting their Parent or Child hooked in the transaction (2, 3, and 4).

Attention must also be given to relationships between people at different levels in the hierarchy (5). "Oughtmanship" is sometimes used by both supervisors and subordinates in reaction to work problem situations. Familiar examples include:

- If management around here wants to solve the absenteeism problem, they *ought* to show more interest and concern for the employees!

- Employees around here *ought* to be interested in coming to work and doing their part; there's no excuse for this absenteeism!

- You employees *ought* to be more cost conscious in your work! Don't you know there's a profit squeeze?

- Supervisors *ought* to make it easier for the employees to talk to them. We have lots of good ideas, but they'll never listen to us!

Each of these statements makes a judgment or assumption about other people being responsible for the problem or its solution. Oughtmanship does not lead to problem solving since it involves the Parent rather than the Adult.

If oughtmanship has become a traditional way of reacting to organizational problems, the focal point of organizational climate must also receive attention (7).

To Give An OK To The Natural Child

Although this objective is difficult to achieve by planning specific OD actions, its importance has been recognized by behavioral science researchers. Drs. Robert Blake and Jane Mouton in developing their "Management Grid"[7] approach to organization development found that the use of humor within a work group influenced its effectiveness. Other behavioral scientists have confirmed their findings. Organizational focal points affected by this OD objective will minimally include the individual (1), relationships between individuals (2), relationships between different hierarchy levels (5), and organizational climate (7).

To Identify and Untangle Quickly Crossed Transactions

The identification and resolution of conflicts within an organization involve all seven organization focal points. An understanding of TA by individuals at all levels of the organization is a specific OD activity which will expedite conflict resolution.

To Minimize Destructive Game Playing

Games can seriously interfere with an individual and a work group. When individuals or groups of individuals intensely play a specific game or cluster of games, several undesirable consequences occur:

- Other people are often driven away from the game players. This results in fewer individuals being around to supply essential strokes, and it may cause the players to experience even more intense not-OK feelings.

- Psychological pollution containing high levels of not-OK feelings is created. This "poisoned" atmosphere makes it more difficult for a healthy Adult to survive. And healthy Adult ego states are essential for problem solving.

- Most people work in situations in which teamwork is important; however, intensely played games tend to isolate the players from others. This isolation, in turn, creates breakdowns in communication between team members and other groups that is essential for effective problem solving.

Although many different kinds of interpersonal games can be identified inside most organizations, six specific games appear to be the most common.

- *Harried*
- *If It Weren't for Him (Them)*
- *Ain't it Awful*
- *Now I've Got You, You S.O.B.*
- *Why Don't You? . . . Yes, But*
- *I'm Only Trying to Help You*

These six games can influence the following organization focal-points: the individual (1), relationships between individuals (2), work groups (3), relationships between work groups (4), relationships between hierarchy levels (5), and organization climate (7). Systems, tools, and procedures (6) can sometimes be used by individuals to help them achieve game payoffs.

To Maximize Authentic Encounters (Intimacy)

I have found that many businessmen react with varied not-OK feelings to the term *intimacy*. These same individuals, however, more easily accept the concept of *authentic encounter*, even though it is synonymous with *intimacy*.

Within the TA way of looking at what happens in organizations there are two different kinds of problem solving.

1. Task problem solving involves the Adult processing and computing data about things or nonhuman problems. In terms of the six means for time structuring, this type of problem solving is an activity.

2. Interpersonal problem solving involves the Adult managing of transactions. In terms of time structuring, this type of problem solving is an authentic encounter (intimacy).

Sometimes task problem solving is not accomplished because of interpersonal problems which exist between two or more people involved in the decision making. Therefore, authentic encounter between these people is essential for the resolution of their interpersonal problems before the task problems can be resolved. Since authenticity is risky for most people, they may attempt to substitute games or some other form of time structuring (withdrawal, pastimes, etc.). The inevitable result will be organizational, work group, and individual hang-ups.

To Develop Supportive Systems, Policies, and Work Climate

Work climate (focal point 7) affects the kinds of results that the individual, group, and organization produce just as the way the atmospheric climate affects the quality of crops that a farm produces. Work climate is comprised of values, attitudes, and underlying assumptions that determine how work gets done (or not done) and how problems get solved (or not solved).

Systems, tools, and procedures (focal point 6) can also be examined with the following questions in mind.

- What underlying assumptions have been made about people and work groups in the design of these systems, tools, and procedures?

- What values and attitudes do (will) these systems, tools, and procedures tend to reinforce? Which ones will they tend to discourage?

TRANSACTIONAL ANALYSIS ASSUMPTIONS REGARDING OD

Many TA-based assumptions related to organization development can be made. The following list is by no means intended to be comprehensive.

- Time is not controlled rationally within an organization. All individual and work-group time is spent in one or more of the following ways:

    Withdrawal

    Rituals

    Pastimes

    Activities (Tasks)

    Games

    Authentic Encounters

- Individuals who work in groups that do not encourage stroking will spend much of their time trying to obtain strokes through:

    Withdrawals

    Rituals

    Pastimes

    Games

- Crossed transactions between people are natural. Forbidding or not recognizing these conflicts is denying the natural. One goal of OD is to untangle crossed transactions in a minimum amount of time.

- When individuals are faced with single-choice alternatives, the probability of Ⓒ and/or Ⓟ responses to that choice increase.

- Conversely, when individuals are faced with multiple-choice alternatives, the probability of Ⓐ responses increases.
- When an individual or work group is presented with data about itself, it may react in one of the following ways:

> Withdrawal (Ignore data)
>
> Rituals
>
> Pastimes
>
> Activities
>
> Games
>
> Authentic confrontation

- The manner in which an individual or work group reacts to data about itself is an important source of *new* data.
- When individuals are faced with taking action when they have minimum data regarding the action to be taken:

> The probability of their reacting with Ⓟ or Ⓒ responses increases.
>
> The probability of their reacting with Ⓐ responses (problem-solving) decreases.

This is sometimes labeled resistance to change.

- The manner and form in which data are presented to an individual or work group can influence its reaction to the data.

> Data presented as tentative perceptions have higher probability of stimulating Ⓐ reactions.
>
> Data presented as unchangeable "truth" have higher probability of stimulating Ⓟ or Ⓒ responses.
>
> Data heavily loaded with negatives have a higher probability of generating "bad feelings" in the individual or work group receiving them and therefore generating Ⓟ or Ⓒ responses.
>
> Too many data may tax the capacity of Ⓐ to deal with them effectively due to overloading.

SOME TENTATIVE CONCLUSIONS ABOUT TA APPLICATIONS WITHIN BUSINESS ORGANIZATIONS

After three years of experience in testing and applying TA concepts within a large business organization, I have reached the following conclusions. They are both personal and tentative. I am eager to compare them with the experiences others have had within different organization contexts.

1. *The transactional analysis conceptual system of human behavior has a potentially important role to play in the evolution of OD.* I have found that TA concepts can be easily taught to, and understood by, businessmen. For many of them who have learned TA, the concepts have become important tools for analyzing daily problems and predicting employee reactions to situations and changes. Many, if not most, businessmen are more at home living in their heads than they are in their guts or hearts. For them, TA provides a "head language" for discussing emotional issues and problems.

I have also found that TA can be a useful integrator of various management theories. Before becoming familiar with transactional analysis, I only suspected that Likert's System IV, Blake's 9,9 management style, Herzberg's motivators, and McGregor's Theory Y all had more things in common than was immediately apparent. With TA concepts, I was able to identify more specifically their relationships. [8] This characteristic of TA may in the future prove helpful to management theoreticians and OD practitioners.

2. *Individual scripts, particularly those of key business executives, have hidden high-potential influences on what happens in organizations.* Although I am not a qualified TA script analyst, my continuing study of script concepts has made me increasingly aware of the dominant role that individual scripts can play in an organization's life. This experience has led me to speculate about organizational scripts.

Some departments (suborganizations) within large organizations are regarded differently from others by individuals both within the department and outside. Some are seen as aggressive, problem-solving, high-status groups (winners), whereas others may be seen as low-morale, passive, *If It Weren't for Them* nonachievement groups (losers). One department may be seen as low stroking, hard *Now I've Got You, You S.O.B.* playing, with a high level of *Ain't It Awful* pastiming. Another department in the same building may be viewed as consistently playing *Why Don't You? - Yes But, I'm Only Trying to Help You,* and *Schlemiel* with a low performance contribution to the overall organization.

If these observations are valid, what explanation might be offered?

I suggest that a key executive with primary departmental responsibility will often be managing from his own individual script. After time passes, his own personal injunctions become a part of the culture of the department he manages. The games he plays and the payoffs for which he plays them become important dynamics in his organization. When he selects individuals to work for him, he will tend to select those who are compatible with his games. His rackets, what he does when the going gets tough, become models for others to follow during work crises. Members of the department adopt similar corporate heroes, for example, tough SOB's or bright humanistic bosses, etc. His script payoff may become undistinguishable from the "fate" his entire department seems to be headed for.

Admittedly, this organizational script concept does not fit into a TA operational model as neatly as does the individual script. It does, however, provide a starting point for additional organization analysis.

3. *It is both essential and difficult to establish specific individual contracts within groups working on organization development.* My experience to date with OD efforts has been that specific, mutually understood contracts with work group members are rare. Often OD work is initiated by a key executive of a department who may imply, "If It Weren't for Them (subordinates), we would be getting better results." Subordinates, on the other hand, may agree that their department could benefit from some OD work, but they may indicate that many of their problems could be resolved "If It Weren't For Him" (the boss).

Another closely related issue is "How far can the OD consultant legitimately go in establishing a contract with work group members?" I'm convinced that a business or OD consultant, even if qualified, should not engage in any individual script analysis, even though one or more individual scripts may be primarily responsible for many of the difficulties the organization is experiencing. On the other hand, the dilemma still remains: How will organizations and the people within them become winners rather than nonwinners or losers? Is this to remain a personal and private concern for individual members to resolve outside their working hours?

4. *Business organizations are not rational in much of their behavior, and TA can help businessmen understand some of this irrationality.* Although rationality is perhaps the dominant god worshiped by most businessmen, irrationality often pronounces the benediction. In my experience, TA has been one of the most potent tools I've found to deal with this issue. I'd like to close by sharing one of my poems on this subject.

THE CORPORATE STATE

If organizations were rational,
Would they bury themselves under paperwork?
Or have headquarters in New York City?
Or rupture into bitter strikes?
Or hire people they later fired?

If organizations were rational,
Would they ever make dumb decisions?
Or just plain not decide on important things?
Or name three more Vice Presidents
While reducing the steno pool
To save money?

If organizations were rational,
Would they ever protect the few
While the many suffered from their hollow games?
Or spend 100 thousand
For an annual report
That tells how they lost ten million
Since last year?

If organizations were rational,
Would they ever buy computers
To eliminate paperwork?
Or hire outside experts
To tell them what they already knew?

If organizations were rational,
What would all of us people do
For work and spending time
And dreaming up new ways
To make those damned organizations
More rational?

FOOTNOTES AND REFERENCES

1. *Journal of Applied Behavioral Science*, 5, No. 1 (1969): 111. Reprinted by permission.

2. *Ibid.*, p. 110. This poem was written two years before I became familiar with duplex transactions and games such as *If It Weren't for Him* and *If It Weren't for Them*. Reprinted by permission.

3. Lyman K. Randall, "Common Questions and Tentative Answers Regarding Organizational Development," *California Management Review*, 13 (Spring, 1971): 45. Reprinted by permission.

4. Drs. Robert Blake and Jane S. Mouton, "OD — Fad or Fundamental?" *ASTD Journal*, (January, 1970): 17.

5. Lyman K. Randall, "OD — Fad or Fundamental" (edited by Phil Chase), pp. 10-12. Published by ASTD, July, 1971 (for limited circulation).

6. Although TA people in other contexts often use various color stamps (dirty brown stamps representing "inadequacy feelings," red stamps referring to saved-up anger, etc.), we use the label "dirty stamps" to refer to all collected not-OK feelings. Several years ago a group of black employees strongly

objected to the term "dirty brown stamps" since it represented to them one more instance of "Whitey" putting not-OK labels on the skin color. As one black pointed out, "Why not call them dirty white stamps since you can more easily see dirt on a white background than on brown?"

7. Drs. Robert Blake and Jane S. Mouton, *The Managerial Grid* (Houston, Texas: Gulf Publishing Co., 1963).

8. "The Transactional Manager: An Analysis of Three Contemporary Management Theories" by Lyman K. Randall, May, 1971.

APPENDIX

AMERICAN AIRLINES TACT PROGRAM POST-EVALUATION

1. How sample was selected — random

2. Total N = 502

3. Comprised of following employee groups:

    Discussion Leaders
    CTO Ticket Salesmen
    ATO Ticket Salesmen
    Skycaps
    Passenger Service Representatives
    Ticket Lift Agents

4. Timing: 3 months post-evaluation

    TACT training completed approximately May, 1971
    Questionnaires completed August, 1971

TACT SURVEY

Please check only one answer to each question.

1. When I was attending the TACT Program I thought it was

    | 71% | 1. | very interesting and informative. |
    | 28 | 2. | moderately interesting and informative. |
    | 1 | 3. | not very interesting or informative. |
    | 0 | 4. | boring and obvious. |

2. In discussing my job performance now, my Supervisor

    | 23% | 1. | frequently uses TACT language or concepts. |
    | 34 | 2. | occasionally uses TACT language or concepts. |
    | 9 | 3. | seldom uses TACT language or concepts. |
    | 8 | 4. | never uses TACT language or concepts. |
    | 26 | 5. | has not discussed job performance with me recently. |

Behavioral Science Research
August, 1971

3. In dealing with difficult customer situations,

   53%   1. I frequently try to work them out using TACT
             concepts.

   44   2. I sometimes try to work them out using TACT
             concepts.

   3   3. I rarely or never try to work them out using TACT
             concepts.

4. In dealing with other employees on work-related issues, I

   33%   1. frequently use TACT language or concepts.

   56   2. sometimes use TACT language or concepts.

   11   3. rarely or never use TACT language or concepts.

5. In dealing with friends and family, I

   27%   1. frequently use TACT language or concepts.

   56   2. sometimes use TACT language or concepts.

   17   3. rarely or never use TACT language or concepts.

6. After participating in the TACT Program, I

   34%   1. often consider which of my ego states is "in charge"
             of a given transaction.

   47   2. occasionally consider which of my ego states is "in
             charge" of a given transaction.

   12   3. seldom consider which of my ego states is "in
             charge" of a given transaction.

   7   4. never think about ego states or transactions.

7. Destructive and time-consuming "games" such as *Why Don't
   You? — Yes But!*, *If It Weren't for Them*, and *I Was Only Trying to
   Help You*

   12%   1. are never played at this station.

   28   2. are seldom played at this station.

   49   3. are occasionally played at this station.

   10   4. are a way of life at this station.

   1   — No response.

8. If I had an on-the-job opportunity to learn more about Transactional Analysis,

   71%   1. I would be very interested in doing so.

   22   2. I would be moderately interested in doing so.

<u> 6 </u>   3.   I would have little interest in doing so.

<u> 1 </u>   4.   I would have no interest, whatsoever, in doing so.

9. If station/office "library" copies of *I'm OK — You're OK* were available,

<u>50%</u>   1.   I would definitely want to borrow a copy.

<u> 27 </u>   2.   I might want to borrow a copy.

<u> 10 </u>   3.   I doubt if I would borrow a copy.

<u> 1 </u>   4.   I would not want to read it.

<u> 12 </u>   5.   I have already read the book.

10. If special Guest Presentations of the TACT Program were arranged locally,

<u>43%</u>   1.   I would like to invite my family or friends.

<u> 30 </u>   2.   I might invite my family or friends.

<u> 20 </u>   3.   I doubt if I would invite my family or friends.

<u> 7 </u>   4.   I would not want to invite my family or friends.

11. In my opinion, the TACT Program is about

<u>59%</u>   1.   matters that strongly influence my life.

<u> 37 </u>   2.   matters that sometimes influence my life.

<u> 4 </u>   3.   matters that rarely or never influence my life.

12. Since completing the TACT Program, I now see myself

<u>13%</u>   1.   very differently than I did before.

<u> 53 </u>   2.   somewhat differently than I did before.

<u> 21 </u>   3.   a little differently than I did before.

<u> 13 </u>   4.   no differently than I did before.

13. Since completing the TACT Program, I now see others

<u>24%</u>   1.   very differently than I did before.

<u> 48 </u>   2.   somewhat differently than I did before.

<u> 20 </u>   3.   a little differently than I did before.

<u> 8 </u>   4.   no differently than I did before.

14. Since completing the TACT Program, my feelings about my work

<u>32%</u>   1.   have become much more positive.

<u> 46 </u>   2.   have become somewhat more positive.

<u> 21 </u>   3.   have not changed at all.

<u> 1 </u>   4.   have become much more negative.

15. Apart from technical procedures, what I learned in the TACT Program has resulted in my doing my job

<u> 8% </u>   1.   very differently from the way I did it before.

<u> 49 </u>   2.   somewhat differently from the way I did it before.

<u> 31 </u>   3.   a little differently from the way I did it before.

<u> 12 </u>   4.   no differently from the way I did it before.

16. What I learned in the TACT Program has resulted in my doing my job

<u> 58% </u>   1.   more efficiently.

<u> 37 </u>   2.   about the same way.

<u> 0 </u>   3.   less efficiently.

<u> 4 </u>   4.   Don't know.

<u> 1 </u>   —   No response.

17. What impact do you think the TACT Program has had on customer treatment at your location?

<u> 13% </u>   1.   In general, passengers receive much better treatment.

<u> 52 </u>   2.   In general, passengers receive better treatment.

<u> 34 </u>   3.   In general, passengers are treated in about the same way.

<u> 0 </u>   4.   In general, passengers receive worse treatment.

<u> 0 </u>   5.   In general, passengers receive much worse treatment.

<u> 1 </u>   —   No response.

18. Overall, I believe the company made a good investment in developing TACT and in exposing people like me to this program.

<u> 50% </u>   1.   I strongly agree.

<u> 32 </u>   2.   I agree.

<u> 13 </u>   3.   I am uncertain.

<u> 4 </u>   4.   I disagree.

<u> 1 </u>   5.   I strongly disagree.

8

USING TRANSACTIONAL ANALYSIS IN SEMINARS FOR CAREER WOMEN

by Dru Scott

Dru Scott's special achievements include solving problems in a number of areas using the transactional analysis (TA) method. These areas include using TA in training for managerial communications, executive effectiveness, time management, and personal development for career women.

Ms. Scott has designed and conducted numerous training courses, three of which have been adopted nationwide. Her Career Women's Seminar, Interpersonal Communications for Managers, and Office Management courses have been presented to managers and employees from New York to Honolulu.

She designs and conducts most of this training as part of her work with the U.S. Civil Service Commission. As associate director of their Communications Training Institute, she regularly presents these seminars throughout the western United States and Hawaii. She also does private management consulting through her own company, the Key Development Center.

Ms. Scott is a faculty member of the University of California Extension where she teaches Women in Management, Women at Work, Transactional Analysis in Management, Introduction to Transactional Analysis (a credit course), and Advanced Transactional Analysis. She is a frequent speaker for other private and governmental groups.

Dorothy Jongeward and Dru Scott are co-authoring two new books to be published by Addison-Wesley in 1974: The Trouble with Women: Positive Change Through Transactional Analysis; *and* Affirmative Action for Women: A Practical Guide.

INTRODUCTION

This article summarizes another TA success story — the integration of TA with training for working women. The article looks at the combination from several viewpoints: the climate, the course design, and the results.

Right now organizations across the country are taking steps to right the wrongs that may have occurred against working women. The motivation may be a sense of fairness, a response to government regulations, or both. Whatever the motivation, however, the pattern of action often calls for special programs for women. These programs can help women become more aware of their script messages as women and become more aware of steps they can take to help themselves, other women, and employers.

Organizations can meet this affirmative-action need through special training. The following course announcement describes a successful three-day Seminar for Career Women. The seminar can be part of an affirmative-action program or can be presented independently. (Although the model I'm discussing is Federal, this program can be easily adapted to private industry.) This announcement started the ball rolling. The immediate response was enthusiastic. We originally planned for 30 women in a seminar, and we had enough responses for two classes the first time the course was announced. Since the first seminar in the Spring of 1971, these notes have stimulated over 1,500 women to attend Seminars for Career Women. The notes also stimulated over 140 employers of these women to pay the course tuition and travel costs. During those two years I answered a lot of questions. This article includes the answers to some questions that may be coming to your mind also.

THE SEMINAR ANNOUNCEMENT STIMULATED A NUMBER OF QUESTIONS

Who sponsors the seminars?

These seminars were presented as part of the curriculum of the San Francisco Regional Training Center of the U.S. Civil Service Commission. The training center is one of eleven similar operations across the country serving the training needs of Federal, state, and local government agencies. All courses operate on a cost-shared basis, with the sponsoring governmental agency paying tuition. The seminars, as well as other Training Center courses, are held in a number of cities in California, Nevada, Arizona, and Hawaii.

The original development of the seminars included input from Dorothy Jongeward and Muriel James, who have both been active in women's programs for many years.

THE COURSE ANNOUNCEMENT

SEMINAR FOR CAREER WOMEN

<u>What's the approach?</u>

This course is designed to help you answer these questions:

> Do you discriminate against yourself?
>
> Who are you at work?
>
> How did you get that way?
>
> What do you do with and to others?
>
> What psychological games are played at the office?
>
> Where are you going with your job and your life?
>
> What do you need to change to get there?
>
> What should you know about the President's Federal Women Program?

<u>Who may attend?</u>

You, if you are a career-minded woman*

in a managerial, professional, technical, administrative, or clerical position

and work for a Federal, state, or local government

<u>Purpose</u>

To help you make a more effective contribution to your agency and get more job satisfaction

---

*The course has been expanded and is now open to men also.

Dorothy Jongeward and I later developed the seminar so that others could lead it. Most of the training aids are included in the course design section. Much of the material reflects Dorothy Jongeward's experience in training over 6,000 women since 1960. Her training experience not only reaches many women (and men), but it also covers a wide range of levels. The levels extend from high school to university graduate school, from evening adult education to on-the-job training, and from beginning clerical training to corporate vice-presidential seminars.

Who is a career woman?

A career woman is any woman who sees working in paid employment as a significant part of her life. She is any woman who wants to achieve organizational goals, and who sees work as a way of expressing her potential as a human being.

Who comes to this seminar?

Women in the groups range from clerk-typists to district managers, from secretaries to engineering project managers, and from attendance clerks to mathematicians. The women range in experience from 1 to 25 years in their jobs. Organizations range from the City of Pleasant Hill to the U.S. Army in Hawaii to the Social Security Payment Center in San Francisco.

Although the seminars appeal to a diversity of women, they primarily attract women who are just starting to think through traditionally prescribed sex roles and new life and work possibilities.

Many different attitudes are represented in the seminars.

Some women come to the seminars knowing exactly who is responsible for the woman's problem. They know that men cause the problem. And they know that their role is to fix blame and complain loudly about what men have done to them.

Other women come feeling that something needs to be changed, but they are not sure what or who.

Other women come ready to take positive steps to help themselves and other women better use their talents.

Still others wonder what the fuss is about.

Are the courses women's lib or people's lib?

Shortly after the seminars began they were nicknamed courses in "people's lib," and the nickname stuck. The term is a natural, since a goal of the course is women winning and men winning. Winning for men and women means that both must live and use their potential. Winning means all people getting what they want out of life without hurting themselves or others. [1]

Does the seminar teach that every woman should work?

The course stresses giving each woman a chance to make her own decisions. No one tries to cram one person's expectations down another person's throat. Each woman is encouraged to make her own Adult decisions and to take charge of her own life. She often uses the talents and ideas of other people in the seminar to help her, but the final decision is hers.

Many women decide to strive for higher-level jobs. Many women decide to take their work more seriously. On the other hand, some women decide they really do not have to work, they really do not want to work, and they are working merely because of social pressures.

Other women feel better about continuing to do what they have been doing already. For example, some women, without consciously deciding, do things that are quite constructive and productive in their lives. However, they sometimes feel uncomfortable about these things because of vaguely felt pressures from society. By getting factual information and becoming aware of their decisions, they can deal with any vague feelings of uneasiness. Often, women are scripted to feel guilty about their accomplishments. The TA training helps women feel better about things they have already achieved.

THE COURSE DESIGN

This section lists materials, a sample schedule, and a lesson brief keyed to each title in the sample schedule. The course design highlights practical guides that will help you as a trainer conduct similar sessions.

Materials

Using *Born to Win: Transactional Analysis with Gestalt Experiments* [2] speeds learning before, during, and after the actual workshop.

The first six seminars were presented before the book was published. The remaining seminars used the text. In the later seminars we had to spend two to three hours less on basic TA concepts. Also, participants having the advanced study assignment were immediately more confident about the usefulness of course material.

Before the course

Two or three weeks before the seminar, we send each woman a copy of *Born to Win* and "The Myth and Reality," an article by the Department of Labor's Women's Bureau. We ask each participant to study all of the four-page pamphlet and the first three chapters of the book. We ask them, as they study the book, to think about defining these terms: Parent, Adult, and Child ego states; complementary, crossed, and ulterior transactions; and psychological games.

During the course

Using the text in class makes Adult-Adult teaching easier. Participants have other sources of information than the workshop leader and each other, and using reference material in class helps sharpen the habit of actively seeking new information. During an agree-disagree exercise participants first jot down their individual decisions. They then come to a consensus in a small group. The consensus stage frequently involves checking out information in *Born to Win* or other books in the classroom. (See Appendix A at the end of this chapter.) The first evening we ask the women to study Chapter 4; the second evening, to study any chapter they are particularly interested in.

Afterwards

After the training session, the text serves (1) as a summary of the transactional analysis material covered in class; (2) as a means of sharing some of the information to co-workers; (3) as a guide to a study group; (4) as a study source of chapters not covered in class; and (5) as a quick reference for individual participants.

Other materials are helpful

You can give each participant a program schedule; a portfolio with notepaper, pen, and name plate card; and a roster of the persons attending the class.

Use of an overhead projector, chalkboard, or flipchart can add visual interest.

If you decide to use the Mass Media and Your Image of Women unit on the first afternoon, each participant needs one or two magazines. If you use the Putting It All Together unit on the second afternoon, the group needs 18 sheets of 2' × 3' poster board, 6 bottles of rubber cement, and 6 pairs of scissors.

If you as a trainer are interested in participative TA teaching materials, look at *Winning with People: Group Exercises in Transactional Analysis* by Dorothy Jongeward and Muriel James. [3] It is full of workable involvement ideas.

SAMPLE SCHEDULE

Day One

A.M.   Program Objectives and Introduction
        Four Growth Paths to Personality Development for Women
        Transactional Analysis Overview

P.M.   Analysis of Personality: Winner or Loser Compulsions
        Four Psychological Positions
        Mass Media and Your Image of Women

Day Two

A.M.   Ego State Contamination
        Women: A Historical Perspective
P.M.   The Midpoint Checkout
        Putting It All Together: A Workshop

Day Three

A.M.   Time Structuring
        Psychological Games People Play at Work
P.M.   Changing Back on the Job
        Summary, Evaluations, and Presentation of Certificates

The seminars begin at 8:30 A.M. and end at 4:00 P.M. with an hour break for lunch.

LESSON BRIEFS

Day One, A.M.

Lesson Brief Title: Program Objectives and Introduction

Objectives

> Demonstrate to participants they won't be embarrassed, talked down to, or bored.
> Give participants a chance to get some Child-Child strokes.
> Convey the importance of the Child getting strokes for Adult functioning.
> Give participants permission to take responsibility for their own learning.
> Give participants permission to learn without hurting.

Time: 30 to 45 minutes

Lesson Brief

> During the first part of the seminar we review the program objectives printed on the back of the schedule. These are the same questions that appear in the course announcement.

Throughout the seminar each participant can measure her own progress toward the goals of the course. This approach avoids the Parent-Child "I'll give you a test, and then I'll tell you how well you measure up."

Besides measuring her own progress toward clearly defined and accepted goals, each woman takes responsibility for her own learning. I usually say, "Most women in our culture learn over a period of years that the way to live is to be passive and wait for someone to come along and do things for you. Just as that rarely works on the job, it rarely works in training classes. Some time ago at the end of a three-day management course, a woman wrote me a note saying, 'I couldn't see very well the last three days. My chair was in an awkward spot.' "

I assure the current group that Mother Drusilla will not be around to move anyone's chair. The permission to take responsibility for one's own learning and to do something about any problem that blocks learning does work, but the results are sometimes funny. In one seminar in Los Angeles, immediately after talking about this permission, three people immediately stood up and left for the rest room.

In a group in San Francisco, one woman stood up and said, "I'm bothered by smoke. Can we use the airplane seating system? The smokers sit on the port side and all the nonsmokers on the starboard side." All of a sudden everyone started moving.

An introductory discussion of ego states and strokes tests how well the women understand the advance reading. The discussion also leads into the importance of making sure the Child is getting plenty of strokes.

Here is an opening exercise that provides Child-Child stroking and facilitates later Adult data processing. Two participants who don't know each other work through three one-minute steps. Before the steps begin, each two-person team decides which person will be an "A" and which will be a "B."

Step One: A imagines out loud what she feels the other person is like. For example, she might say, "I imagine that you hate Chinese food, you like to get up early in the morning, you like Herman Hesse . . . ." During this step B has the hard job — staying quiet.

Step Two: The roles are reversed. B does the one-way imagining. A does the listening.

Step Three: A and B check how accurate their imagining was. [4]

At the end of this exercise the participants discuss what happened
and how they felt. They find a collection of 30 stiffly sitting
strangers taking a big step toward becoming a fully functioning
learning group. They find a group that feels better and a group that
has fewer not-OK Child feelings detracting from Adult learning.

Lesson Brief Title: Four Growth Paths to Personality Development for
Women

Objective

Present a framework for understanding how people learn to see
themselves.

Time: 40 to 60 minutes

Lesson Brief

Four paths to the development of personality serve as a framework
for much of the material that evolves later in the seminar. This unit
concentrates on bringing out special scripting American women
often learn.

- *Personal identity* is how women identify themselves in
  nonsexual capacities. Some examples are the sense of ability,
  intelligence, competence, and personal worth.

- *Sexual identity* for many women comes from a relationship
  with a man and from taking care of others. Women are often
  first defined by their sexual roles, such as wife or mother,
  rather than as a person who is also a wife or a mother.

- *Life goals* for a woman are frequently in terms of getting
  married or having children. As was pointed out in the first part
  of this article, these goals are often achieved by the middle of
  a woman's life.

- *A value system* for a woman that is culturally approved is
  likely to revolve around taking care of someone else and
  getting satisfaction from others' achievements to the exclusion
  of her own achievements. Also, values women frequently
  adopt, such as being constantly submissive, are unproductive
  on the job.

This unit is largely lecture with some questions and answers. Information in the "What Do You Do When Your Script Runs Out?" article mentioned earlier fits into this segment.

To conclude this section, you can ask participants to make up a list of what a little girl growing up in America today would likely hear about each path.

Lesson Brief Title: Transactional Analysis Overview

Objective

Make sure participants understand some basic TA terms.

Time: 45 to 75 minutes

Lesson Brief

This unit opens with a brief discussion of the functions of each ego state. Participants contribute ideas until there is a list of two to five functions for each ego state, written where everyone can see them. For example, the list for Parent would include criticizing and nurturing.

Women working in groups of two to four comprise the next step. They pick three situations and develop a Parent, Adult, and Child response to each situation. We ask them to be prepared to act out their situations and responses.

The time breakdown is about one-third to discussion of ego state functions, one-third to small group work, and one-third to role-playing and analyzing the examples.

You can follow the same pattern for transactions. A lecture-discussion brings out the characteristics of complementary, crossed, and ulterior transactions. The next step is diagraming some transactions and asking the small groups to prepare to role-play a transaction that fits each diagram. As a team is presenting one set of transactions, the other teams check to make sure the role-play fits the diagram.

The final step of this unit is a discussion of what characteristics must be present for a set of transactions to be called a game. This session is brief, since games are discussed in greater detail on the third day.

Day One, P.M.

Lesson Brief Title: Analysis of Personality: Winner or Loser
Compulsions

Objectives

Establish the validity of the concept of script.

Present script types — winning, nonwinning, and losing.

Present examples of common nonwinning scripts for women.

Have the women start identifying their own script.

Time: 45 to 60 minutes

Lesson Brief

"What goes into a dramatic script?" is a good opening question for
this session. As participants suggest elements of a dramatic script,
these ideas can be related to a psychological script. Developing this
analogy helps define how a psychological script works. The next
step is verifying the definition. One way to do this is to describe a
person living out a destructive, or losing, script. Then ask the
participants if they know anyone personally who seems to be living
out this pattern. You can use the same approach for a winner, and
then a nonwinner. By this time most people are nodding and
saying, "Yes, that's really true." Although we don't directly ask for
a personal assessment, many participants start figuring out what
kind of a script they are living out.

This introduction generates high interest — more than enough
interest to carry you through a 30-to 40-minute lecture. During
this presentation we cover the ways in which scripts are developed
and examples of common nonwinning scripts that women frequently adopt. Cinderella, Sleeping Beauty, and Mother Hubbard
are all good examples. At this point it's useful to let participants
pick out common threads in the sample scripts. Usually, most of
the women quickly spot the passivity and the waiting for a magical
rescuer. Some of the women will notice that all the samples
portray women who give more strokes than they receive. Frequently, the discussion centers on the harmful implications of
women constantly giving strokes to others and getting very few
themselves.

The next step concentrates on helping the women think through
their own scripting. One way is to ask each person to jot down the
specific things she learned about key subjects, subjects such as

mental ability, physical ability, personal appearance, education, woman's place, femininity, and sexuality. Before participants start jotting down script messages, point out that learning can be from verbal messages or nonverbal examples. I stress that answers are for their personal use only.

Lesson Brief Title: Four Psychological Positions

Objectives

Define strokes.

Discuss how positions are developed.

Summarize key characteristics of

I'm not-OK — You're OK,

I'm OK — You're not-OK,

I'm not-OK — You're not-OK,

I'm OK — You're OK.

Have participant think through how a person operating from each position acts.

Time: 30 to 90 minutes

Lesson Brief

The concept of strokes and their life and death necessity is a powerful opener for this unit. If you think someone may not clearly understand what a stroke is, you can briefly review some definitions. One definition that I find people grasp quickly is: A stroke is any way we let other people know we know they are alive.

Participants should have this concept, at least, firmly in mind at the end of this unit. There are both positive and negative strokes. Strokes may be either physical or symbolic. Without strokes, an infant will die. If an infant gets negative strokes, he will not die, but he will grow up emotionally ill in some way. A person intuitively knows that negative strokes are better than no strokes at all and will work to get negative ones if not enough positive ones are forthcoming.

At this point, the women will have some understanding of the importance of strokes. The film *Second Chance* extends the understanding to a feeling level. This fifteen-minute film shows how a lack of strokes has slowed the growth of 22-month-old Susan to the height and weight of a child less than half her age.

Susan's retardation is temporarily arrested when, during her hospitalization, she is given stroking and loving care for over six hours a day for two months. [5]

The film also leads into a discussion of the development of psychological positions. You can mention the different ways the same position may be arrived at. For example, a child may learn to feel, "I'm not-OK — You're OK," if a parent frequently yells, "You dumb kid! You can't do anything right. Why, your sister Helen was toilet trained by nine months, and look at you at a year and a half." A child might arrive at the same position by frequently hearing, "Oh, don't bother your head with those old nasty shoelaces. I'll tie them for you."

Looking at the four psychological positions: I'm not-OK — You're OK; I'm OK — You're not-OK; I'm not-OK — You're not-OK; and I'm OK — You're OK is a useful framework for helping women examine their own self-image.

After discussing each position, you can ask the participants to work on the next project individually or in small groups. The worksheet grid includes a list of the four positions, with a number of characteristics that applies to all four. For example, how would a person with an I'm not-OK — You're OK position

1. be described by close acquaintances?
2. give and get strokes?
3. collect feelings or stamps?
4. deal with conflict?
5. manage?
6. receive supervision?

The small teams then answer the same questions for another position, until all four are discussed. [6]

Lesson Brief Title: Mass Media and Your Image of Women

Objectives

Point out how women are portrayed in magazines and how these portrayals may effect women's image of themselves.

Focus on using the insights to make positive changes rather than just fixing blame.

Time: 30 to 45 minutes

Lesson Brief

We use this lesson only when there is a low level of awareness of women's portrayal in the media. Before the course, we ask each participant to bring one or two magazines with her to the seminar. During the exercise on Mass Media and Your Image of Women, the participants look closely at how women are portrayed. They look for generalizations about how a woman should look to be OK in the eyes of Madison Avenue. What size? What age? What roles? What should she be doing to her body? How should she relate to other people? to men? to other women? to children?

Most of the women have not thought about the impact of the media on their own roles and how they picture themselves. This exercise ends with women saying, "No wonder I feel not-OK every time I look in the mirror. I'm not an 18-year-old size 5 with two spotless children, three-inch-deep carpets, and an impeccable house." Many of the women are vaguely aware of how women are stereotyped by the media, but they have not felt the force of this representation before.

A few words of instruction, plus a group of women with some magazines, equals an explosive, insightful exercise.

At the conclusion of the exercise you may want to stress, "What are you going to do about it?" This helps avoid the "If It Weren't for Madison Avenue" game. Again, the goal of this exercise is to develop insight that leads to action, and not just insight that leads to fixing the blame.

Day Two, A.M.

Lesson Brief Title: Ego State Contamination

Objective

Help participants identify cultural contamination relating to women.

Time: 20 to 30 minutes

Lesson Brief

A question that comes to many women's minds after the information on scripts and growth paths is that, with all of this information, why are so few changes being made? Looking at how Parent thinking may contaminate an Adult explains why change is so slow. It explains why "facts" may not change someone's mind, even though that person is a clear thinker in many other areas.

Here is an exercise that points out cultural contamination about the role of women. We ask each team to make up a list completing this sentence: "Women are . . .," and another list for the sentence, "Men are . . ." In this exercise they don't ask "Is this statement true?" but "Would a child growing up in our culture commonly hear these statements?"

The contrast between the "women are" and the "men are" lists jumps out when the lists are summarized on a transparency or chalkboard. Frequently, the first response women have is "The men have all the good things and the women have all the bad things." After looking at the lists a little longer, they may decide that it isn't that good to have cultural scripting to always be the leader, always be strong, never show feelings, etc.

After looking at how the Parent can contaminate Adult thinking and produce prejudice, we look at Child-contaminated thinking or delusion. A form of delusion women frequently have is waiting for a rescuer. The group discusses how a woman might live out the rescuer delusion.

Lesson Brief Title: Women: A Historical Perspective

Objectives

Spotlight the history of women acting from subordinate roles.
Create an awareness of the role of women played in the struggle for equal rights.

Time: 1 to 3 hours

Lesson Brief

At this point, most of the participants are aware of the importance of a sense of history. They realize that before you can get where you want to go, it's important to know where you've been and where you are.

The opening for this exercise is a six-question quiz. Just to get the feeling, you may want to answer the quiz yourself right now.

> 1. What happened to the women delegates who crossed the Atlantic to attend the World Anti-Slavery Conference in London in 1840?
>
> 2. What happened at Seneca Falls in 1848?
>
> 3. Who was Susan B. Anthony?
>
> 4. Who was Carrie Chapman Catt?
>
> 5. When were women given the right to vote?
>
> 6. Who was Sojourner Truth?

We ask the women to complete the quiz and, after doing this individually, to talk about their answers with other team members. One or two minutes of strained silence is usually followed by three or four minutes of embarrassed conversation. "I've never even *heard* of Carrie Chapman Catt," "I think Susan B. Anthony was a wierdo I saw in a history book someplace," and "I'm not sure when women got the vote." Suddenly, the realization of how ignorant most women are of their history as women hits the group. These few questions create an awareness of the need for more knowledge about the history of women, and a willingness to seek out more facts. Usually at this time, we show the film, *Women on the March: The Struggle for Equal Rights*, part I, by the National Film Board of Canada. [7] The film includes actual film clips of the feminist movement in England in the early 1900's. Although the film features England, the struggle there closely parallels the American struggle for "votes for women."

After the film, women in the class talk about their feelings and observations about the film. The reactions consistently are, first, a great deal of pride and appreciation for what has been achieved for women, and second, a new or renewed sense of the importance of women taking positive action. Usually at this time, the information we've covered on how women are scripted to be passive starts coming together with how the equality that has been achieved was won by women who were active and not passive.

Direct quotes and examples from the lives of outstanding women in history add feeling and power to this section. You may want to jot down specific ideas as you prepare for the unit. *The Century of Struggle: The Woman's Rights Movement in the United States* by Eleanor Flexner is an excellent source book on the history of the struggle for the right to vote in the United States. The "And ain't I a woman?" quote from Sojourner Truth is particularly moving. [8]

We conclude this unit by summarizing the Federal Women's Program. Part of this summary is a short report by participants who are involved with this part of the Federal Equal Employment Opportunity effort.

Day Two, P.M.

Lesson Brief Title: The Midpoint Checkout

Objective

Clear up some frequently misunderstood TA details.

Time: 30 to 60 minutes

Lesson Brief

Exercises in this section give participants a chance to do Adult-Adult self teaching. [9] The Ego State Checkout list and the Agree/Disagree handout summarize and reinforce important transactional analysis concepts covered so far during the course. Participants individually complete the exercises, then discuss them as a team.

The most valuable part of the learning is in sharing and evaluating the ideas with each other. The terms *agree/disagree* further stress Adult learning, rather than the Parent *right/wrong* learning. This lesson also portrays women learning to facilitate other women's personal growth rather than competing with other women.

The Ego State Reaction Quiz closes this unit. Since participants generally can quickly identify the appropriate answers, the quiz gives success at the end. (The Agree/Disagree Sheet takes more time to analyze and is more difficult.)

Lesson Brief Title: Putting It All Together — A Workshop

Objectives

Sharpen participant's ability to identify Parent, Adult, and Child ego states.
Sharpen participant's ability to see how women are portrayed in magazines.

Time: 60 to 75 minutes

Lesson Brief

During this exercise each five-person team builds three collages. One collage represents Parent ego state, another Adult, and the last, Child. The examples are taken from magazines the women brought with them to class.

This exercise reveals several different things. The team members find out quite a bit about their styles of leadership and followership. (We deliberately do not give any instructions on how to go about building the collage, so they have the chance to experience and examine the process.)

In addition to observations about process, the participants increase their ability to figure out which postures, positions, etc. represent which ego states. They also figure out that it's difficult to find examples in the media of women functioning from the Adult. The limiting implications of this on scripting women for Parent or Child roles comes through clearly.

During 1971 we used this unit in all of the seminars. As a result of an evaluation after that time, we dropped it from some. We now use it only when the group needs more work in recognizing ego states and in seeing how women are portrayed in the media.

Day Three, A.M.

Lesson Brief Title: Time Structuring

Objectives

Present enough information so that participants can
1. define each time structuring method,
2. estimate how much time they are investing in each method,
3. estimate what kind of strokes they're getting.

Time: 30 to 60 minutes

Lesson Brief

We use our time to give, get, or avoid strokes in these six ways:

Withdrawal	Games
Rituals	Activities
Pastimes	Intimacy

After discussing each method of time structuring, the women evaluate each method and decide which one provides the strongest intensity of strokes and which provides the most readily available strokes. For example, rituals provide easily available strokes but strokes of low intensity. Games provide easy-to-get strokes that are strong, although negative. And games are a two-for-one sale — twice the ego state involvement with the same number of transactions.

You can lead from this discussion with any one of a number of questions. Here are a few.

1. What percentage of your time do you spend in each time-structuring method?
2. What percentage of strokes do you get through each method?
3. What are your favorite pastimes?
4. Who gives you negative strokes?
5. Who gives you positive strokes?
6. What kind of strokes do you usually give to others?
7. Do you get more than 20% of your strokes from any one source?
8. When did you last experience psychological authenticity or intimacy? What feelings did you have from your Child ego state?

An excellent way to use this material is to give each of the participants a printed list of these questions. Ask them to pick one and concentrate for sixty seconds on answering it. Pick another for the next sixty seconds. Keep going for three or four questions. It's surprising how much people can figure out and jot down in sixty seconds. (I've tried this exercise for an unlimited time, and Parkinson's Law prevailed. Work did expand to fill the time available for its completion.)

These last two questions are not optional.

9. Is there anything you want to change?
10. What are you going to do about it?

Lesson Brief Title: Psychological Games People Play at Work

Objectives

Review general dynamics of games.

Give participants a chance to analyze an on-the-job game, identify roles and the payoff, and experience stopping the game from any role.

Time: 90 to 120 minutes

Lesson Brief

The first step in this lesson is to make sure all participants understand and can identify the requirements for a set of transactions to be a psychological game. Since some of the participants will already have a good TA background, this is usually done in teams, with the more advanced participants helping to teach the less knowledgeable ones. Working in teams, the groups identify what the necessary characteristics are. They usually say there must be

1. a predictable payoff,

2. involvement of more than two ego states,

3. an ulterior transaction,

4. a repetitive pattern of transactions,

5. a period of discount.

A brief review of the Karpman Drama Triangle introduces the approach we take toward games. We stress the importance of understanding the roles in games, rather than being able to attach a name. Talking through two or three sample games shows how the roles are played and switched. To give the participants a better idea, you can have them play a practice round of *Why Don't You?-Yes, But.*

After this, participants look at the game sheet developed by Dorothy Jongeward (See Appendix C at the end of the book). The sheet lists a number of games by predominant roles: Persecutor, Rescuer, or Victim. The people in the class then pick out any games they would like more information on.

The training class breaks into groups of three to five participants to discuss examples of games they observe on the job. After a few minutes of talk about game playing that they have observed or participated in, they select one example to concentrate on.

Deciding how to portray this example is the next step for the small groups. After the first role-play in front of the entire class, a group demonstrates how the game can be stopped. With the entire class's help the group may run through the example two or three times, showing how the game can be stopped from any role.

This portrayal of games in front of the entire group is one of the most valuable parts of the seminar. Participants get practice in spotting roles in realistic situations. They also get practice identifying exactly what a game is.

The last game we discuss is *Psychiatry*. It's often tempting for participants to leave a training session and go back to their jobs as experts in the game of *Psychiatry*. This game uses TA information and terms to put down others. To avoid this, we role-play examples of how the information learned in the seminar can be communicated in a nonjargon, nongamey way. Rather than a participant going back to the job and saying, "Oh, you're always being Parent," we discuss ways to present the information. For example, "When you shake your finger at me when evaluating my reports, I feel put down." This ability to communicate the same information in a nonthreatening way helps speed the transfer of skills to the job. It also eliminates the problem of people returning and creating more hostility with the techniques learned.

Day Three, P.M.

Lesson Brief Title: Changing Back on the Job

Objective

Show participants they can increase the usefulness of the course on the job by planning now how to start applying the material.

Time: 20 to 30 minutes

Lesson Brief

This session concentrates on the critical problem time — the two weeks immediately following the training. Former course participants from a variety of training subjects tell me the first two weeks after the course is the make-or-break period. If they do not apply the material on the job during those two weeks, they usually never apply it.

This unit helps bridge the gap between classroom and job performance and creates an Adult-Adult contract for taking action.

It also creates a new positive stroke source to make up for a possible decrease in strokes from giving up old behavior.

"Two by two by two" is the subtitle for this unit. The unit takes two people two steps in two weeks. Here's how it works: Each person selects a partner she feels comfortable working with. The two people brainstorm together. From the ideas developed in the brainstorming, each woman picks two steps she can take during the next two weeks. The steps must be ones she can take on her own initiative.

Here are some sample steps participants have selected during this exercise:

"I'm going to level with John about my feelings toward the way he frequently gives me work at the last minute."

"I am going to play *Uproar* with subordinates not more than once a week."

"I am going to speak up in staff meetings rather than be quiet and collect feelings of resentment."

After selecting the two steps, most of the two-person teams make a contract to help each other achieve their goals. A major benefit of the contract is providing an alternative stroke source. For example, if a participant stops getting strokes from playing *Uproar* with her staff, she will need some strong strokes from another source. Her partner can give these strokes, and positive ones, to fill the new need.

I have found this two-person exercise more useful than having an individual participant decide on a plan of action and turning in a card to the instructor. The participant-participant contract emphasizes Adult-Adult, whereas the participant-leader contract tends to be more Child-Parent. (Since I have 90 to 120 new participants each month, I'm not going to be able to give many individuals strokes for change.)

Lesson Brief Title: Summary, Evaluations, and Presentation of
Certificates

Objectives

Get a sense of closure on course material.

Get reactions of participants about effectiveness of training.

Time: 10 to 20 minutes

Lesson Brief

The summary is made by participants rather than the workshop leader. We sit around informally, and if a woman wants to mention what changes she is going to make, she just speaks out. The comments are typically brief, but pointed. They touch all aspects of the course from the history of women to time structuring, and from strokes to psychological games.

During the closing exercise, participants receive a certificate and a feedback form. On the form we ask the following questions.

1. In terms of how well the course objectives were achieved for you, how do you rate the course? Not at all achieved = 1. Fully achieved = 20.

2. What part of this training session will be the most useful to you on the job?

3. What part will be the least useful to you on the job?

Although this feedback does not measure on-the-job results, it does provide a useful guide to methodology or subject matter to be changed.

THE FOLLOW-UP SURVEY REPORTS SEMINAR SUCCESSES

This section outlines how the survey was conducted, the conclusions from seminar participants and their supervisors, detailed answers from the participants' survey, and detailed answers from the supervisors' survey.

How We Made the Survey

Participants in five classes held between October 1971 and early March 1972 received a follow-up survey two to seven months after they participated in a seminar.

This anonymous survey was divided into two parts: (1) for the participant to complete, and (2) for the participant to give to her immediate supervisor. Supervisors and participants were asked to return the anonymous surveys independently. Of 130 participants receiving the survey, 85 returned the forms. Seventy supervisors returned the questionnaires.

What We Concluded

Our conclusions summarize first the findings of the participants' survey, and then the findings of the supervisors' survey.

Highlights From the Survey of Participants

The survey findings agree that the seminar greatly benefited participants. The responses to the key questions were very enthusiastic. We found that:

> 72% of the participants agreed that they were more effective on the job as a result of participating in the seminar.
>
> 67% agreed that they now got more job satisfaction.
>
> 93% agreed that they now have more Adult control in their interpersonal relationships.
>
> 77% said they had stopped playing psychological games or played at a lighter degree. (Some believe that most people spend 50 to 90% of their waking hours playing psychological games. If so, this one area alone can result in major dollar savings.)

One group of questions deals directly with discrimination — men against women, women against women, and individual women against themselves. Here we found that:

> 88% agreed that they recognized subtle forms of discrimination more readily as a result of the seminar.
>
> 86% were more aware of stereotyping of women by women.
>
> 88% of the women agreed they are more aware of how some women learn not to succeed.

The last statement is probably the most significant. We found that:

> 85% of the women felt that the seminar had a great effect on their lives. (Several commented further on this point in the open-end questions.)

Highlights From the Survey of Supervisors of Participants

The statements on this survey were less emphatic than on the survey for participants. None of the statements ranked higher than 64%, while on the participant survey one statement ranked 93% and five ranked in the 80 to 90%'s.

Although none of the statements was as high on the supervisors' survey, the most important question ranked almost two-thirds. That was the following one.

64% of the supervisors said they believed their subordinate (a class participant) was more effective on the job as a result of the seminar.

Answers to the open-end survey questions were the most revealing part of the supervisors' survey. There were several concrete examples of major improvements. One problem in this part of the survey, however, was that the supervisors were not familiar with the seminar terminology and details. This, combined with the diversity of job classifications and levels represented by participants, made it difficult to get accurate supervisory feedback.

Survey Details in the Appendix

The survey questionnaires, and responses are included in Appendix C at the end of this chapter. [10]

SUMMARY

For many reasons, the need for special training for women is now. The need is great. Organizations need training that helps women make more of a difference back on the job. Using TA in special training for women avoids the problem of just giving information and defining what's wrong, but not giving a workable method for change. The evaluation survey of the Seminars for Career Women gave us evidence that we'd only suspected before. The seminars did help improve on-the-job performance. Participants and their supervisors alike recognized and reported the improvement.

FOOTNOTES AND REFERENCES

1. This definition of winners is developed in *Born to Win: Transactional Analysis with Gestalt Experiments*, by Muriel James and Dorothy Jongeward, (Reading, Massachusetts: Addison-Wesley, 1971), pp. 1-6.

2. The course tuition includes a copy of this book.

3. Dorothy Jongeward and Muriel James, *Winning with People: Group Exercises in Transactional Analysis* (Reading, Massachusetts: Addison-Wesley, 1973).

4. I first saw Kris Hayes, a training director at McClellan Air Force Base in Sacramento, use this approach.

5. Film, *Second Chance*, Hoffman-La Roche Laboratory, Nutley, New Jersey, 07110.

6. See also *Winning With People* by Jongeward and James. This book contains a similar worksheet and several other instruments that can be used in Seminars for Career Women.

7. Film, *Women on the March: The Struggle for Equal Rights*, Part I, by the National Film Board of Canada. We didn't find Part II of the film which features more contemporary women pertinent to the course.

8. Eleanor Flexner, *The Century of Struggle: The Woman's Rights Movement in the United States* (New York: Atheneum, 1971) pp. 90-91.

9. The Ego State Reaction Quiz is reprinted with permission from *Winning With People: Exercises in Transactional Analysis.* This quiz, the Agree/Disagree sheet, and the Ego State Checkout are in Appendix B of this chapter.

10. Sally Keen, a training officer with the U.S. Social Security Payment Center in San Francisco, contributed many valuable ideas when I was developing the questionnaire.

APPENDIX A: REFERENCE BOOKS

We have a copy of some useful reference books displayed in the training room. As the course progresses, participants borrow and add books to the collection. The following books listed in recommended order are a good start.

About Women

Flexnor, Eleanor, *The Century of Struggle: The Woman's Rights Movement in the United States* (Cambridge: Belknap Press, Harvard University, 1959).

Friedan, Betty, *The Feminine Mystique* (New York: Norton, 1963).

Morgan, Robin, ed., *Sisterhood is Powerful* (New York: Vintage, 1972).

Gornick, Vivian and Moran, Barbara K., eds., *Woman in Sexist Society* (New York: Vintage, 1972).

About Transactional Analysis

Harris, Thomas A., *I'm OK — You're OK* (New York: Harper & Row, 1969).

Ernst, Ken, *Games Students Play* (Millbrae, California: Celestial Arts Publishing, 1972).

Berne, Eric, *Games People Play* (New York: Grove Press, 1964).

Berne, Eric, *What Do You Say After You Say Hello?* (New York: Grove Press, 1972).

APPENDIX B: EXERCISES

Part 1: Agree? Disagree?

Will you individually go through the list, marking each statement "Agree" or "Disagree." After everyone in your group has finished, discuss the answers in your group.

Key: *P* - Parent ego state   *A* - Adult ego state   *C* - Child ego state

_____ 1. The main use of TA is to change the people around you.

_____ 2. An 8-year old boy has only a C.

_____ 3. A depressive life position is based on I'm OK – You're not-OK.

_____ 4. I'm not-OK – You're OK is a hostile position.

_____ 5. It's bad to act from your C.

_____ 6. A person should never do what the P says.

_____ 7. The A checks out or validates current reality.

_____ 8. The natural C is self-centered and rebellious.

_____ 9. The A makes new decisions.

_____ 10. You can change through your P.

_____ 11. The adaptive C is spontaneous.

_____ 12. Cultural traditions are passed on through the A.

_____ 13. The P is best at solving problems.

_____ 14. Script is based on a decision made in early childhood and is a compulsion to live life in a certain way. A script ends in a predictable manner.

_____ 15. You can become I'm OK – You're OK through A decisions and positive experiences.

Part 2: Ego State Checkout

Decide individually which ego state would be most frequently associated with the following behaviors. Then discuss your choices with your group.

1. Being affectionate
2. Doing what you're told

3. Being self-centered

4. Passing on traditions

5. Worrying that people will be critical

6. Nurturing

7. Procrastinating

8. Quickly judging

9. Being authoritarian

10. Testing current reality

11. Acting protective

12. Having fun

13. Being intuitive

14. Making decisions to change

15. Being seen and not heard

16. Making new decisions

17. Rebelling

18. Estimating

19. Gathering facts

Part 3: Ego State Reaction Quiz

Identify each reaction to the situation as either Parent, Adult, or Child (P, A, C). There will be one of each in each situation. Naturally these will be educated guesses, since you can't hear the tone of voice or see the gestures.

1. A clerk loses an important letter.

    a.   "Why can't you keep track of anything you're responsible for?"   _____

    b.   "Check each person who may have used it in the last two days and try to trace it. Perhaps Mrs. Smith can help you."   _____

    c.   "I can't solve your problems. I didn't take your old letter."   _____

2. A piece of equipment breaks down.
   a.   "See if a repairman can come this morning."   _____
   b.   "Wow! This machine is always breaking down. I'd like to
        throw it on the floor and jump on it."   _____
   c.   "Those operators are so careless. They should know
        better."   _____

3. The boss is not satisfied with a letter his secretary wrote in
   reply to a memo from another department.
   a.   "Golly, Mr. Smith, I read that memo three times and it's
        so bad I just can't figure it out. He must be a jerk."   _____
   b.   "I found the memo contradictory, Mr. Smith. I'd
        appreciate your telling me what you see as his main
        question."   _____
   c.   "We shouldn't have to answer this memo at all. That man
        clearly doesn't know what he's talking about."   _____

4. Coffee break rumors report a co-worker is about to be
   transferred.
   a.   "Boy, tell me more. I'd like to get something on George.
        He gives me a pain in the neck!"   _____
   b.   "Let's not spread a story that may not be true. If we have
        a question, let's ask the boss."   _____
   c.   "We really shouldn't talk about poor old George. He has
        so many troubles — financial, marital, you name it."   _____

5. The boss has had an important proposal rejected.
   a.   "Poor Mr. Brown, you must feel terrible. I'll fix you a
        little cup of tea to cheer you up."   _____
   b.   "You think you feel bad! Just listen to what happened to
        me!"   _____
   c.   "I'm sorry about the reversal, Mr. Brown. Let me know if
        there is anything you want me to do."   _____

6. A buxom secretary appears on the job in a very tight sweater.
   a.   "Wow, look at that!"   _____
   b.   "Tight sweaters should not be allowed in the office."   _____
   c.   "I wonder why she chose that to wear to work."   _____

7. Someone unexpectedly gets a promotion.

   a. "Well, Mrs. White deserved it. After all, with all those children to feed, she needs that extra money. Poor thing."   ____

   b. "Oh brother! She got that for buttering up the higher-ups."   ____

   c. "I thought I was more qualified for the promotion than Mrs. White. But maybe I haven't given her enough credit."   ____

8. A reduction in personnel is announced.

   a. "What will I do if I'm laid off?"   ____

   b. "This damn company isn't worth working for anyway."____

   c. "I believe that all women should be fired first. They don't need the money. They're just taking jobs away from men."   ____

APPENDIX C: FOLLOW-UP SURVEY

DETAILS THE PARTICIPANTS REPORTED

Questionnaire for Participants

Seminar for Career Women Training Evaluation

For each statement, circle which of the positions at the right most aptly describes your present thinking.		
SA	Strongly Agree
TA	Tend to Agree
NSO	No Strong Opinion
TD	Tend to Disagree
SD	Strongly Disagree

As a result of participating in a Seminar for Career Women, I	Percent	Percent	Percent
	SA and TA	NSO	TD and SD
1. ＿＿＿ am more effective on the job.	72	26	2
2. ＿＿＿get more job satisfaction.	67	27	6
3. ＿＿＿ have more adult control in my interpersonal relationships.	93	6	1
4. ＿＿＿ find working with overly dependent persons increasingly frustrating.	27	27	45
5. ＿＿＿ more effectively handle authoritarian or bossy persons.	75	20	5
6. ＿＿＿ am less sure of exactly what is expected of me at work.	1	18	81
7. ＿＿＿act more often from the ego state most appropriate to the situation.	80	9	11
8. ＿＿＿ find myself in more "it was the only thing I could do" situations.	5	18	78
9. ＿＿＿ have stopped playing, or play at a lighter degree, psychological games.	77	15	8
10. ＿＿＿have an increased consciousness of how some women are programmed to be losers and non-winners.	88	8	4

	Percent	Percent	Percent
11. ＿＿＿ understand more clearly subtle patterns of discrimination.	88	8	4
12. ＿＿＿ am more aware of stereotyping of women by women.	86	7	6
13. ＿＿＿ see fewer psychological games played in the office.	2	25	73
14. ＿＿＿ see less stereotyping of women by men.	12	15	73
15. ＿＿＿ believe the seminar has had little effect on my life.	6	9	85

Participant Question

1. *Considering all training courses you have attended, how would you rate the seminar in terms of its value to your job performance?*

   61% of the participants ranked the seminar in the top 10%.

   87% of the participants ranked the seminar in the top 20%.

   97% of the participants ranked the seminar in the top 30%.

   4% of the participants ranked the seminar lower than the top 30%.

The following are typical answers to these open-end survey questions.

Participant Question

2. *What is your most important learning from this course?*

   "The realization of the subservient role which women have accepted without question, and the fact that it can be changed, and that changes are taking place today. Becoming more interested and active in bettering the present conditions for women and myself."

   "A new awareness of myself on the job and the roles that I play, and the things I can do that will give me more job satisfaction and advancement in my career."

   "Learning to adjust to job situations and coping with demonstrative and unreasonable personnel."

   "An awareness that people are programmed for certain behavior patterns, and that reprogramming is possible."

   "Beginning of an awareness of people's problems — analyzing and understanding behavior. Realization of the power to direct one's own life."

   "To operate from the ego state that is most appropriate to the situation. My attitude needs changing."

"I was quite impressed by the statistics on length of time a woman works and this has definitely made me take my own job more seriously. Also, I think I will reeducate my daughter to place more emphasis on career choice."

"A more rational approach to my job performance. Analyzing myself and solving problems."

"My own smugness in thinking I was such a super manager came in for some critical analysis."

"I had begun to believe my own stereotype. I learned I could change myself — that there was no reason I couldn't be a leader in the organization, instead of a secretary, and to get off my duff and break out of the stereotype, instead of simply feeling frustrated."

Participant Question

3. *What is your least important learning from this course?*

"Learning about the psychological games people play."

"That there is prejudice against women by both sexes. I already knew that."

"Not applicable. The course was meaningful and well planned in its entirety."

"I felt the entire course was very informative and helpful. It was so well planned that I felt every woman left with a new awareness of her future as a career woman."

"Can't think of anything that fell into this category — all seemed succinct and important. The collage making didn't teach me much — I would have preferred more time to discuss."

Participant Question

4. *What subjects would you like added or covered more thoroughly?*

"How we as women put down ourselves and other women."

"How to have mini-classes in TA when we get back to work."

"A little more history of women perhaps."

"How much of our makeup is the result of upbringing and/or subjects pertaining to the individual's personality."

"How women themselves discriminate against women."

"How to deal with discrimination against women."

"How women are their worst enemies in getting ahead in business."

"It was already very thorough."

"Life scripts — how to change."

"Games people play. More information about the female role in American society."

"Developing self-control and personality development."

"How one can change from a loser to a winner."

"We didn't have time to cover all the material in *Born to Win*. Also I was sorry I had not read the entire book before the beginning of the seminar. I would strongly urge that it be mandatory for attendees to read and thoroughly understand the material in the book before going to the seminar."

"Games and game thwarting and how to cope with other's games."

"More on games played and which ego states are involved."

"History of women was fascinating. Would have enjoyed more time spent on this part as a background for the course."

"Turning a 'man's world' into everyone's world is so much easier when everyone is trained for this."

"I can suggest no changes. The course could not be improved in any way. Let a good thing alone."

DETAILS THE SUPERVISORS REPORTED

Questionnaire for Supervisors of Participants

Seminar for Career Women Training Evaluation

For each statement, circle which of the positions at the right most aptly describes your present thinking.		
SA	Strongly Agree	
TA	Tend to Agree	
NSO	No Strong Opinion	
TD	Tend to Disagree	
SD	Strongly Disagree	

As a result of participating in a Seminar for Career Women Training Session, do you believe the participant	Percent SA and TA	Percent NSO	Percent TD and SD
1. _____ is more effective on the job? Please job down any examples.	64	34	1
2. _____ gives evidence of getting more job satisfaction? Please jot down any comments or details.	61	34	4

	Percent	Percent	Percent
3. _____ is less conscious of tradi- tional and new roles for women at work?			
Any comments?	19	37	44
4. _____ demonstrates less initiative on the job?			
Please list examples of actions that suggest this conclusion.	1	13	86

Here are some sample comments from the open-end questions on the survey of supervisors.

Supervisor Question

1. *As a result of participating in a Seminar for Career Women Training Session, do you believe the participant is more effective on the job?*

"Appears to be less argumentative in presenting her opinions and making compromises where necessary, without sacrificing any of her ideas."

"Assumes more responsibility."

"More understanding with other people and understands their problems."

"Used to have constant chip on her shoulder. Highly critical of everyone else. Much better attitude now. More compassionate towards fellow employees. Actually has some understanding for the boss, too."

"Seems to get along a little better with people she supervises."

"Participant uses a more relaxed and less defensive approach when working with others. Participant's self-confidence has increased."

"Gets along better with subordinates, appears to understand their problems more. Doesn't overreact as much as she used to."

"Is becoming more career minded and has a higher degree of dedication."

"Participant seems to be more receptive to points of view other than her own."

"More prone to acceptance of more responsibility and personal career planning."

Supervisor Question

2. *As a result of participating in a Seminar for Career Women Training Session, do you believe the participant gives evidence of getting more job satisfaction?*

"Have noticed she initiates more actions on her own and with less skepticism."

"Seems to be more eager to get the job done pronto. Has launched a couple of new projects on her own."

"Volunteers readily for additional assignments."

"Enjoys accomplishing assigned tasks to a greater degree."

"Her attitude has improved, as evidenced by a decrease in her complaints and a willingness to tackle more complex assignments."

"Present position is designed for women and fulfills their satisfaction needs."

Supervisor Question

3. *As a result of participating in the Seminar for Career Women Training Session, do you believe the participant is less conscious of traditional and new roles for women at work?*

"If she has been conscious that there is a traditional role for women, she hasn't transmitted it to me. We both believe that if there are traditional roles for women, it's because of the organization and its hierarchy."

"Freely counsels women employees within the organization. Has prevented/settled some minor gripes. Feels free to discuss things with boss, knowing her ideas will be considered on merit."

"Participant focuses on work accomplishment and ability and not on past traditional male/female roles to evaluate a situation."

Supervisor Question

4. *As a result of participating in a Seminar for Career Women Training Session, do you believe the participant demonstrates less initiative on the job?*

"She works more independently and with a minimum of guidance."

"Appears to seek more responsibility."

"With increased confidence she has increased initiative in her own job, but does not feel the need to solve other person's problems outside her job."

"In spite of the fact that she is overworked, she still exercises a great deal of initiative."

"After training, I observed several instances of looking for opportunities to help others with backlog."

"Always has demonstrated high initiative."

"Participant has always been leader in the office, and no observable change has been noticed."

"Active on EEO Committee to set our station goals for next year. Nontraditional women's roles are being added for the first time because of her."

9

BANKING ON PEOPLE AND TA

by Mae Bass

Mae Bass is an Affirmative Action officer with the Bank of America in San Francisco. She worked as a secretary and executive secretary during her first six years with the bank. After participating in an in-bank management training program, Ms. Bass spent four years in the training department as assistant coordinator for the bank's Banking on People (NAB) program. Most recently she has served in the Equal Opportunity section of Personnel dealing with programs for both women and minorities.

In addition to her banking and family responsibilities (Mae has two daughters), she leads seminars for government, community organizations, and leadership institutions. These presentations and seminars deal with careers in business, the changing role of women in business, and the use of transactional analysis in training programs for the economically disadvantaged.

Mae received most of her formal education in Phoenix, Arizona. She has an Associate Arts degree in Secretarial Science from Phoenix College and has taken many specialized courses in counseling and management at San Francisco State University and the University of California at Berkeley.

INTRODUCTION

Transactional analysis has become an integral part of the Banking on People Training Program [1] at Bank of America in California. Why? Consider the statement below made by one of our trainees while participating in a classroom session in preparation for a full-time clerical position in the bank.

"I can't do nothing Mrs. Medearis, maybe I have to go home because I am donkey — I am never going to learn nothing."

It was this and similar statements that displayed the same defeatist attitudes and negative self-images. Such statements impel our staff — as counselors and instructors for "disadvantaged" adults — to explore concepts, ideas, techniques, theories, and methods with the objective of finding workable techniques for inclusion in our counseling sessions. Our desire is that these techniques will open new avenues for the trainees to use — if they desire — to build more positive psychological self-images.

Although people are born to win, they are also born helpless and totally dependent on their environment. Winners successfully make the transition from total helplessness to independence, and then to interdependence. Losers do not. Somewhere along the line they begin to avoid becoming self-responsible.

As we have noted, few people are total winners or losers. Most of them are winners in some areas of their lives and losers in others. Their winning or losing is influenced by what happens to them in childhood. [2]

That is to say, we think of ourselves as plain, pretty, or ugly and as smart, mediocre, or dumb, depending on our experiences and the way others react toward us. Our interpretation of others' actions and reactions toward us influences our self-image. Our self-image, in turn, influences our attitudes and behavior.

These concepts have a direct bearing on the training program. In our guidance function to foster growth through methods that will actualize human potential, one of our primary concerns is to provide those trainees who have developed negative self-images with an awareness of self. We provide them with information and alternatives to *help them help themselves* develop positive psychological self-images.

This concern is well-founded because most of our trainees are members of our society's minority groups, and many of these persons have developed negative psychological self-images as a result of what they have been told about themselves. They have been told these things by significant people in their lives (i.e., loving but untrusting parents, unbelieving and discouraging teachers, etc.) and by the prevalent beliefs of our society as a whole. These persons have been labeled as failures, school dropouts, social dropouts, and other negative labels.

Up to this point, I have shared with you only our trainees' psychological profile. Though we are working with our trainees in a work-oriented setting, in order to deal effectively with these negative concepts, we cannot and do not lose sight of the need for *total counseling.* We must provide these new employees with tools to deal with work-related situations or procedures, such as operating an NCR machine or a full-key adding machine, and with getting along with supervisors and co-workers. In addition to providing the tools for vocational success, we must also aid employees in such personal situations as attempting to deal with spouses, children, relatives, friends, merchants, and landlords.

Transactional analysis has provided the staff with one of the workable tools we were seeking that would bring about ways and means of aiding and counseling the total life style and attitudes of our trainees.

Before I continue to discuss how we use TA in the Banking on People Program at Bank of America, I will provide you with an introduction to the total program.

BANKING ON PEOPLE TRAINING COMPONENTS

Since June 1968 Bank of America has participated in the National Alliance of Businessmen Program. The program is jointly funded by the bank and the U.S. Department of Labor. It is an intensive statewide training program set up in the Training Department to hire, train, and provide promotional opportunities for persons from disadvantaged backgrounds who are unemployed or underemployed. It is basically a work-study program which includes English usage, mathematics, grooming, environmental survival skills, office machines, and interpersonal relations. The training lasts eight weeks. This includes four weeks in the classroom and four weeks on-the-job training. For those foreign-born students who need or desire it, an additional two-and-a-half weeks is spent in the classroom to study English as a second language.

PROGRAM OBJECTIVES

The overall goals are to produce efficient employees capable of

1. following directions,
2. using clerical skills effectively (bookkeeping, math, grammar, filing, etc.),
3. presenting a pleasant appearance and good work attitudes,
4. continuing and appreciating learning,
5. doing self-initiated work,
6. dealing with their personal problems.

The trainees are trained for such jobs as general administration clerks, typists, NCR operators, tellers, file clerks, and mail clerks.

THE PARTICIPANTS

Earlier in this chapter I gave you a psychological profile of persons with a negative self-image. Shown below is the profile selection criteria furnished and required by the U.S. Department of Labor. The participants are "disadvantaged" persons, mostly minority group members. They must be from a low income family (using the Labor Department's definition of low income) plus be one of the following:

1. a high-school dropout,
2. a welfare recipient,
3. handicapped, or have special obstacles to employment.

HOW CANDIDATES ARE SELECTED

Applicants are referred only through the Human Resources Development Centers in the state. They are selected on the basis of interview only. We are primarily concerned that the applicants have a sincere desire to work and have some degree of stick-to-itiveness.

Once the 13 to 15 candidates are selected for the training session, they are provided with training in the following areas:

1. *Orientation*
   a) Bank history
   b) Bank objectives
   c) Partial tour of bank's World Headquarters Building
   d) What the bank expects of its employees
   e) What the employees can expect from the bank (benefits)
   f) Bank reference aids
   g) Review of the banking system
2. *English usage*
   a) Word building — suffixes
   b) Parts of speech
   c) Bank vocabulary building
   d) Spelling rules
3. *Mathematics*
   a) Percentages
   b) Parts of speech
   c) Bank vocabulary building
   d) Spelling rules

4. *Environmental skills*
   a) Consumer math
   b) Personal money management
   c) Use of personal checking account
   d) Use of savings account, interest
5. *Reading*
6. *Office practice*
   a) Typing practice
   b) Full-key and ten-key adding machines and calculators (instruction and practice)
   c) Filing practice
   d) Other simulated office duties
7. *Personal development*
   a) Grooming and personal etiquette
   b) Good impressions and positive attitudes
   c) Personal hygiene
   d) Interpersonal relations through transactional analysis

TRANSACTIONAL ANALYSIS IN THE BANKING ON PEOPLE PROGRAM

TA has been used in this program since June 1971.

The theme of our one-day session is winners and losers as discussed in Chapter I of *Born to Win*. Our approach uses discussions and exercises dealing with the concepts of the life script, how it is developed, and *how it can be changed*, if desired.

The other basic TA concepts presented to the trainees during the introductory session are life positions, the ego states, transactions, games, breaking up games, and psychological stamps.

The session is presented by two members of the staff acting as co-leaders, with the aid of overhead projection slides. Each slide presents a central theme. Once each central thought or concept is presented, the staff members expand upon the subject and then ask the trainees to participate by relating their personal experiences or thoughts. Each trainee is presented with a printed copy of the information contained on the slides. (Some trainees have returned the day after the presentation and related enthusiastic discussions they had with their husbands or friends as a result of sharing the booklet with them and talking about their day's activities and instruction in TA.) In addition, each trainee is provided with a copy of *Born to Win* to use during the four weeks in class.

The class is asked to divide into groups of three or four persons after their session on transactions and to develop their own examples of the different types of transactions. They are then asked to discuss their examples as a class. In a later session they are given a worksheet, Getting to Know Your Ego States, and are asked to fill it in. These sheets provide the staff with feedback on their grasp of the concepts.

The staff was initially concerned with its ability to present the TA concepts in a one-day session so that the trainees could grasp the basic concepts and gain enough knowledge of TA to use it in their relationships, and so that their interest would be sparked in continuing to learn about TA and the many ways they could use it in their everyday lives.

Though we would still like to be able to devote more time to TA in the training program, we have been gratified with the impact the one-day sessions have made on many of the trainees. (This impact is beautifully and rewardingly demonstrated by an anonymous letter left on the desk of the instructor one day and quoted at the end of this chapter.)

Our desired goals for this one-day session are reflected in our instructional and behavioral objectives stated below.

1. If desired, the trainee should be able to know the steps to take to begin changing from a loser script to a winner script.

2. When confronted with an attack of "I'm not-OK," the trainee should be able to use knowledge gained in PAC training to rid himself (or herself) of these feelings.

3. The trainee should be able to define the goal of transactional analysis.

4. When asked, the trainee should be able to define and recognize the three ego states, as defined by Dr. Berne, and be able to determine which ego state he (she) or the person he (she) is dealing with is operating from and which life position he (she) is practicing.

5. When confronted with a problem in interpersonal relations, the trainee should be able to recognize the type of transaction in an effort to deal tactfully and/or effectively with the person.

6. The trainee is to be able to recognize when he (she) is playing a game or a game is being played.

7. When a game is recognized and thought to be undesirable by the trainee, he (she) should be able to use some of the TA techniques to break up the game.

Some of the comments from the critique sheets completed at the close of each session indicate that most of the session objectives were met. In answer to the question:

"Do you think the information gained in this session will be helpful to you? If so, explain in what way."

some of the comments have been:

"Yes. I understand a little better why I feel and think as I do about myself."

"Yes. It helped me to set a goal for myself, and to try to reach it; to see what I really want out of life. Also, it helped me to be a better person."

"Yes. It made me have more confidence."

"Yes. It helped me understand how I can guide my life much better. It has given me a guide to help me, not only in this class, but in my home life."

"Yes. It made me know I'm OK and I must hope other people are OK."

It is statements like these and the letter quoted below that make our involvement with the Banking on People Training Program and transactional analysis a very rewarding experience.

June 27, 1972

Friend Lilly,

I have been wanting to speak to you . . but not knowing where to start, or really what to say, I deceided to write it in plain "ENGLISH". (So will you please excuse any misspellings or wrong puncuation, you may come across)? Thank You.

I wanted to tell you, first of all, that if I would have had you for one of my teachers in high school, I think that maybe I would have stayed there and grauduated. But seeing as how I diden't well . . . you know how it is . . .

Mrs. Medearis, you make everything seem so interesting, even though it's terribly "BOREING". The things we do and learn here is really something! ! ! You are an excellent teacher. I'm thankful and proud that I had the pleasure to meet you, and be taught by you.

I am so glad that I am now begining to understand myself. Mrs. Bass did a wonderful job of teaching us to understand ourselves along with our present ego states. Now that "I" know which ego state I'm coming from and where to start making changes, I have noticed the difference already ! ! ! (I'm really happier, and more confident in myself). And I'm still working on me!

I had almost forgotten I had the will to really buckel down and learn, but being in your class has brought this out again. You know, if I had known when I first entered this class what I know now, some avoidable differences could have been avoided. Ego state? Well, anyway, it's a lesson to me.

I still don't like myself (Your O.K. I'm not O.K.) but I feel after I get all the bugs out . . . ALL the BUGS . . . I will not only like myself, but others will be fond of me also!

You know, the understand of myself, of other persons, the english, office pratice, class disscusions and everything else that goes with it, no-one will ever be able to take that knowledge from me. No matter how many jobs I have in my life-time, the knowledge that I take with me from this class will remain mine forever.

I would really like to give my personal thanks to Mrs. Bass, Cheryl, Mr. Wilson, and to you Mrs. Medearis, for your time, patience, and especially your understanding !

I will never forget any of you. *"NEVER"*

Sincerely,

New Employee

FOOTNOTES AND REFERENCES

1. This refers to the Bank of America's participation in the National Alliance of Business Men's Training Program.

2. Muriel James and Dorothy Jongeward, *Born to Win* (Reading, Massachusetts: Addison-Wesley, 1971) p. 3.

10

TRANSACTIONAL ANALYSIS APPLIED TO MOUNTAIN BELL

by Kathy O'Brien

After pondering over her two childhood ambitions to become either a psychologist or a snake, Kathy decided to attend the University of New Mexico to study psychology and interpersonal communication. After two hungry years, she went to work full-time for Mountain Bell as an operator while she completed her undergraduate studies. Within the next two years, Kathy was promoted to Assistant Manager of Operator Services in the traffic department. Once established in this position, she returned to UNM to do graduate work in organizational communication. During that time Kathy discovered TA and many corporate applications of the theory. She was so excited about the many possible uses of the theory in the Bell System that she wrote a paper about it and presented it to some of the higher level managers in the organization. Since most managers in the Bell System are continually bombarded with "papers," this method of introducing TA into the organization was not too productive. The following year was spent turning ideas into realities. The Mountain Bell TA workshop was conceived, developed, and conducted within the management ranks.

Since that time, Kathy has transferred to the Wisconsin Telephone Company as a Business Service Counselor, and to Marquette University in Milwaukee to complete her graduate studies. Since TA is a big part of Kathy O'Brien, the workshops have also moved on to Wisconsin. Mountain Bell, however, is still using TA in many of its management seminars.

APPRAISAL OF MANAGEMENT TRAINING

After doing extensive research in the field of transactional analysis, a training session based upon this theory was designed to facilitate the internal communication in the Bell System. The program was initiated at Mountain Bell, in Albuquerque, New Mexico, a southwestern subsidiary of the American Telephone and Telegraph Company. As in most large organizations, there are many communication problems which are recognized but which remain unsolved. The ease and effectiveness with which TA can be applied to these problems within the organization was the primary motive in the development of this training session.

Dr. Napoleon N. Vaughn, President of Urban Market Developers, Inc., in a recent study of attitudes of employees made this comment in discussing internal communication within the Bell System:

The American Telephone and Telegraph Company is the largest communication system in the world, and yet its internal organization suffers outright confusion in the communications area. The irony of the individual employee isolated within the massive system is everywhere apparent . . . No direct line is open, so the employee is marooned on an island of limited access . . . No personal consideration is really expected in a network that is too powerful to be challenged from within. [1]

The concept of an individual employee isolated within the massive system may be more ironic than Dr. Vaughn realized. As the common nickname "Ma Bell" implies, the Bell System has traditionally been a Parent-oriented organization. The "lost" employee is like a child smothered by a big parent. There is often a tendency in a boss-subordinate relationship to conduct transactions in a Parent-Child manner. A supervisor expects adult behavior and responsibility from his subordinates, while he, at the same time, treats them as small children.

An example of this may be seen in the traffic department, which is composed primarily of the operator force. Until recently, if an operator needed to be excused to go to the restroom, she was required to seek permission from the chief operator. While the rules have become more lax — now an operator need only flip on a light or turn over a sign as a signal to others to await her return before they go — this indignity is not unlike the hand-raising of grade-school children. In this case, however, the company is dealing with grown-ups. This system does serve the purpose of maintaining the required work force at all times. It does seem, however, that there could be a more adult approach to the problem, perhaps by placing the responsibility on the employees and trusting them not to abuse their privilege.

For many years, management trainers in the Bell System have applied the behavioral sciences to their organization. Understanding the value of these theories and teaching better techniques with which to apply them is only a part of the task of bettering employee relations. Due to the complexity of the organization, actual implementation of these theories has been limited. A manager needs more than cognition of the theories. He needs to have an understanding, based on his own experience, of how these theories will fit into his own behavior and his own job.

The Bell System offers new managers several theories for study, among them McGregor's Theory X and Y, [2] Blake and Mouton's Managerial Grid, [3] Herzberg's "Work Itself," [4] and many internally developed theories. Much can be gained from a theorist's point of view in studying these assumptions about people and managerial techniques. The problem in implementing any of these theories is that their success is contingent upon an atmosphere within the work environment supportive of the principles which they proffer. As seen in the International Harvester training programs, most trainees, upon returning to the job from the training situation, revert to the behavior that previously met with their bosses' expectations. [5]

These very real problems of practical adaptation of existing management programs serve to reinforce the value of TA as the missing link in the process of learning, internalizing, and applying managerial principles. Although TA has been used primarily in groups, it can be effectively utilized by the individual for personal growth and understanding. Its effectiveness and implementation is not contingent upon the knowledge, acceptance, or use of its principles by any other member of the organization.

This is not to discount the value of the above-mentioned theories in management training — they can add to the cohesiveness of the organization, as well as facilitate the flow of information within it. TA however, can supplement these theories, since an individual can evaluate his use of them from his own experience, as well as gain insight and knowledge which will better enable him to evaluate his role and responsibilities in organizational transactions.

A TA workshop was held for the New Mexico employment supervisors who had already participated in the majority of the company-sponsored management training programs. At the conclusion of the workshop, the comment was made that, had the group experienced TA prior to the company "team development" program, it would not have taken them eighteen months, as it did, to implement the program. The employment supervisors were able to gain a greater understanding of themselves as individuals and as members of a team through the experience and knowledge gained in the TA workshop.

At the conclusion of another TA seminar, a member of the engineering department explained that he was working on a presentation of a "Management by Objective" program for his department, and was looking for a session to precede his. He commented that, "in looking at the department one-and-a-half to two years into Management by Objective, we need to do something to improve boss-subordinate communication. I've diagnosed the problem; now I want a treatment. TA is the best tool I've seen so far."

If the impression is being created that TA is the cure for all problems, and is popular with everyone, it is not intentional. TA is a theory about people and "Ma Bell" exists because of people. While other existing managerial philosophies advocate the theory that people have common needs and motives, TA gives a person permission to be unique and to develop his individuality in a manner which gives strength to the organization. If this application of TA appears to be a cure-all, the following notes and illustrations from the actual Mountain Bell (and American Telephone and Telegraph) workshops will seem like a miracle.

THE WORKSHOP

The workshops were designed to accommodate a minimum of six participants, and a maximum of fourteen. [6] It is asked that each participant be accompanied by another person with whom he works closely. The rationale was that upon returning to the actual job environment, each participant would have another person from his training class with whom he could discuss what was learned, and who could reinforce the use of the principles taught. With the exception of a few interdepartmental sessions, all of the workshops as of this writing have been conducted with entire work groups, including the supervisor and the management personnel who report directly to him. After presenting several sessions to this type of group, it was felt that the way the sessions were conducted was the most effective. Many of the workshops proved to be an outlet for suppressed hostilities, as well as a tool for building a more cohesive group.

Illustration

Two second-line supervisors had a conflict over the sloppy manner in which the employees were strewing their personal belongings in the employee lounge. The conflict had evidently been raging for several months. One of the supervisors (Fred) had stormed into the office of the other supervisor (Maria) during a meeting and demanded that she remove all of the employees' coats from the lounge. After Fred left, Maria continued her meeting. After only five minutes had elapsed, Fred walked into the meeting carrying all of the coats, dropped them in the middle of Maria's desk, and left.

The two supervisors appeared to have collected many brown stamps (bad feelings) over this little incident, judging by the warmth displayed between them. During an exercise which involved the exchange of "warm fuzzies," [7] these supervisors experienced a very intimate and moving moment in which they both realized the futility of harboring resentments over this matter, and they gave up their stamps.

The effect of this experience on the supervisors and on the whole group was delightful. Having experienced the initial disagreement, even the trainer thought a miracle had occurred. A less dramatic example can be seen in the feedback received after a session conducted for A.T.&.T. Long Lines division in El Paso, Texas. Jaak Aulik, Operations Manager, wrote to me:

> My supervisors and I were discussing Management by Objectives, a system of results measurement where each supervisor prescribes his areas of responsibilities and the *specific* items that he expects to accomplish, as well as the times by which he will have them completed. The supervisor and the next-level manager then meet initially to see if the objectives are mutually acceptable, and later to see how many of the objectives have actually been accomplished. The percent of success (and perhaps the degree of difficulty) determines his appraisal.

> One supervisor brought out a reservation which was then voiced by several of his peers that this system relied upon each supervisor telling of his own accomplishments and that in turn offended his values inasmuch as he did not believe in bragging about the things that he did. At this point, the meeting threatened to come to an abrupt halt, either by way of saying that we will go to the Management by Objectives and everyone *will* comply, or by pointing the accusing finger and saying that the supervisor's position was merely a clever rationalization for avoiding any appraisal based on fact and potentially injurious to his ego as well as his paycheck. Luckily, though, the knowledge of Transactional Analysis that you passed on in your seminar, we opted for a third alternative that was educational as well as beneficial.

> We analyzed that bragging was offensive to us because it has been *taught* to us as being offensive. Telling of one's accomplishments is only a lesser degree of bragging because it has been *taught* to us as being undesirable. Every mother's son has been *taught* — that is, has been given the injunction — that modesty is a virtue and that it is far better to have others find out about your worth rather than

telling them about it. Now, however, we are confronted with a business which functions on information and its timely receipt. In order to make sound decisions, each manager must have a thorough knowledge of the activities that are taking place within the business and of lower levels of management that are making decisions. This counters, however, the injunction we have received in childhood — to be modest, don't give information of your accomplishments to others — and the result is a dilemma to the supervisor caught between his mother's guiding principles and values, and the needs of a well-informed business management. Without the knowledge of injunctions and counterinjunctions, this problem would have been a stumbling block to my organization . . . and might have resulted in a serious rift between levels of management. As it was, we merely exposed what we had been taught, recognized what was valid — that is, don't brag — and retained what was of value — communicate with others in business by giving Adult information. [8]

Not only have the principles of TA helped managers in working out existing problems, but the exercises in the workshops have also helped the participants to see each other in different roles (or ego states), thus shifting the interpersonal emphasis from a superior-subordinate level to an understanding of the individual as a person.

Since every workshop involves different work groups whose jobs vary considerably, the content and presentation of the session also varies somewhat to make it more relevant to each group. Therefore, the following description of the workshop is a chronological breakdown of the basic format of the session.

WORKSHOP INTRODUCTION

The majority of the participants who attend the workshops have little or no previous knowledge of TA. Because of this, a brief description of the development of the theory as it was first used in psychotherapy, as well as the more recent applications of the theory, are presented. This information is then related to the concepts behind the development of the Mountain Bell workshop and its objectives. These objectives are best expressed by Dorothy Jongeward and Muriel James in their Instructor's Manual for *Born to Win*:

1. *To stimulate an awareness of how personality affects communication patterns.*

2. *To improve management communication.*

3. *To understand the principles of transactional analysis.*

4. To stimulate an awareness of how the decisions a person makes about himself early in childhood relate to and influence his behavior and attitudes as an adult — particularly as a manager. [9]

During this introduction, the group members are given a chance to collect "real" gold and brown "trading stamps." These are psychological trading stamps, and are the currency of transactional rackets. The color of the stamps are representative of the feelings a person collects — in this case, gold represents good feelings and brown represents bad feelings. Just as with the grocery store type of stamps, these can be cashed in for a prize, only with TA stamps, the prize is a psychological one. For example, a manager who has collected three books of brown stamps can cash them in for a guilt-free chewing out session of an employee, thus releasing his pent-up bad feelings; or three books of gold stamps earned by several days of hard work and overtime can be cashed in for one day of loafing in the office.

Throughout the workshop, the trainer passes out little pieces of paper labeled gold and brown "trading stamps" to the group members without explanation of their meaning. (Actually, the brown stamps are labeled with an "S" for manure.) If someone makes a comment which gives the trainer a good feeling, such as displaying exceptional interest in what is being said or done, he is "paid off" with a gold stamp. Likewise, behavior which gives the trainer a bad feeling earns a brown stamp.

Although this exercise is done in jest, it is interesting to observe the participants' reactions to the trading stamps both before and after they are explained.

Illustration

Paula had a truly refreshing Natural Child. When she was in good form, she was really good, and when she was bad, she was awful. She had been making frequent humorous but sarcastic comments to her co-workers during the session, each one being followed by a brown stamp from the trainer. Paula was very bright and alert, and had a quick wit and a faster mouth, so in the course of the workshop she amassed a considerable number of brown stamps. Probably because she had collected so many, Paula didn't spend much time figuring out what the brown "S" stamps represented, and was successfully trading all of them off for her co-workers' gold stamps. When asked by the trainer what she was doing, Paula replied, "I've been getting brown stamps all week from everyone, so now I'm giving them back."

Later in the session, when trading stamps were explained, this incident received many laughs, but it also reinforced the principles which the stamps represent.

STRUCTURAL ANALYSIS — THE PAC

In explaining the PAC, it took the leader only one session to realize that most people have a compulsion to take notes (or perhaps what was being said was particularly noteworthy), so the figure below was printed and handed out to alleviate the need for notes and to save the participants' time for listening to what was being said. As the ego states are being explained, the group members are asked to give examples of messages they received as a child, or stimuli which consistently activate a particular ego state. These messages are then examined to see what relationship they have to the individual's behavior as a manager.

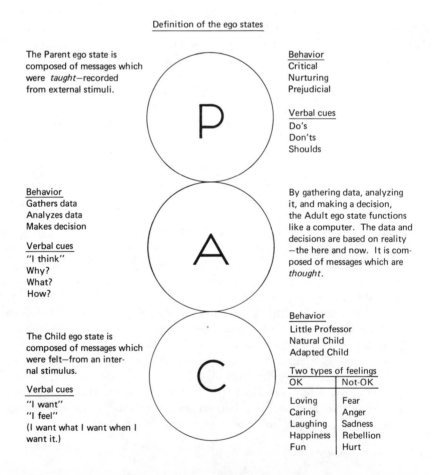

Definition of the ego states

The Parent ego state is composed of messages which were *taught*—recorded from external stimuli.

Behavior
Critical
Nurturing
Prejudicial

Verbal cues
Do's
Don'ts
Shoulds

Behavior
Gathers data
Analyzes data
Makes decision

Verbal cues
"I think"
Why?
What?
How?

By gathering data, analyzing it, and making a decision, the Adult ego state functions like a computer. The data and decisions are based on reality —the here and now. It is composed of messages which are *thought*.

Behavior
Little Professor
Natural Child
Adapted Child

The Child ego state is composed of messages which were felt—from an internal stimulus.

Verbal cues
"I want"
"I feel"
(I want what I want when I want it.)

Two types of feelings

OK	Not-OK
Loving	Fear
Caring	Anger
Laughing	Sadness
Happiness	Rebellion
Fun	Hurt

Illustrations

Message: If you want something done right, do it yourself.

Effect: Manager has problem delegating work to his subordinates. He works many overtime hours doing the work himself so that it will be done right.

Message: A woman's place is in the home.

Effect: (In male manager) Has never recommended a woman for a promotion because he believes they cannot make managerial decisions since they are overemotional, and "only good for making babies and dinner."

(In female manager) Has a tendency to act "motherly" toward her subordinates to compensate for the guilt she has for not staying home with her children.

This analysis of messages also enables managers to realize that their co-workers have many of the same, or similar, messages, but they have developed a different response to them.

Each member of the group is given an Ego State Reaction Quiz [10] which was designed to show three possible reactions, representing the three ego states, that an individual can have to the same stimulus. The quiz illustrates how a chronological adult (most managers are one) can respond in an ego state other than his Adult, which is sometimes difficult for participants to believe.

At this point in the session, the participants have a relatively good understanding of the PAC, so to give them a chance to see all of the ego states in action on the job, a slide-tape presentation is shown. The presentation shows employees in all of the ego states, first in the Adult, then in the Parent, then in the Child. There is a juxtaposition of shots taken in a family situation which illustrates how behavior is transferred from the home to the job. The last half of the presentation shows the transition of an individual from the Adult ego state to the Parent, and then to the Child.

The next exercise is a role-played meeting during which the participants discuss a topic which they might normally discuss in an actual meeting. Before the meeting is started, each person is given a card marked either P, A, or C, and is asked (given permission in some cases) to conduct all of their transactions from the ego state indicated on their card. At the conclusion of the meeting, each participant is asked to determine what ego state he felt his fellow group members were assuming. He is then asked to make a note of the type of behavior he was trying to emulate in his role-playing (i.e. critical, nurturing, or prejudicial Parent; gathering data, analyzing it, or making a decision in the Adult; or Little Professor, Adapted Child, or Natural Child). After each participant has described the ego state assumed, the other members of the group have an opportunity to tell their perceptions of the same ego states. Therefore, one participant who may have perceived himself as being Adult as indicated on his card may have been perceived as being Parent by the other members of the group. The majority of the group members get completely involved in the mock meeting and need to be reminded that this is pretend. At the end of the meeting, these are the ones who are most astonished at the ease with which they change from one ego state to another.

In discussing the PAC, an explanation of contaminations in the ego states is presented. This enables the participants to see how recorded messages will automatically replay, contaminating the Adult analysis of the stimulus.

Illustration

In accordance with the current trend in organizations today, Mountain Bell has been avidly supporting and participating in the Equal Employment Opportunity movement. In attempts to lessen the existing stigma in individual philosophies toward racial or ethnic groups, the company has developed a cultural awareness program which every employee is required to attend. By explaining in the TA workshop the acquisition of prejudicial attitudes and behavior, the participants were able to examine their own Parent tapes for archaic messages. If these messages were seen by the individual as being archaic, they could then be rejected, thus eliminating some of the unconscious discriminatory tendencies a manager might have. The possibility of a manager examining prejudicial messages and deciding they are still relevant to reality was also discussed so as not to imply that awareness of prejudicial feelings will eliminate them.

The presentation of the principles of transactional analysis is perhaps the most important part of the meetings, in terms of the needs of the organization. The presentation and exercises utilizing the principles of structural analysis fill a large part of the workshop in order to allow the trainees to internalize the information and increase their understanding of their role in determining the outcome of transactions which occur in their jobs. Before explaining transactions, the relationship between structural and transactional analysis is given to explain what happens when two PAC's get together.

A felt board with stick-on arrows and PAC letters is used to define the four types of transactions: complementary, crossed, and angular and duplex ulterior transactions. The jargon used to describe the transactions is not emphasized, but rather the implications in the communication environment are stressed. In a complementary transaction, the trainer explains that communication can continue; in a crossed transaction, communication is blocked; and in ulterior transactions, the outcome may be counterproductive.

After defining the various transactions, the group members are asked to discuss transactions they recently had which went either particularly well or very poorly. The following illustration was one which was offered for discussion.

Illustration

Toni, a clerk in a department which was, out of necessity, very concerned about absence and tardy time, had established a trend of late arrivals. Neel, a new supervisor in the office in which Toni worked, and the one to whom she reported, noticed these late arrivals since she and Toni worked closely throughout the business day. The following is part of the transactions which took place between them concerning the tardy time.

Neel: Do you know why we need you to be here right at eight o'clock?

Toni: I don't know why you make such a big deal about tardies. No one gets upset if I get off work late.

Neel: You know what you need to do each day, so it's your responsibility to pace yourself and your work so that you will be through by five. However, we're not discussing the time you leave work; we're discussing the time you come in to work in the morning.

Toni: Well, I guess the fact that I have a four-year perfect attendance record doesn't make any difference.

Neel: Yes, that does make a difference, but not when we're talking about the trend of tardy time you have established.

Toni: Now I'm so upset I can't work. I should have reported off all day.

This example, and any others that are brought up in the workshops, was discussed and diagramed. Neel, who had some exposure to TA prior to the workshop and the discussion with Toni, had made a conscious effort during the entire transaction to remain in her Adult. She added that during the contact, she was constantly fighting the urge to allow her Parent to be hooked. After continually getting defensive Child responses from Toni, she kept hearing a voice inside her saying,

"This TA isn't working. It's just not working." Fortunately for the trainer in that session, the story had a happy ending — Toni was never tardy again. By refusing to accept Toni's Child behavior, Neel was able to establish a new Adult rapport and a productive working relationship.

After analyzing the transactions contributed by the group, replays of the mock meeting are discussed. This is done because it is less threatening than analyzing real situations, especially real ones that have a bad ending. (Many of the participants offer "real life" examples of transactions by starting with, "A friend of mine had a problem once. . .") In the mock meeting, the participants have been given permission to have crossed or ulterior transactions as well as complementary ones.

The part of the workshop devoted to transactions is a natural lead into the next section on life positions and stroking, mainly because everyone always wants to know why "they" are like that.

LIFE POSITIONS

The four life positions:

1. I'm not-OK — You're OK
2. I'm OK — You're not-OK
3. I'm not-OK — You're not-OK
4. I'm OK — You're OK

have been explained best in these workshops briefly, with many examples. Not only does the trainer get tongue-tied, but the note-takers confuse the matter even more with their "Run that by agains."

Illustration

(The number of the example corresponds with the number of the life position from above.)

1. "I knew my work had gotten worse. I'm just not as fast as the other operators."

2. "Why in hell didn't you do that the way I showed you? I should have known the only way to get this done right was to do it myself."

3. "I thought I was the only incompetent person in this department, but I was wrong as usual. The whole damned department is full of incompetents!"

4. "Thank you for the appraisal of my work. I think you were very fair and honest in your evaluation."

It is difficult to talk about life positions without discussing stroking and its effect on the development of the life position a person decided on early in life.

Stroking

Before the discussion on stroking begins, the trainer takes time to share with the group her favorite fairytale called "A Fairytale" by Dr. Claude Steiner. [11] After the story, the group usually takes a few minutes to discuss the story's implications and to exchange a few fuzzies with each other. The fuzzies are instructional as well as fun, however, for they serve as a good introduction into stroking — the very real need to receive strokes, negative or positive, to keep the spine from shriveling up, and to keep from dying.

Illustration

Neel was having a monthly review with one of her employees (Ann) about her work during the past month. Ann had at one time been an outstanding employee, the quality and quantity of her work being exceptional. For several months prior to this particular work review, her work had decreased in both areas, and Ann had become very hostile toward her supervisor and her job. At the beginning of their discussion, Neel was almost talking to herself as Ann did not appear to be listening to anything that was said, much less making any responses. After only a few minutes of talking, Neel asked Ann to go back to work if she was not going to participate in the discussion. Ann knew immediately that something was wrong since she hadn't gotten the whole report on her work yet. This turn of events got Ann interested in the conversation. Ann and Neel were then able to discuss the work results in a productive manner. After talking for a short while, Ann blurted out, "Who cares what I do? I'm just a number here."

This may be a dramatic illustration, but it is a significant one. Ann was dying of stroke deprivation, something which is commonplace in many large organizations. An employee receives a great deal of supervisory help as part of his development into a productive worker. Once he reaches the productive stage, those wonderful strokes are withdrawn and given to someone who may not be doing quite as well.

Everyone knows a negative stroke is better than no stroke at all, so when the positive strokes were no longer available to Ann, she let her work slip, since this would surely bring a negative stroke. Neel, the same supervisor who thought her TA wasn't working, knew that Ann needed a lot of stroking, particularly the positive type, and was able to help Ann maintain a high work level.

Each workshop usually has its skeptic who believes he is above stroking. The skeptic's attitude is based on the rationale that the more education one has and the higher one rises in the hierarchy of the organization, the less stroking one needs from outside sources, because at that point the most rewarding strokes come from self-stroking. But this is not as good as strokings by others. By its absence, one develops an appreciation for warm fuzzies (positive strokes).

The warm-fuzzy story seems to be the most contagious part of the workshop. After an A.T.&T. workshop, the trainer received a copy of the group's district newsletter in which the following remark appeared.

Recently El Paso acquired two new supervisors, J.L. and K.R. — the latter has a very fuzzy face, and we would like to know if he is a warm fuzzy or a cold prickly? Would someone in the district please let us know?

Jaak Aulik, Operations Manager in the El Paso district, also sent the following comments on the effect of fuzzies in his plant.

I've found an instance personally where I have been able to use the story: a breakdown of communications between two groups was prevented from escalating into open hostility by assembling the factions and telling them the story. Each of the individuals took the story as it was intended and began to show some empathy for the other party's position. [12]

One final illustration of Steiner's "fairytale" in action follows.

Illustration

Neel used the warm-fuzzy story in counseling an employee who was a good worker as far as the quantity and quality of her work was concerned, but had, on many occasions, a rather curt tone when dealing with the customers. The employee, Barbara, recognized the problem herself, but attributed the tone she used when dealing with the customers to the mood she was in when she came to work. After hearing the fuzzy story, Barbara commented "The more warm fuzzies you give out, the more you get." The following week, Barbara received two customer letters commending her on the way she handled their business and citing her courteous manner. In this case, Barbara got some nice warm fuzzies in return for the ones she gave out — great reinforcement for her new attitude.

With all the excitement the warm fuzzies have created around the Bell System, the trainer is suggesting that the public relations department adopt the slogan "Ma Bell gives warm fuzzies."

To understand the human need for stroking is great, but how does this understanding relate to organizational behavior? How do people get strokes? What do they do with them? Knowledge of stroking is not enough. One must also understand life positions, rackets, stamp collecting, the structuring of time, and the role the organization plays in determining these factors. If Ann was basically OK, she might merely have asked her supervisor for a stroke for her work. But in an organization which places considerable emphasis on levels of organizational hierarchy and appropriate behavior for each level in relation to its level-conscious superiors, this is usually not an acceptable procedure. Note the following example.

Illustration

One third-level supervisor (in a hierarchy of five) reported that he asked his fourth-level supervisor for a work appraisal, to which his supervisor replied, "If I didn't like the way you did your job I would have told you by now. You can assume you are doing your job right until you hear otherwise from me."

This maintenance stroke (if it can be classified as one) probably maintained the third-level employee at least until he got back to his office.

A person's life position will also determine how he accepts incoming strokes. For example, the OK supervisor says: "You did a good job on your presentation of the study results." Not-OK subordinate: "Ah, it was nothing. Joe did most of the work."

Although the TA workshop is not a package of miracles for turning not-OK employees (frogs) into OK employees (princes or princesses), it does increase sensitivity toward fellow members of the organization, a fact which, in turn, might diminish the need for the Anns of the company to seek negative strokes when positive strokes are available.

The life position one has decided upon will also be apparent in the rackets one uses. An employee who collects brown stamps probably has been collecting them long before his employment by TPC (The Phone Company), but many new rackets for collecting brown stamps may be learned within the organization.

Illustration

One fifth-level department head (that's the biggie) reportedly asked a mere first-level employee to comment on some ideas he had for managing his department. After the first-level man so boldly made his comments, and added a few more that weren't asked for, he went back to his own little desk to work, undaunted by the experience and not realizing that the fifth-level man had collected a whole big bag of brown stamps in that one brief encounter. When the time came for the cash-in of the stamps, the first-level man was caught totally off guard when he learned he was going to be fired. The fifth-level man later ate his stamps, and all turned out well, but the experience was valuable to the first-level man as he now had first-hand information on the power possessed in one big bag of brown stamps, particularly if it is held by the boss. [13]

Experience is thought to be a good teacher, and with each workshop, the trainer's realization of the importance of the six ways of structuring time also increases. There is a real danger in a supervisor first becoming enlightened to the games he has been playing with his subordinates and co-workers, and then ending the games without replacing with something else the time the games filled. This leaves the employee at a loss, for not only does he have to restructure that time, but also he must find a new source for the strokes he is not now receiving, be they positive or negative.

The following examples of ways to structure time have been brought up in the workshops, and have a direct influence on the effectiveness and behavior of the manager.

Withdrawal

Since the assumption is often made that because an employee is good in a job he will also be good as a supervisor of others who perform the same job, many employees find themselves in a position in which they are not only uncomfortable, but unsuited. Feeling not-OK in a position may cause a supervisor to withdraw from having contact with those he supervises and to fill his time with paper shuffling — amazing as it may seem, for some people this alternative is more desirable than face-to-face interaction. On the other hand, some people interact with others very effectively on the job, but are not-OK with the same people in a social situation. They may withdraw to their own thing during the lunch hour and after work. The first case is destructive withdrawal for it affects the job performance of the supervisor and of those who depend upon his supervision. The second case can be constructive withdrawal if that is what makes the employee happy.

Rituals

Rituals are good because they provide mutual stroking with no real commitment. The significance of a ritual is usually not apparent until the ritual, or some part of it, ceases. A boss can use this as a way of telling an employee how insignificant he really is by not providing a reciprocal stroke when the employee says "Hello" to him in the corridor or cafeteria.

There is another danger for the individuals who go from office to office partaking in rituals and/or pastimes, and later get promoted because they are "good guys." The danger isn't really there for the one who can effectively get away with it and still do his job, but it is there for the guy who is working hard to master his job and develop himself for a new one. He may become apathetic when he learns that socializing and "exposing himself" is more effective for getting promotions than for developing his own qualifications.

Pastimes

Pastimes are a great way to feel another person out as to his interests, and to determine if there is enough in common between you to warrant further interaction. Like rituals, pastimes, too, can be misused. An ambitious, aggressive female learns that her boss is not particularly interested in an afternoon session of "wardrobe" or "diapers" but may be very interested in killing time with a session of "Arnold Palmer" or "Joe Namath." [14]

Pastimes can also be counterproductive if used as an alternative to work.

Activities

Of all the management jobs which were represented by a member of the group in the workshops, there was no job that did not require activities (work) at some level, so this would appear to be a good way to fill some of the time between eight and five, particularly for managers in TPC whose merit increases depend upon it. Activities can become destructive when an employee overloads himself at the expense of others in the organization — doing everybody's work and leaving them idle time to fill, or becoming so engrossed in the activities that he neglects the rituals and pastimes his supervisor and subordinates are depending upon.

Games

While Eric Berne says some games are better than others, it is obvious that games can consume a great deal of time and produce very little. [15] The organization has as many ongoing games as it does managers. While a list of the examples of games mentioned in the workshop is beyond the scope of this chapter, many of the games described in the groups had the same basic theme. It seems that some members of the organization save up a lot of information about the job performance (or personality conflicts) of an employee until he has enough to justify a verbal lashing, a demotion, or even termination of employment (*NIGYSOB*). [16] Job appraisals are infrequent, or at best irregular. A surprising number of supervisors reportedly set their employees up for the big *NIGYSOB* game by collecting information — true or false — for the great moment of accusation which causes some red faces or a few tears. Sometimes a demotion or a promotional block is the result. One group participant reported having been told, "Write that in his record, give him a warning the next time he does it, and then keep watching until you catch him again. Then we'll let him have it." Of course, many of the group members admitted to having the moves of the game "down pat," including the victims. There are some drawbacks however. The *NIGYSOB* game being as popular as it is has created many paranoid employees who will jump into a game of *Stupid* if someone even looks at them. The game of *NIGYSOB* is retarded while *Stupid* is being played-out. In the end some very good aggressors emerge but some simply quit playing by quitting their jobs.

The Bell System is no worse than any other large organization in the game-playing department. Organizations are run by people, many of whom have structured their lives around the playing of games — including their corporate lives.

After several workshops had been conducted, we realized that it was necessary not only to discuss the organizational games, but also alternatives to them. If a manager becomes enlightened about a game he has been playing with an employee (or employees) and makes a decision to end that game, he needs to replace the time the game filled with something else. Unless the time is restructured, the possibility exists that the players will either switch roles in the game or start playing another one.

Illustration

Two weeks after a manager (Ron) had attended one of the first TA workshops, he called the trainer about a problem which had him perplexed. After the session, he realized he had been playing *Why Don't You? — Yes, But* [17] with one of his employees and decided to end the game. The next time the employee (Dick) came to him with a problem, Ron told him to work out a solution and then discuss it with him again. Dick left the office very confused and didn't come back to talk with Ron for several weeks. By that time a decision about the problem had been made — a very poor one at that — and the results were nearly disastrous. Ron tried to discuss the reasons for the decision, the reasons that Dick hadn't discussed it with him, and the outcome. But he then realized that Dick was now playing a new game *See What You Made Me Do*. [18]

Since Ron cut off the game without building a new level on which to communicate, Dick found his own way, with unfortunate results for all of those involved.

Intimacy

Hopefully, as a result of the TA workshops, many more intimate working relationships will form in the organization. This is not to suggest that the trainees spring forth from the session and form sexual liaisons with one another, but that they try establishing honest, open relationships with their co-workers, their subordinates, and their supervisors, enhance their communication efforts interdepartmentally, and increase goal-directed behavior.

Scripting

The presentation of the principles involved in life scripts has received a variety of reactions. Some see its value in helping "sick" people but see no use for it in the organization. Others recognize some facets of life script examples in themselves and seek individual counseling from the trainer — either after work hours or at a time when their co-workers are not present. This type of counseling has been avoided thus far by the trainer, because in a management training seminar, such behavior from the trainer is considered inappropriate and unethical. Individuals seeking therapeutic sessions are referred to non-Bell-related sessions.

Illustration

Donna has five children, one in a home for the emotionally disturbed, one in a home for wayward girls, one an alcoholic at 15, one a drug addict, and one who is "normal" but has an unusual relationship with her cat. Donna always attributed her children's problems to the "now" generation, but she began feeling responsible for their conditions after the workshop — particularly the part on life scripts. She recalled telling the drug-addict son that he was exactly like her husband, a "no-good bum" whom she divorced. The alcoholic son was always said to be like Donna's brother — an alcoholic himself.

Donna started bringing a child or two in for counseling without forewarning the trainer. Since the trainer and her superiors felt this was not within the realm of her job, it had to be stopped.

Many people (including some in organizations) need help in confronting and working out problems, but because of other incidents similar to the incident with Donna, scripting is no longer presented in depth as originally planned. It should be mentioned that the presentation of scripting has been very constructive for many participants. However, other more powerful members of the organization have felt it could be too threatening for some to handle.

Following the discussion on scripting, the session is opened to questions (actually it is never closed to them); then the meeting is summed up and concluded. The conditions under which the workshops have been run have not been ideal. The session was first presented to top management for approval and acceptance during the peak of the annual "austerity program." The first expenses usually cut are training expenses. The fact that the sessions were allowed to be conducted at all was amazing in itself.

One of the selling points in favor of the sessions was that they could be conducted in a one-day period of time. Since the trainer's belief in the sessions was so strong, the decision was made to conduct them under whatever conditions were possible. Fortunately, the feedback from the participants indicated that the information presented in the workshops was not only valuable, but was being used. (One manager reportedly stopped a meeting abruptly and said, "God, that was a Parent thing to say.")

The long-range goals for these sessions are to incorporate them into the Bell System "Initial Management Training" as well as other existing programs. It is not intended to be *the* answer to whatever ails the organization, but to be simply a tool for understanding and applying methods of management and communication theories.

The first series of workshops did not allow for follow-up sessions for discussion and reinforcement of the applications of TA on the job. This is slow in changing, but the need for these sessions is in the discussion stage. In any large organization, change is never quick. Change in managers' behavior which took a lifetime to develop will also be slow. The trainer has learned to accept the small corporate blessings as they come, but not to give up fighting for the miracles. If only one person can be spared the organizational pressures which can turn a creative mind into a piece of driftwood, all the efforts, frustrations, and time involved in putting together this workshop is justified.

It cannot be said that no one listens to the little guys at Mountain Bell and A.T.&T. The system listened to this trainer, saw something of value, and allowed the sessions to be run. But what happened to the managers who shouted when no one listened? They grew silent and accepting. Why do so many of them grow old and apathetic and say, "I had new ideas once, but back then no one listened"? Maybe no one listened then, but people are beginning to listen now because they know that unless those minds can be reached and restimulated, the System will continue to mold "Ma Bell's *Children*" into tomorrow's Parents — the managers.

FOOTNOTES AND REFERENCES

1. John A. Howland, "Talking At or Talking With," *Bell Telephone Magazine*, March/April, 1971: 5-9.

2. Douglas McGregor, *The Human Side of Enterprise* (New York: McGraw Hill, 1960).

3. Robert Blake and Jane Srygley Mouton, *The Managerial Grid* (Reading, Massachusetts: Addison-Wesley, 1969).

4. Frederick Herzberg, *The Motivation To Work* (New York: John Wiley, 1962).

5. Edwin A. Fleishman, Edwin F. Harris, Harold E. Burdt, "Leadership and Supervision in Industry" (Columbus: Bureau of Educational Research, Ohio State University, 1955).

6. I was taught in school that a group such as this should always have an odd number of people. In accordance with this, the workshops always have an odd trainer.

7. Warm fuzzies (good feelings), plastic fuzzies (counterfeit warm fuzzies), and cold pricklies (bad feelings) are terms created by Dr. Claude Steiner and appear in his story "A Fairytale," which was printed in the *Transactional Analysis Bulletin*; (Berkeley, California: International Transactional Analysis Association) 10 (No. 36, October, 1970): 146.

8. Correspondence from Jaak Aulik, A.T.&T. Long Lines Department, Operations Manager, El Paso, Texas, dated May 21, 1972 and addressed to Kathy O'Brien, Mountain Bell, Albuquerque, New Mexico. Reprinted by permission.

9. Muriel James and Dorothy Jongeward, "Transactional Analysis and Management Practice," Instructor's Manual for *Born to Win: Transactional Analysis with Gestalt Experiments* (Reading, Massachusetts: Addison-Wesley), 1971, p. 1.

10. Muriel James and Dorothy Jongeward, "Ego State Reaction Quiz," Instructor's Manual for *Born to Win: Transactional Analysis with Gestalt Experiments* (Reading, Massachusetts: Addison-Wesley, 1971), pp. 8-10.

11. See footnote 7.

12. See footnote 8.

13. It might be added that in the workshop, when the truth comes out about the meaning of the gold and brown stamps, since they were given out as a learning experience, no one has yet tried to cash them in on the trainer. Thus, this exercise remains unchanged in the sessions.

14. Pastimes are superficial exchanges between people about common topics. They are used to pass time with someone a person does not know well, and offers a chance for those involved to "feel" each other out to see if the relationship has more potential.

15. Eric Berne, *Games People Play* (New York: Grove Press, 1964).

16. *NIGYSOB, Now I've Got You, You S.O.B.* is a game described by Berne which has the aim of justification. An example of this would be a young executive who plays *NIGYSOB* as he observed his father doing when his father waited for people to make a mistake and then felt justified in exploding with rage.

17. *Why Don't You? – Yes, But* is another game described by Berne in his book on games. In this game a person solicits for solutions to a problem only to

later reject them with some excuse. The payoff comes when no more solutions are offered, and the Child of the player can marvel in the Parent inadequacy to do anything for him.

18.   *See What You Made Me Do* is a game in which the player can relieve himself of all blame for things that go wrong by rationalizing that the other guy made him do it.

11

TA IN SELLING

by Ed Musselwhite

Ed Musselwhite began his sales career with the Data Processing Division of the IBM Corporation after graduating from Northwestern University. During his career with IBM, he earned numerous awards for outstanding personal sales performance, and was promoted rapidly to become one of IBM's youngest sales managers. In addition, he was a top-rated guest instructor at IBM sales schools.

Ed is one of the founders, and Executive Vice President, of DELTAK, Inc. DELTAK is a multi-million-dollar producer and direct marketer of its own text-, audio-, and video-based multi-media training programs for industry, specializing in the fields of data-processing education and human relations training.

DELTAK utilizes transactional analysis extensively in its various human relations courses for customer contact personnel, supervisors, managers, and salesmen.

Ed's personal interests in transactional analysis and its business applications have made him a featured speaker at numerous seminars and conferences.

Even if you are not a salesman*, some part of your job probably requires you to seek out and engage in mutually successful transactions with other people. But if you are a salesman, your job is to spend every possible minute of the working day in such transactions. Consequently, I'm convinced that transactional analysis provides one of the most powerful sales training tools ever made available for most of us.

The success of a sales organization depends on how realistically each salesman understands his customer's needs, how clearly he communicates the value of his products or services in light of those

---

* The word "salesman" is used in this chapter to refer to any person, male or female, whose prime job responsibility involves the selling of goods or services.

needs, how confident and secure he is in his feelings about himself and his organization, and how effectively and profitably he uses the time and dollars allocated to marketing activities. For the salesman, TA provides productive skills in all of these areas.

If you are not a salesman or sales trainer, TA's application in selling is still important to you. First of all, if you are in a position in which you must make recommendations for change, you are a salesman when you make those recommendations. If you must implement programs which involve change, you are at that moment a salesman. (If you don't like the idea of being called a salesman, don't feel lonely; lots of salesmen don't like it either, for reasons I'll mention later.) When you must convince others to adopt your ideas and take action (as salesmen do), TA is a great help.

Second, if you are not a salesman or sales trainer, TA's applications in selling can assist you in measuring its potential value in other areas of your organization. Sales training provides one of the most measurable applications of TA in business. The performance of your company's salesmen and sales managers has probably been quantified, chartered, graphed, and analyzed more often and in more ways than any other statistical data about your company. For this reason, the behavioral changes and performance improvements which TA generates in your marketing operations can be readily compared to past performance.

PARENT MESSAGES AND LIFE POSITIONS IN SELLING

You may have some very emphatic Parent messages about salesmen. Most of us do. How would you describe a salesman? Think about that for a moment and jot down some of the adjectives you would use. How would these messages affect a salesman's work today?

Did you come up with words like "egotistic," "arrogant," "pushy," "smooth-talker," "unethical" — or maybe "confident," "out-going," "independent," "a people person"? If your mental image of a salesman falls into the "arrogant" or "pushy" category, I'm sure you didn't like my earlier statement about all of us being salesmen at one time or another. (Salesmen with similar images miraculously become "marketing representatives.")

The fact is, our unanalyzed messages about salesmen are probably wrong, just as they probably are about other professions and races, and the other sex. If I asked your organization's salesmen, clerical staff, or top executives to write down their messages about your profession, how close do you think they would come to defining you. Chances are, they would miss by a mile!

TA is a powerful training tool because it forces us to look beyond the stereotypes and address the human needs and motivations of people as they really exist. Salesmen, trainers, secretaries, accountants, managers — all of us — have one thing in common. We are all human beings who were domesticated by parents, and — as a result — each of us has a life position, with a script, which will operate like a perpetual-motion machine unless we recognize it and choose to change it. With our script tucked under our arms, we bounce around transacting with other people, choosing to selectively accept and give positive or negative strokes for recognition in the ways in which we've learned to reinforce our feelings about ourselves and others.

The sales profession and the people in it have only one element that makes them different. That's the fact that they must transact constantly with other people in a job that publishes the successes and failures of their transactions almost daily. To reinforce whichever life position he chooses, all a salesman has to do is look at the salesmen's performance ranking chart on the wall of the sales office.

For example, here's how five competent salesmen recently reacted to their relative performances. What do these statements tell you about the life position each is reinforcing?

> "There I am, ranked at the bottom again. I'm just not worth a damn!"

> "Another lousy month. I've got the worst territory and the cheapest bunch of customers in the office."

> "Well, I'm still number three in the office, but I know it's just luck; it won't last."

> "Things haven't been going so hot so far this year, but I think that the prospect seminar I gave last week, plus the work I've done on polishing my presentation, should get me back on target."

> "Yes siree, that proves it again, I AM A STAR!"

Selling, like no other profession, gives the opportunity to keep a minute-to-minute scoreboard. A salesman faces numerous quantifiable opportunities each day to prove to himself that he is OK or not-OK, whichever he chooses. If he feels not-OK, he can reinforce that life position repeatedly at great expense to the organization, and at great monetary and emotional expense to himself.

TA can help a salesman recognize and reduce the nonproductive effort he may be expending every day reinforcing unrealistic Parent messages about himself or his profession. This effort can then be focused on productive activities which can bring real success to him and his organization.

HOW TA CAN BE USED TO IMPROVE INDIVIDUAL
SALES SKILLS

You can find libraries of books that present successful selling techniques. Within these volumes, successful salesmen have documented the simple techniques that they have used to become wealthy, and even famous. These techniques have worked for them and most should work for other salesmen as well.

Even in the face of these success stories, many salesmen find it frustratingly difficult, or impossible, to use these techniques. This is true even though these same salesmen may verbalize the value of these techniques almost as well as the authors themselves. TA helps to explain this phenomenon and also suggests practical ways of transposing these skills from theory to everyday use.

Let's start by listing some of the techniques that most successful salesmen would agree are vital to sales success. (If you are not in sales, you may be surprised to find that these techniques are not manipulative ploys or trade secrets; rather, they are straightforward activities which maximize clear communications between the salesman and his customer, keep the salesman focusing on the customer's needs, and make the best of the salesman's time.)

1. Know your product or service thoroughly. Be an expert, not a con man.

2. Spend every available minute talking with people who are prospects for your product or service. (Your pals in the office aren't going to buy anything.)

3. Qualify the prospect. Make sure the person you are talking to has a real need for your product so that you don't waste his time or yours.

4. Make sure you thoroughly understand the customer's environment and his specific needs before you present your product.

5. Always present your product in terms of its benefits to the customer, not in terms of the product's features. The customer does not buy features, he buys the benefits that those features will provide him.

6. Be sure you know the real feelings of the customer at every step in the sales cycle so you do not mislead yourself.

7. Answer questions and objections straightforwardly. Objections can become advantages.

8. Ask for the order!

Although there are dozens of techniques that could be added to this list, most successful salesmen would agree that the consistent use of those listed above would insure an above-average sales career.

If it's that easy, why do so many salesmen find it difficult to follow these rules? Why is it a truism that "in most companies, 20% of the salesmen sell 80% of the revenue"? These questions have sent sales managers stumbling home talking to themselves ever since Diogenes invented the first territory review.

Let's look at the sales techniques listed above in terms of the attitudes a salesman would have to have about himself and other people to comfortably follow these rules. Translated, the rules say:

1. You've got to really know what you're talking about.

2. You've got to purposely get yourself into as many transactions as time will allow, where the potential outcome of the transaction will affect your pocketbook, reputation, and self-image. (You'll probably fail more times than you will succeed, but don't let that get you down.)

3. You've got to be a person who feels comfortable asking open and level questions about another person's needs and feelings, and possibly finding out that you have nothing in common.

4. You've got to care about his needs, and he's got to sense your honesty so you both can openly communicate; not because you are a social worker, but because it is to your mutual advantage.

5. You've got to be more listener than orator in these transactions because you must communicate effectively from the other person's point of view.

6. You must be in the "here and now" every moment during transactions so that you can sense the other person's positive or negative feelings, and respond directly to them.

7. You must take what you know about yourself and what you have learned about the other person and convert this knowledge into positive solutions to differences of opinion.

8. You must be self-assured enough to risk asking for approval from another person when that approval might be refused. If it is refused, you must not view the refusal as a personal rejection; rather, you must see it as a simple indication that more information, communication, and understanding are required.

Translated into attitudes, the rules to sales success are not so simple. To be this "put together," more than memorizing simple rules is necessary.

Without TA or some other understandable analytical tool, salesmen and sales managers are forced to focus on the symptoms and not the causes of personal selling difficulties. For example, sales managers have been beating up salesmen since time began to make more sales calls. (The serpent peddling apples in the Garden of Eden probably caught hell from his boss for calling on just one prospect.) This technique sometimes has a positive effect temporarily; but generally, the salesman with this problem finds himself very shortly staring at empty days or weeks on his calendar. TA allows a salesman with this selling difficulty to understand "why" he might be avoiding customer encounters and gives him the tools to do something about it if he chooses. This is dramatically more effective than just being told to "make more calls."

To illustrate, let's take three common selling technique problems that many salesmen face and see how TA concepts might help a salesman understand why he has these difficulties.

1. Why do many salesmen make only a few personal sales calls during a day and spend so much time shuffling papers, organizing their files, socializing in the office, and using other plausible means to avoid talking to people who might buy from them? Could it be that they feel not-OK about themselves, while feeling that the customer is OK? If so, it's only natural that they should postpone customer encounters which in the salesmen's mind probably won't work out very well anyway. By concentrating on busy-work that is available, they can postpone the next anticipated rejection as long as possible.

   Could it be that these salesmen are using their job to act out a loser's script? Since a customer who doesn't see them probably isn't going to buy, this is a way of assuring failure.

   Or could it be that these salesmen get most of their strokes from their office environment. They may not have learned how to get or accept strokes from their selling activities, therefore they get them from their associates and the secretaries. (I suspect they don't get many positive strokes from their managers this way.)

2. Why do so many salesmen immediately jump into their "canned" pitch without really investigating and specifically addressing the customer's particular environment, needs, and desires? Maybe it's because these salesmen have great difficulty asking open questions at all. This could be another I'm not-OK — You're OK dramatization.

   This lack of openness may indicate that they are using the "canned" sales pitch as a ritual to avoid productive activities in which they assume they'll fail, or to avoid an open transaction where they feel very uncomfortable and threatened.

3. Why do so many salesmen have to struggle so hard to get up the courage to ask a customer to buy their product? (If you're not in sales, you might not have guessed that this is a widespread sales problem, but many sales managers will retire, mumbling to themselves "If Charlie had only asked them for the order, I'd have a vice president's pension now.") Here again, the salesman's not-OK feelings may make him certain that the customer will say no; so why give him the chance? "As long as he hasn't said no, he might say yes." (Unfortunately, unless he is asked, the customer and the salesman may grow old, poor, and frustrated together.)

There may also be some loser messages in the salesmen's scripts. By not asking for the order, they can live that script to its natural conclusion with no detours.

The salesman with sales technique problems may intellectually accept the need to apply the rules of successful selling. Without the analytical tools TA provides, however, the cause and affect of his inability to carry them out cannot be easily connected. Consequently, real behavioral changes are extremely difficult or impossible.

TA provides a salesman with the tools he needs to understand why he may be having difficulty applying the sales techniques he knows will be successful for him. With TA, he can begin to recognize and discard (if he chooses) the negative messages that may be crippling his sales career.

TA also provides sales managers with the insights necessary to understand how a specific salesman can reach his potential, and how the sales manager can help in that task.

HOW TA HELPS SALES COMMUNICATIONS

Now that TA has helped us discard some of our previously unrecognized negative messages and we are confidently and openly getting where the action is, what do we do when we get there? Well, TA isn't through helping us yet.

A salesman must be able to conduct mutually productive transactions with his customers. Whether we are salesmen or not, we all run into those moments when open communications start to degenerate into stressful and unproductive encounters. Many times, we seem hopelessly locked into these negative encounters, and we leave them feeling frustrated and confused.

None of us really like these transactions when they're painful, and they generally are. To a salesman, they're not only painful, but they can also cost him a sale.

TA provides us with a method of analyzing transactions while we are in the midst of them. It also provides the tools that can help us get our communications back on a productive track again.

If a salesman thoroughly understands the TA concepts of ego states and transactions, he will have a workable method of knowing when the communication lines are open, and when they are breaking down. This knowledge can keep him out of heaps of trouble.

With proper instruction, all of us can learn to adequately recognize the ego states which are being used in our transactions. Without playing the game of *Psychiatry*, we can learn to recognize these changing ego states by carefully observing facial expressions, postures, words that are being used, and tone of voice. The most important ego states to recognize in day-to-day business transactions are the most commonly discussed ones. Here's an easy way for salesmen to remember which is which.

Critical Parent:	All salesmen drink too much!
Nurturing Parent:	But he works so hard, he needs to relax.
Adult:	Do you have any statistics on that?
Adapted Child:	I'd be afraid to drink with a salesman.
Little Professor:	So that's how they make all their sales!
Natural Child:	I wish I could drink like a salesman!

Once we can recognize these ego states, the TA concept of analyzing transactions starts to play a practical role in maintaining open communication. The rules are simple, and they work.

1. The communication lines are broken in a crossed transaction. (It's almost impossible to interest a bank robber in opening a savings account.)

2. Complementary transactions can continue indefinitely as long as both parties choose to keep the transactions complementary. ("Rapiers or pistols, Mr. Hamilton?" "Pistols please, Mr. Burr.")

From a sales and business point of view, some complementary transactions, although potentially continuable, do not foster open communication. For example, I can't think of a situation where you would want to have either party trying to conduct honest business from his Critical Parent or Adapted Child, even if the transaction is complementary. If either of these ego states is involved, you are probably headed for trouble rather than real communication.

There are three complementary transactions that are most productive in selling and/or general business situations.

1. Adult to Adult. This is the most obvious and common transaction in business. In this transaction, both parties are constructively using their Adults to openly proceed with the business at hand.

2. Natural Child to Natural Child. Sometimes we overlook the fact that getting the Natural Child involved in business can be productive from the standpoint of breaking the pace. It can give us the energy and enthusiasm to carry on until the work at hand is completed.

3. Nurturing Parent to Adapted Child. Now and then in business, it's appropriate for us to use our Nurturing Parent to comfort the fears of another person. This is not a transaction in which logical and perceptive decisions are made; nevertheless, it is sometimes necessary before Adult to Adult communications can resume.

   The Nurturing Parent ego state should be used with great care. Nurturing an Adapted Child in a manner unacceptable to the tapes of that unique Child ego state can bring on a Rebellious Child response. This can create even more trouble. If the use of the Nurturing Parent sounds at all condescending, watch out; it may receive an unexpected and shocking Rebellious Child or even Critical Parent response. Sorry indeed is the salesman who said, "Don't you worry about that at all, Mr. Murray, we've had more experience than anyone else in the business of installing these engines." He wasn't prepared for, "Well if you're so good, wise guy, why is your company being sued over in Pittsburgh for a half-a-million bucks in damages for default of contract?"

Those are the three most productive transactions, but what happens if the other person jumps into his Critical Parent or Adapted Child ego state and wants to stay there? Well, the worst thing that can happen is for us to get hooked into our Critical Parent or Adapted Child as a result. Avoiding this takes practice, but it's worth it. (The old counting to ten routine isn't bad.) We've got to keep our Adult in control and stay that way until we know the "All clear" has been sounded. Our Adult can then hook the other person's Adult and things can become productive again. There are two good ways to bring this about.

1. Ask relevant Adult questions that require thought on the part of the other person. In the face of such questions, the Critical Parent and Adapted Child can't logically respond. Many times, responses from these ego states don't make a whole lot of sense in relation to the question that was asked. The person you are talking with will

generally realize this fact and get back into his Adult to answer so he won't sound illogical. When he's there, keep his Adult functioning by your own Adult questions, manner, and tone.

2. When Adult questions are not enough because of the emotion of the moment, active listening (sometimes called reflective listening) is a popular technique which can do wonders for defusing emotional situations.

Volumes have been written on this technique, and I strongly suggest that you learn more about it and its use. Simply stated, active listening feeds back verbally to the Adapted Child or Critical Parent "the feelings" that you hear in their words. The key to successful active listening is the word "feelings." Simply parroting back to the sender his terminology will only get you into deeper trouble.

The intelligent use of active listening successfully gets communications going again because it says very clearly that you are really listening, and that you care. Some of the better active listeners that I have observed have also worked into their active-listening responses the Nurturing Parent feeling that "I hear you, I care, and also, you have 'permission' to express your feelings and I won't threaten you." That's a tremendously positive stroke and can many times open the communication lines wider than they ever were before.

Many salesmen have finally found out what a prospect's real objections were to his proposal through the use of active listening. For example, here's how a salesman using active listening could have handled the engine installation problem mentioned earlier.

Mr. Murray: I don't think you guys are good enough for this job!

Salesman: It sounds as if you're concerned about our ability to meet the time schedule we've agreed to, is that right?

Mr. Murray: Yeah, I've heard that you guys got into a lot of trouble over in Pittsburgh for missing an installation date.

Salesman: You're concerned that the same thing will happen here?

Mr. Murray: You bet I am; if I agree to your new approach to generating power here at the plant, I'm putting my job on the line.

Salesman: You feel our success or failure will reflect on you personally?

Mr. Murray: You bet. If this works out like I hope it will, I may become general manager. On the other hand, I could be in real trouble.

Salesman: Well, Mr. Murray, I can understand why you'd be so concerned about installing on time. Let's take a few minutes right now to brainstorm together on how we can minimize every possible delaying factor. Would that make you feel more comfortable with your decision?

Mr. Murray: It sure would. In fact, I've got a couple of ideas about. . . . .

This time the salesman was not just listening to the words that were being said; he was also listening to the feelings that were being expressed. Through active listening, he was able to find out what the customer's real concerns were and proceed to address them. Moreover, the customer probably felt that this salesman was not just a "cliché tosser" but a man who listened and cared. Active listening led to a much more productive situation for both parties.

The ability to analyze transactions with TA can provide a salesman with the means to keep the communication lines open between him and his customer. That's one of the most productive skills a salesman can possess.

OTHER USES OF TA IN SELLING

You know by now that I'm convinced TA can improve a salesman's performance considerably. It can help him generate more business and, equally important, help him enjoy the tremendous number of positive strokes that selling can provide.

I have just skimmed the top of a few TA concepts to illustrate how they apply to selling. There is, of course, much more benefit to be gained. The whole analysis of stroking and time structuring (particularly games and rackets), for example, is important for salesmen to understand. Discussion in other sections of this book concerning games, strokes, and time management contain helpful ideas that a salesman can put to immediate and profitable use.

There's an old proverb that says, "If you don't know where you're going, any road will do." Unfortunately, this has been the road map that most salesmen have followed in the past while struggling to understand human behavior. TA has helped to change all that.

Now, with TA, a salesman can begin to understand why people act the way they do, and that understanding is just as important when he looks at himself as it is when he looks at a customer. Some salesmen and sales managers may brush TA aside after only a superficial look, feeling it is inconsequential, but most salesmen I know who have been exposed to TA in any depth have the reaction, "That makes a lot of sense!" It helps to change the old proverb to, "I know where I'm going, and I also know the quickest and most enjoyable way to get there."

Part III

TA APPLIED TO MANAGEMENT STRATEGIES AND THEORIES

TA CAN IMPLEMENT SUPERVISORY EFFECTIVENESS AND OTHER MANAGEMENT THEORIES

TA can give us a handle on some of those ticklish problems in supervision. With the awareness that TA often stimulates, a student can begin to see options. None of us have to be "stuck" with behavior patterns that are ineffective. By processing more of our actions and words through the Adult, change in management style can occur.

In addition, the theories of such management writers as McGregor, Blake and Mouton, Likert, Maslow, etc. can often be put in a practical frame of reference with TA. Before people can actualize their human potential through their work, as Maslow and McGregor suggest, they may need to understand what inhibits the actualizing process. For example, psychological games reinforce negative past experiences and therefore inhibit self-actualization. Game players' energies are invested in the past, not in the present. If people choose to give up games in favor of authenticity, they are encouraging their own growth. They are beginning to self-actualize by experiencing more of their possible selves.

12

TA APPLIED TO SUPERVISION

by William C. Bessey and Robert M. Wendlinger

*William Bessey is an Assistant Vice President
and head of Management Development at Bank of
America. He is an experienced teacher, adminis-
trator, and program designer in the field of
supervisory and executive development.*

*Dr. Bessey obtained his B.S. and M.S. degrees
in psychology at the University of Oregon and
returned thirteen years later to get his
Doctorate in Business Administration.*

*He has served on the faculty at Portland State
University, was Director of Business School
Conferences at the University of Oregon and
for seven years worked at Tektronix, Inc.
where he started and headed the educational
and training section.*

*He serves now on the MBA faculty at Golden
Gate University in San Francisco. He is a member of the American Psychological Association
and the American Society of Training and
Development.*

*Robert Wendlinger is an Assistant Vice President
in the Communications Department at Bank of
America.*

*He has been a staff member or consultant in
communications for such organizations as New
York Life Insurance Company, American Petroleum
Institute, American Telephone and Telegraph
Company, and the United Hospital Fund of
New York.*

He is co-author of Effective Letters: A Program
in Self-Instruction *(McGraw-Hill, 1964) and has
contributed to books on managerial and
supervisory practices.*

He has spoken on communications before various
university and business groups and is a board
member of the Industrial Communication Council,
a national organization of corporate
communication managers, as well as a member of
the International Transactional Analysis
Association.

THE SUPERVISOR

The effective supervisor has his or her Adult ego state in control when it counts, both with subordinates and in transactions with peers and superiors. The one problem that takes most of the supervisor's time, causes the most stress, and costs the most sleep, is the Child ego state in conflict with the requirements of the working world. The conflict ranges from a bank teller resenting an 8 A.M. starting time to a research director's angry outburst at a budget cut.

This chapter is concerned first with the supervisor's own ego states and how important it is for him or her to use the Adult ego state at the right time. It is especially concerned with what the supervisor can do to encourage employees to move from the Child ego state to the Adult ego state when this is necessary — in other words, to *grow*.

Our two concerns — (1) the Adult ego state in supervisors, and (2) moving employees toward more frequent use of their own Adult ego states — are of course closely related. As we analyze the transactions between supervisor and employee, it will become clear that supervisors are in a unique position to encourage growth. But the supervisor's Adult ego state must be in control to encourage the employee toward more frequent use of his or her own Adult.

The Supervisor's Adult

The Adult ego state is defined by Eric Berne as:

. . .an independent set of feelings, attitudes, and behavior patterns that are adapted to current reality and are not affected by Parental prejudices or archaic attitudes left over from childhood. . .

. . .concerned with the autonomous collecting and processing of data and the estimating of probabilities as a basis for action.

. . .organized, adaptable, and intelligent, and is experienced as an objective relationship with the external environment based on autonomous reality testing. [1]

James and Jongeward further explain:

Reality testing is the processing of checking out what is real. It involves separating fact from fantasy, traditions, opinions, and archaic feelings. It includes perceiving and evaluating the current situation and relating the data to past knowledge and experience. Reality testing allows a person to figure out alternative solutions. [2]

How do these Adult ego state characteristics compare to the traits of a good supervisor? Here are the traits listed in one highly regarded text on supervision:

A sense of mission
Self denial
High character
Job competence
Good judgment
Energy [3]

The Performance Record, an appraisal form for foremen and supervisors, lists the following factors:

1. Developing responsibility and teamwork in employees

2. Helping employees improve their job performance

3. Giving employees reasons and explanations for action

4. Alertness to employees' special problems

5. Seeing that employees are treated fairly

6. Planning and scheduling work

7. Showing judgment and resourcefulness in getting work done

8. Checking quantity and quality of work done

9. Taking responsibility and initiative

10. Cooperating with staff and others in higher management [4]

When we compare TA's Adult ego state and "good supervision" traits, we see obvious Adult characteristics: judgment, giving reasons, planning, checking work, and taking responsibility. But do we see more than simply Adult ego state? How do we categorize such traits as sense of mission, high character, helping employees, resourcefulness, and alertness to employee problems? Certainly not in what James and Jongeward call the Constant Adult ego state:

If a person excludes his Parent and Child using only his Adult, he may be a bore or a robot without passion or compassion. Berne describes the

*excluding Adult as "devoid of the charm, spontaneity, and fun which
are characteristic of the healthy child, and. . .unable to take sides with
the conviction or indignation which is found in healthy parents.* [5]

If there is more to the good supervisor than just the Adult ego state,
what traits from the other ego states are important to the supervisor-
employee reltaionship?

The Child Ego State

The Child ego state contains basically all the impulses that come
naturally to an infant. It also contains the recordings of his early
experiences, his responses to them, and the "positions" — that is, OK?
not-OK? — taken as a very young person about himself and others.

At any one moment, supervisors and employees may think or act
from any one of the *three parts* of the Child ego state:

> The *Adapted Child* is the part that has been trained by significant
> authority figures. He may do as he is told. He may sulk, blame, or
> withdraw from confrontation. He sometimes feels not very OK.

> The *Little Professor* is the "smart little kid" in the very young
> Child — sometimes called the Adult in the child — who, with
> limited experience and data, still manages to be intuitive, creative,
> and sometimes manipulative of others.

> The *Natural Child* contains the basic natural emotional responses
> of an infant — fearful, self-centered, and aggressive on the one
> hand; affectionate, expressive, and sensuous on the other —
> provided its needs are met.

The expressiveness, charm, and playfulness of the *Natural Child*
can help to create pleasant working relationships and add humor and
spice to a routine day. But the supervisor who is controlled by the
Natural Child may be self-centered and self-indulgent, be hurt by
employee indifference, act without thinking, or try desperately to be
liked. He may try always to control a situation. Any of this behavior
presented in more than a small degree will give the supervisor trouble.
The *Adapted Child* in an OK person is aware that social
organizations require rules and regulations, that the wishes and needs of
others need to be considered, and that patience is necessary in dealing
with complex issues involving people and systems. So an individual with
a healthy Adapted Child is likely to be courteous and considerate of his
co-workers and his employees.

A supervisor whose Adapted Child has been repressed, on the other
hand, is likely to lack confidence and to be inhibited. He may comply
with organizational policies and procedures even when Adult data
suggests that they are unworkable in a changing world and need

revision. This supervisor may simply conform, even if it is harmful to himself and his employees. Or the supervisor may sulk and blame others, sometimes withdrawing altogether from rational Adult confrontation and decisions.

Finally, because such a supervisor wants to rebel and doesn't dare to, the Adapted Child may decide to stall. In business organizations, this can mean avoiding decisions, being late to meetings, missing deadlines, or avoiding difficult personnel situations like counseling, appraisal, or disciplining sessions. A supervisor with a not-OK Adapted Child is not likely to be effective.

The intuitive power and creativity of the *Little Professor* will, on the other hand, add significance to the relationship between supervisor and employees. The Little Professor may help a supervisor to

- intuitively sense the causes of a long-standing problem before all the data is in,
- find new and creative approaches and solutions to problems,
- soothe over difficult personnel situations,
- win employee cooperation,
- relieve a threatening situation.

The Little Professor, admitted to the world of work at the proper times and combined with the dependable behavior of the Adult, can mean a healthier and more creative supervisory-employee relationship. James and Jongeward say:

The Adult and the Little Professor make a good team. Together they can design a new building, write a book, compose a musical score, improve human relationships, make a home attractive, create relevant curriculum, develop a mathematical formula, and so forth. [6]

With his Adult in control, an individual — supervisor or subordinate — can authorize the use of his Little Professor. This is appropriate at times when creativity and new ideas are needed, or when limited data is available to help solve a problem. One useful technique to stimulate the Little Professor is "brainstorming." When using brainstorming, *all* ideas that are offered, no matter how unorthodox, must be accepted without criticism until a list of ideas is long enough to be discussed realistically, i.e., by the Adult.

The Parent Ego State

In many minds the Parent ego state is the one most readily associated with the supervisors, i.e., an authority figure who tells people what to do. There are occasions when this is likely correct — in times of emergency, with new employees, and in a limited number of other situations. As Berne says:

Many things are done because "That's the way it's done." This frees the Adult from the necessity of making innumerable trivial decisions, so that it can devote itself to more important issues, leaving routine matters to the Parent. [7]

Some fortunate supervisors display a "natural" authority — a comfortable expectation developed over years of experience that things will go their way. This can be productive for the supervisor and the employee, provided the supervisor lets the employee do for himself or herself when able.

We are in our Parent ego state when we feel and act as did our actual parents, or significant authority figures in our lives. Depending on what we copied from Parent figures, we may be critical, punitive, or prejudicial ("Why can't you ever get it right?"), or nurturing ("It has been a bad day. Let's take it easy today and talk about it tomorrow.")

There is little doubt that the *Critical Parent* ego state is ill-suited to supervisors. It activates that not-OK Child in an employee with the resulting self-deprecating or rebellious feelings. The critical supervisor, never satisfied and seeing only weaknesses, will in the long run damage even the strongest Adult. He chips away at self-respect and can eventually restrict an employee's entire outlook. The supervisor whose Critical Parent is in control for a significant portion of the workday is disqualified for the supervisor's job.

The *Nurturing Parent*, on the other hand, can be a constructive influence in the supervisor-employee relationship. It would seem particularly useful at those times when the employee needs support to work through a crisis or difficult problem. From the Nurturing Parent, the supervisor might say things such as:

"It's a tough job."
"Come on in if you get stumped."
"Give it a try — I'll back you on it."
"Let me get you started."
"I know how irritating customers can be."

Through nurturing, the supervisor establishes a climate that can encourage an employee to try something new or to recoup after a failure. But the right amount of nurturing is an elusive supervisory skill. Nurturing, as a steady diet, can keep the employee in a Child ego state, and will no more build independence and self-respect than critical parenting. The supervisor should be in the Adult ego state a good share of the working day but can use both the Nurturing Parent and Child ego states at the appropriate times. The question ever before the supervisor, however, is: When are the appropriate times?

THE SUPERVISOR'S ADULT AS EXECUTIVE OF THE PERSONALITY

James and Jongeward help to resolve this question of appropriate time in their concept of the Adult as executive:

Each person has the potential to put his Adult in executive control of his ego states. If freed from negative or irrelevant influence from his Parent and Child, he is emancipated to make his own autonomous decisions.

...He evaluates before acting and takes full responsibility for his thoughts, feelings, and behavior. He assumes the task of determining which of the possible responses in his ego states are appropriate, using that which is OK from his Parent and his Child. [8]

The Adult ego state as executive does not mean that the person is always acting from the Adult. It means that the Adult allows appropriate expression of all ego states because each has its contribution to make to a total personality. [9]

The supervisor's Adult decides the issue and keeps control of the Parent and Child ego states at appropriate times. The feeling of, say, compassion may have its source in the Parent ego state but it is controlled by the Adult and is displayed with Adult control.

Stated another way, the Adult as executive can be regarded as *empathetic* rather than *sympathetic*. The sympathetic supervisor will feel sorry for the subordinate and want to help, perhaps by doing something *for* him or her (Parent-Child). The empathetic supervisor has the same feelings, but his Adult as executive tells him that the way to help is to encourage a subordinate to approach a problem from his or her own Adult and not the Child (Adult-Adult).

A supervisor whose Adult is in control can move a subordinate away from the Child ego state into the Adult, i.e., help the subordinate to grow. Many transactions between supervisors and employees present a golden opportunity to encourage employee growth and development. To illustrate what can happen, here are three ways that a stimulus about the subject of expense control might be handled.

Illustration

Jim: Here's an idea I have for avoiding another hassle with the Expense Control Department. (A)

Supervisor: Good! Let's take a look at it. (A)

This was an Adult to Adult transaction with no difficulties.
Here is the same problem presented from another ego state.

Illustration

Jim: What should I do about that problem with Expense
                 Control? (C)

Supervisor: That's OK. I'll take care of it. (P)

Now we have a Child-Parent transaction. It is complementary, i.e., the
employee got the Parent response he expected, so at least there is
communication. But the supervisor has kept the employee in his Child,
himself in Parent, and made some additional work for himself as well.

The supervisor, with his Adult in control, can encourage his
subordinate also to come on Adult instead of Child. While the
employee may *intend* the transaction to be Child-Parent, the supervisor
does not permit his own Parent ego state to be "hooked."

Illustration

1. *Jim:*   What should I do about that problem with Expense
                 Control? (C)

2. *Supervisor:* Yeah, that's a dandy. What do you think you'll do?
                 (A)

3. *Jim:*   I don't know. (Pause) Can *you* talk to them? (C)

4. *Supervisor:* It's *your* expenses they're shooting at, isn't it? (A)

5. *Jim:*   Yes, but what will I say? I didn't know what the
                 procedures were! (C)

6. *Supervisor:* It's a problem. (A)

7. *Jim:*   (Silence)

8. *Supervisor:* Are you a little leery of the Expense boss? (P)

9. *Jim:*   Yes, as a matter of fact. (A)

10. *Supervisor:* He's a stickler. (A)

11. *Jim:*   Well, OK. I'll bone up on the expense manual and at
                 least tell them how I can do it from now on. (A)

In this transaction, the supervisor resists Jim's efforts to put him in
the Parent role (1, 3, 5) and responds as Adult (2, 4, 6). As a result, the
transaction becomes crossed briefly, and communication temporarily
stops (7). Jim is in a difficult spot as he does not want communication

to stop with the supervisor (after 7). So there is "built-in" pressure on him to move to his Adult and deal with the problem. With a little nurturing (8) and consistent Adult on the part of the supervisor (10), Jim moves gradually to the Adult ego state (9, 11).

THE KEY TO GROWTH

The subordinate's Child ego state is the most vulnerable part of his or her personality. It contains all the not-OK feelings that the subordinate has. And when the supervisor is presented as Critical Parent, the not-OK part of the subordinate's Child is sure to be activated, or hooked.

> *Employee:*   I don't think it was fair that I didn't get that promotion.
>
> *Supervisor:*   Well, we gave it a lot of thought. If you're not happy with the way we do things around here, maybe you'd better look around for something else.
>
> *Employee:*   (Silence)

In TA terms, the supervisor's Critical Parent has assumed control of the situation, i.e., "You do what I want and don't ask any questions." The supervisor who consistently comes on Critical Parent to enforce unreasonable standards of performance, or who uses threats "to get things done," may accomplish goals temporarily. But the Adapted Child in the subordinate will rebel, in silence, through lower productivity, or in departure from the organization.

The most damaging aspects of the Critical Parent stimulus in organizations are that (a) the not-OK part in the subordinate's Child is hooked, and (b) the subordinate – as in the above example – cannot deal with Adult reality while under the influence of not-OK feelings.

THE KEY APPLIED TO SUPERVISION

The difficulty in dealing with Adult reality while under the influence of not-OK feelings is recognized in many texts on supervision, which recommend that the supervisor-employee relationship focus on *behavior* and not on the *person*. Imagine, for example, the following situation:

> You've turned in a report to your boss, who says to you, "This is a lousy report." Not good to hear and not good supervision. But suppose the supervisor had said instead, "You are incompetent." Most people would agree that this last is much worse. Why? The first statement is directed at the *report*; you can very well improve it. The second would be directed at *you*; you are incompetent; and

there is nothing you can do to correct it. A real "spinal cord shriveller," in Berne's terms.

The guideline is commonly stated as *Focus on Behavior, Not the Person*. Focus on the lengthy, disorganized report, not on John Smith. Your targets then become tardiness, errors, and late assignments — not May, Sue, or Bill. This principle of avoiding criticism of the person is one of the ABC's of supervision.

In a counseling session, a supervisor might say to an employee:

"You *act* like you disapprove of so-and-so."

"You *give the impression* you don't care."

"You *say* things that get people sore at you."

All of these statements focus on what the person *does*, not what he or she *feels*.

To fully utilize this principle in situations where growth is required, i.e., movement from the Child to the Adult in a particular situation, we need to extend its meaning. An example from family life will demonstrate the extended principle.

> You walk into the playroom and find your three-year-old son hitting his one-year-old sister with a toy truck. Applying the principle, you think, he doesn't like his baby sister — he *wants* to hurt her — and that's OK because his feelings are normal for a three-year-old and you accept them. But his behavior may seriously hurt her, so he's put into his room, or spanked or whatever. You say, "I know you don't like her sometimes, but whenever you hit her you go to your room." You accept his feelings, thereby maintaining his self-respect while correcting his unacceptable behavior.

The extended principle, then, is:

Easy on feelings, i.e., respect the Child ego state.

Tough on behavior, i.e., some behavior is unacceptable by Adult standards.

Illustration

In a supervisory situation, how does the principle work? Let's say you are a bank operations officer and one of your tellers is good on all counts except that, when busy, he is impatient and testy with customers. You've talked with the teller about this several times, but you've had more complaints this week.

1. *Supervisor:*   We've had two more complaints this week. What can you do to improve your customer relations?

2. *Teller:*   Who were they?

3. *Supervisor:*   (Relates the specific incidents.)

4. *Teller:*   Oh, those two. They both were in at the busiest times. That woman wanted me to spend all day telling her about banking!

5. *Supervisor:*   I know what a strain people can be, but she said that you cut her dead! What happened?

6. *Teller:*   I just said, "I can't talk when I'm counting money."

7. *Supervisor:*   That sounds pretty blunt.

8. *Teller:*   You want me to balance, don't you?

9. *Supervisor:*   Yes. *And* be polite. You know the bank practice. Another complaint in 90 days will mean a formal reprimand in your file.

In this example the teller stays in the Child ego state, but the supervisor stays in the Adult ego state with some nurturing (5). The focus is on behavior throughout:

1. What can you *do*?
2. The teller is not *rude*, but *behaved* in a rude way.
7. That *sounds* blunt, not "you *are* blunt."
9. The teller needs *to be* polite, not *feel* polite or like the customers.

The supervisor accepted the teller's feelings of irritation (that's the teller's business) but was clear on what such behavior would lead to. The supervisor addressed the employee's Adult and encouraged the teller to think about the consequences of the unacceptable behavior.

Make It Their Problem

An actual incident will illustrate the approach we feel will best facilitate growth of the Adult ego state.

Some years ago, one of the co-authors participated in an exceptional role-playing session. The class was called *Manager Coaching* [10] and the participants were the ten division heads and the executive vice president of an electronics firm. In this particular session the class was role-playing an appraisal interview between a division head and one of the plant managers. Their roles were explained to the participants in the following way.

Division Head — John Taylor

You've been very busy this last year and you feel you've been losing touch with one of your plant managers, Guy Parks. He's a good man but there have been a few signs that he's unhappy or over his head or letting up or *something* — you're not sure. You hope to use this time to draw him out and see what's on his mind and, to use your expression, "get on the same side of the table" with him.

Plant Manager — Guy Parks (This role was explained to the class members but not to the executive playing John Taylor.)

You have this meeting scheduled with the boss and you're not looking forward to it. He'll want to know what you've been doing and thinking and all about the problems of the plant. He really doesn't understand the plant methods any more. Things have changed. He says he wants to "get on your side of the table," but if you do tell him your thoughts and ideas, he never does anything about them anyhow. You plan to be polite but brief (if you can) and get back to the plant.

The division head, John, studied his role, thought out his approach, and told the class what he hoped to accomplish in the interview. (Guy was out of the room.)

The interview went pretty much as expected — John setting the stage, patiently trying to draw Guy out and establish some genuine communication, with Guy keeping a polite reserve. As it continued, John began to show the strain — Guy's lack of response in front of that particular group put a great deal of pressure on John. The last part of the interview proceeded like this:

John: I hope that we can discuss some of these things, Guy. I'd like to see us on the same side of the table.

Guy: Plant II is in good shape, John.

John: Do we need to discuss the long-term goals?

Guy: If you'd like.

Then note John's reply:

John: *Guy, you act like you don't want to cooperate in this interview.*

Guy: Well, uh, no, John, I don't mean . . .

John: That's the impression you give.

Guy: Oh, no, I think we *ought* to get together on these things.

Guy then began to talk freely and the class broke up the interview by giving John a round of applause.

What happened here? What took place in that brief moment that visibly changed John's whole demeanor and set Guy busily to work "cooperating"? By saying, "You act like you don't want to cooperate," John shifted the problem from himself to Guy, where it really belonged. He presented the subordinate with his own behavior and asked, "How about this?" Because John focussed on behavior and not on the person, he activated Guy's Adult rather than intimidating his Child, as he might easily have done.

He also conveyed another equally important message to Guy: "You're OK — you have the brains and can carry the load."

The application of this approach can cover a broad range of behavior.

Illustration

You have a stubborn employee who consistently resists your authority. In this case, you have asked for a one-page summary of a ten-page memorandum he's written. He asks, "Why?"

1. *Supervisor:*   John, to be honest with you, I need this summary to save my own time and the time of management. How about getting the key points on one page?

2. *John:*   Listen, it just can't be done. I've got to sell them on the idea, plus explain the procedure, plus make the recommendations!

3. *Supervisor:*   They won't read it.

4. *John:*   Yes, but if I shorten it, it won't make any sense to them!

5. *Supervisor:*   John, are you aware that every time I make a suggestion to you, you argue with me?

6. *John:*   You just can't boil down that kind of report!

7. *Supervisor:*   What about the arguing, John. Are you aware of it?

8. *John:*   I was just trying to make a point.

At the end, it's beginning to be John's problem.

In this example, John invited his supervisor to participate in his variation of the game *Yes But*, and to offer solutions (2, 4, 6) that would be turned down. Although the transcript of the *Yes But* game may sound Adult, the player, as Berne says, "is actually presenting himself as a Child who is inadequate to meet the situation and is looking for a Parent anxious to dispense his wisdom. . ." [11] The real point is to prove that the Parent is not so smart after all.

Wisely, the supervisor declined to be Parent and remained in the Adult (3, 5, 7). Moreover, the supervisor leveled about the game with John (5) and focussed on the real problem — not the report but John's arguing (5, 7).

Another illustration

One of your production workers whose quality is not up to standards breaks into tears every time you try to discuss her work with her.

1. *Supervisor:*   Mary, you had three rejects again yesterday. We need to talk about this.

2. *Mary:*   Oh, I know! I've been so nervous lately and my husband is changing jobs and I've really *tried* to do better! (tears)

3. *Supervisor:*   What can we do?

4. *Mary:*   (Tries to talk but can't through the tears.)

5. *Supervisor:*   Mary, every time I talk to you about your work, you start crying. Did you know this?

6. *Mary:*   (Surprised) What?

Mary is behaving in a helpless manner in order to avoid her real problem. The supervisor focuses attention on the real problem (1, 3) and levels with Mary about her game of *Poor Me, See How Hard I Try* (5). Mary's behavior has now been called to her attention, and her Adult is more aware of her Child manipulations. This may or may not solve the problem, but at least the supervisor is talking straight about it with her. He has made it her problem.

What the supervisor does in all three instances is consistently provide Adult input to the subordinate. This is difficult to do. If the supervisor's Adult ego state is not in control, he or she might respond from the Critical Parent. Or, having failed to solve the problem immediately, the supervisor's own not-OK Child might become defensive and would be hooked.

GAMES SUBORDINATES PLAY

Some employees will resist any attempt to "make it their problem" and will actually prefer a supervisor to come on either Nurturing or Critical

Parent. This is because of the basic psychological position — You're OK, I'm not-OK, etc. — that the employee has taken about himself and others, and the kinds of feelings that are collected to reinforce his basic position. An employee who has strong not-OK feelings, for example, may collect feelings of fear, depression, anger, etc., from transactions with his or her supervisor.

James and Jongeward write:

In TA the particular feelings the Child ego state collects are called "trading stamps." The term "stamps" is borrowed from the practice of collecting trading stamps when making purchases and later redeeming them for merchandise...

...When a person collects his stamps, he manipulates others to hurt him, to belittle him, to anger him, to frighten him, to arouse his guilt, etc. He accomplishes this by provoking or inviting others to play certain roles *[author's emphasis] or by imagining that another person has done something to him.* [12]

One way that a subordinate can collect favorite feelings, or "trading stamps," from a supervisor is to play games. These are fairly extended transactions, socially acceptable on the surface, but carrying an ulterior or psychological message underneath, and resulting in a "payoff," i.e., the player's favorite feeling, at the end.

In the game of *Kick Me*, for example, a subordinate may provoke a put-down from the supervisor:

Employee: I had too much work to do yesterday and just don't have that report ready.

Supervisor: This is the second time you've been late on this project. I'm going to have to give it to someone else.

The employee has initiated a socially acceptable transaction, apparently Adult to Adult. But the underlying or psychological message is quite different:

Employee: I'm a bad boy, kick me.

Supervisor: Yes, you are a bad boy and here's your kick.

The employee wins by losing, having collected the favorite feeling of rejection, which reinforces this particular not-OK position.

The effective supervisor, with the Adult in control, and aware of the games that office people play, will be able to recognize such provocations and invitations and turn them aside.

THE SUPERVISOR'S CHILD

Supervisors can expect some problems as they encourage employees to accept responsibility for their own problems. For example, it is difficult for supervisors to keep the Adult firmly in control when involved in emotional counseling sessions. Any supervisor knows how resistant and devious a person can be when the Child is questioned. Some subordinates will follow the adage, "The best defense is a good offense," and attack! That is, they will come on Parent themselves and criticize the supervisor. In such cases, the supervisor may be tempted to counteract with the Parent or become defensive with *his* or *her* own Child.

Illustration

One of your women stenos is at odds with the rest of the office because she won't chip in and work on joint projects. You have kept a record of some specific incidents and have decided to talk to her about it.

1. *Supervisor:*   And then last week when we had to put that mailing together in a hurry, you were in the back room filing your nails.
2. *Mary:*   You mean you were spying on me?
3. *Supervisor:*   Oh, no, I wasn't doing. . .
4. *Mary:*   You were *spying* on me!
5. *Supervisor:*   No, no, I didn't intend. . .

In this example, the supervisor has begun in his Adult (1), but Mary's sharp Little Professor advised her to counterattack (2, 4); she is playing the game of *Now I've Got You, You S.O.B.* [13] The supervisor's Child is immediately hooked (3) and he'll probably have to take this up with her at a later time.

Illustration

You are counseling that good teller of yours who is late twice a week:

Supervisor: You were ten minutes late this morning. That's the second time this week.

Teller: Why do you always *pick* on me? I'm one of your best tellers and you pick, pick!

Here again we are likely to forget the issue of tardiness and defend our own Child against the employee's attack. If we have strong not-OK feelings, it is difficult to remain Adult in these cases. But we can learn to recognize our own and others' ego states, particularly transactions between Parent and Child. The supervisor who recognizes that his or her Child has been hooked can count to ten and give the Adult a chance to intercede.

THE NEED FOR AUTHENTICITY

The supervisor, when attempting to "make it the other person's problem," need not exclude his or her own Child and Parent ego states from all transactions.

There may be times when it is appropriate for a supervisor to act as a firm Parent:

"If you don't wear the safety glasses, you'll be suspended for one week. It's your choice." (That is, it's your problem.)

Here is a statement once used by a supervisor during an argument over emergency overtime:

"You mean you *won't* do it, or you don't *want* to do it?"

If there is a consistent pattern, however, the reasons for undue rebellion on the subordinates' part need close examination.

The supervisor need not hesitate to release Child feelings, provided these feelings are genuine and he or she is not playing a role or attempting to manipulate approval from the other. Sometimes an honest outburst by a supervisor can lead to productive results.

Illustration

Here is a supervisor talking to an office group which tends to let the telephone ring too long.

Supervisor: Listen, every time you let the phone ring three times I'm going to be irritated. I may not always say something, but you'll know that's how I feel. Now, do you *want* an irritated supervisor on your hands?

For good or bad, the employees have been presented with the problem.

Illustration

Here is a supervisor dealing with an overly sensitive subordinate in an authentic manner:

Supervisor: John, sometimes it's like walking on eggs talking to you! I never know when I'm going to set you off.

John: (Alarmed and defending himself) That's really *your* problem, isn't it?

Supervisor: How do you feel about it, John? Do you like having this kind of situation?

John: (Sarcastically) I wasn't aware that I was so touchy.

Supervisor: It's the impression you give — almost every day.

This kind of session is risky. John may have strong not-OK feelings in his Child which are easily triggered. It takes Adult nerve on the supervisor's part to initiate a confrontation. But it can lead to significant growth for both parties and a lasting bond between them if the encounter is *authentic*.

According to James and Jongeward:

The authentic person experiences the reality of himself by knowing himself, being himself, and becoming a credible, responsive person. He actualizes his own unprecedented uniqueness and appreciates the uniqueness of others. He does not dedicate his life to a concept of what he imagines he should be. . .he does not use his energy putting on a performance, maintaining pretence, and manipulating others into his games. . .he can reveal himself instead of projecting images that please, provoke, or entice others. [14]

Not all transactions will be highly charged with emotion, requiring the supervisor to muster up the courage to initiate the session and then struggle to keep the Adult in control. The supervisor can accept the subordinate's Child, encourage an open discussion of the employee's feelings, and then candidly explore the consequences of the subordinate's *behavior*.

This will change the level of awareness that employees have about their actions and give them a chance to think things over with their Adults.

A supervisor can say, for example:

"What do you think about the assignment? Are you a little leery of it?" (The supervisor accepts the possibility of the Child's fear.)

"Do you *like* having me on your back? I guess it's a real bother. How can you get me off?"

"I know you like to work on your own. How can we do it?"

"If you reject these improvement goals, you put me in a position where I *have* to get into it."

IS IT A PROBLEM?

When an employee's behavior in the Child ego state is not important to the requirements of the job, the supervisor has little reason to "make it his problem." Who cares if the night watchman is a grouch? The effective supervisor accepts the behavior along with a hundred other individual characteristics he or she may see during the day. The supervisor is patient with it and may even enjoy it. The painfully shy unit assembler, the boastful college recruit, the "entertainer" at coffee breaks, the technician with the "far out" philosophy are all OK fellow human beings.

Is It Really the Subordinate's Problem?

The effective supervisor will also be certain that the problem is really the subordinate's problem, and not his or her own. This is part of his being authentic. It is "his problem" only when the Child ego state is dominating the *employee* at an inappropriate time. If the *supervisor's* Child ego state is causing the problem, he or she can do little to help the employee.

Illustration

One department head tried to practice the "make it their problem" approach on his staff and supervisors to no avail. The problem, as he perceived it, involved tardiness and casual supervisory practices. At the same time, he was checking in at the office after 9 A.M., taking an afternoon off for golf when the spirit moved him, and playing favorites with the office women. His attempt to change the work habits of his staff was not an authentic I'm OK — You're OK transaction and he failed in his approach.

A supervisor needs to have the Adult ego state in control in order to draw the employee into the Adult.

The Need for Authenticity in "Making It Their Problem"

Some people feel it necessary to their careers or well-being to always take the offensive. Some political leaders confide that they never apologize or admit they're wrong. They simply change the subject or accuse *others* of something. They become experts at the "put down", i.e., discounting others, and at avoiding a defensive position. This approach is not recommended here.

In applying an understanding of ego states and related techniques, a genuine interest in, and respect for, the other person is vital. The subordinate is presented with the problem because *it is truly the subordinate's problem* and cannot be solved by anyone else. The supervisor helps the subordinate to more rewarding behavior, and the superior-subordinate relationship then becomes an authentic I'm OK-You're OK transaction. The supervisor is relieved of a problem and, at the same time, may set into motion a genuine growth process on the part of the employee.

SUMMARY

The effective supervisor will focus on behavior, not the person, respecting the subordinate's Child. The effective supervisor will "make it his problem" whenever appropriate, and encourage subordinates to solve their own problems in a rational and Adult manner. The supervisor will be aware that sometimes the problem may be his or her own and not the subordinate's. If the supervisor — with the Adult in control — can brave the angry outburst and the sharp tongue; resist the flatterer and the "con man," the dependence, tears, and depression; and face the Child ego state in himself and others with conviction and warmth, then a moment of growth can be created that both supervisor and employee will remember for a lifetime.

FOOTNOTES AND REFERENCES

1. Quoted in Muriel James and Dorothy Jongeward, *Born to Win: Transactional Analysis with Gestalt Experiments* (Reading, Mass.: Addison Wesley, 1971), p. 224.

2. *Ibid.*, p. 225.

3. Lester R. Bittel, *What Every Supervisor Should Know* (New York: McGraw-Hill, 1968), p. 74.

4. J.C. Flanagan and R.B. Miller, "Incident Sheet for Foremen and Supervisors," *The Performance Record* (Chicago, Illinois: Science Research Associates, 1955), form 7-2492. Reprinted by permission.

5. James and Jongeward, *op. cit.*, pp. 228-229.

6. *Ibid.*, p. 132.

7. Eric Berne, *Games People Play* (New York: Grove Press, 1964), p. 27.

8. James and Jongeward, *op. cit.*, p. 235.

9. *Ibid.*, p. 249.

10. From the program "Improving the Coaching Practices of Managers," (New York, N.Y.: Mahler Associates, 1961).

11. Berne, *op. cit.*, p. 117.

12. James and Jongeward, *op. cit.*, p. 189.

13. Berne, *op. cit.*, pp. 85-87.

14. James and Jongeward, *op. cit.*, pp. 1-2.

13

A TRANSACTIONAL ANALYSIS OF MCGREGOR'S THEORY X-Y

by Marylynn Goldhaber, M.S.W. and
Gerald M. Goldhaber, Ph.D.

Mrs. Goldhaber is a counselor at Family Counseling Service of Albuquerque, New Mexico and an Associate Member of the I.T.A.A. Dr. Goldhaber is Assistant Professor of Speech Communication at the University of New Mexico. He is a Special Member of the I.T.A.A. and is studying presently for Teaching Member.

The information contained in this article is derived, in part, from a convention program of the International Communication Association, held in Phoenix last April. Panelists for this program were Thomas A. Harris, M.D., and George Sanborn, management professor from the University of Georgia. Dr. Goldhaber served as program chairman.

One of the most persistent and perplexing problems in the management of organizations is that of achieving reasonably optimum use of the talents of individuals in the organization. This is a problem involving not only the individual (who must be motivated), but the characteristics of the organization (which must encourage such motivation). A major question for management, then, is, What characteristics of the organization will best motivate the individual while maintaining operating effectiveness within the company?

In general terms, these characteristics include organizational structure, managerial principles and practices, communication, personnel, and the prevailing atmosphere of the organization itself. One interesting correlate of these characteristics is that management's philosophy may be reflected in its behavior toward superiors, subordinates, and peers.

The basic assumptions that different people have regarding human behavior in industry vary considerably, but there are two generally obverse points of view that have been publicized quite extensively. These have been referred to by McGregor as *Theory X* and *Theory Y*:

Theory X and Theory Y are not managerial strategies: They are underlying beliefs about the nature of man that influence managers to adopt one strategy rather than another. [1]

McGregor explained the basic differences between these two theories:

The central principle of organization which derives from Theory X is that of direction and control through the exercise of authority . . . the central principle which derives from Theory Y is that of integration: The creation of conditions such that the members of the organization can achieve their own goals best by directing their efforts toward the success of the enterprise. [2]

The recent application of TA to organizational, and specifically industrial, settings provides a rationale for comparing contemporary managerial theories of human behavior (e.g., Maslow [3], Likert [4], Herzberg [5], Fleishman-Harris [6], Blake [7], and Hersey-Blanchard [8]) with TA. The purpose of our contribution is to do exactly that; we will compare McGregor's Theory X-Y with TA in an attempt to illustrate what we believe are the common theoretical relationships. We have chosen McGregor's theory because most contemporary theories of management (as cited above) seem to derive from McGregor's basic assumptions. We draw upon our own personal research as well as case and role-played examples to demonstrate the relationships between the two theories.

THEORY X

Under Theory X, management makes the following assumptions about human behavior.

1. The average human being has an inherent dislike of work and will avoid it if he can.

2. Therefore, most people must be coerced, controlled, directed, and threatened with punishment if management is to get them to put forth adequate effort toward the achievement of organizational objectives.

3. The average human being prefers to be directed, wishes to avoid responsibility, has relatively little ambition, and wants security above all. [9]

Behind this conventional theory, there are several additional beliefs — less explicit, but widespread.

4. The average human being is inherently self-centered and indifferent to organizational needs.

5. He is by nature resistant to change.

6. He is gullible, not very bright, and the ready dupe of the charlatan and the demagogue. [10]

THEORY Y

Under Theory Y, management makes the following assumptions about human behavior.

1. The expenditure of physical and mental effort in work is as natural as play or rest.

2. External control and the threat of punishment are not the only means for bringing about effort toward organizational objectives. Man will exercise self-direction and self-control in the service of objectives to which he is committed.

3. Commitment to objectives is a function of rewards associated with their achievement.

4. The average human being learns, under proper conditions, not only to accept, but to seek, responsibility.

5. The capacity to exercise a relatively high degree of imagination, ingenuity, and creativity in the solution of organizational problems is widely, not narrowly, distributed in the population.

6. Under the conditions of modern industrial life, the intellectual potentialities of the average human being are only partially utilized.

7. The essential task of management is to arrange organizational conditions and methods of operation so that people can achieve their own goals best by directing *their own* efforts toward organizational objectives. [1]

It should be apparent to anyone familiar with TA that McGregor's theory bears some relationship to TA. It is our contention that the relationship can best be seen by examining the management assumptions and the communication behavior (oral and written) of both the Theory X and Theory Y manager.

THEORY X-Y MANAGEMENT ASSUMPTIONS AND TA

James and Jongeward, in their book *Born To Win*, describe the "constant Parent" as one who "collects people who are willing to be dependent upon or subordinate to him... He knows all the answers, manipulates others from the top-dog position, and is domineering, overpowering, and authoritarian." [12] Recall McGregor's description of the Theory X manager as one who directs and controls "through the exercise of authority." [13]

Berne says the "Adult" is the ego state which is "concerned with the autonomous collecting and processing of data and the estimating of probabilities as a basis for action." [14] Recall that the Theory Y manager is one who relies upon information from employees which can be integrated with organizational objectives. Furthermore, Maslow's concept of "self-actualization," [15] from which McGregor derived Theory Y appears related to what James and Jongeward call the "integrated Adult." They state, "he has the honest concern and a commitment toward others that are characteristic of a good parent, the intelligence to solve problems that is characteristic of an adult, and the ability to create, express awe, and show affection that are characteristic of a happy and healthy child." [16]

It would appear, therefore, that the assumptions underlying Theory X can be explained partially in terms of TA's "constant Parent" behavior, and the Theory Y assumptions can be accounted for in terms of behavior stemming from the Adult ego state (or the integrated Adult). The relationship between the Theory X assumptions and the "constant Parent" can be seen in the following dialogue between a college president (named Happihour) and a student radical (named Dud).

Happihour: What can I do for you, son?

Dud: Don't call me son! I'm not your son! I've talked to you before and you obviously didn't listen to a word I said. The demands I have represent a majority of the students here. You can't ignore them!

Happihour: I know these demands, I've read them before.

Dud: Do you understand them?

Happihour: Yes, I understand them, and for your own good, I can't accept any of these demands.

Dud: You and your pompous friends had better start listening to us, because we're going to sit in your office forever!

Happihour: O.K., I will listen to you, but I'll tell you right now, before you begin, that for your own good these demands are not being met.

In the above example, Happihour assumed that the students could only be controlled by his authority, direction, and responsibility; he was unwilling to discuss a new approach or listen to new ideas; he was, in other words, operating directly from the Theory X assumptions. Additionally, he was treating Dud as a child; he even called him "son." The crossed transaction resulted because Dud was unwilling to play the role of the compliant child. Both parties were assuming the I'm OK — You're not-OK position with Dud's "rebel kid" responding to Happihour's "constant Parent."

THEORY X-Y COMMUNICATION BEHAVIOR AND TA

According to Redding and Sanborn, the typical Theory X organization maintains a downward-directed communication system with little or no opportunity for subordinate feedback to be sent upward to higher management. [17] Theory Y organizations, on the other hand, constantly monitor feedback by suggestion systems, group decisions, telephone hot lines, gripe sessions, etc. Common to all of the above feedback systems is the element of listening. It would appear, therefore, that the Theory Y organization listens.

Good listening is also fundamental to the understanding of TA. James and Jongeward state that "listening is one of the finest strokes one person can give another . . . when a person has been listened to, he leaves the encounter knowing that his feelings, ideas, and opinions have been really heard." [18] They go on to conclude that good listening is a function of the Adult ego state (from where the Theory Y manager is programmed).

In the above dialogue, it is apparent that Happihour was not listening to Dud. Even when Happihour said, "O.K., I will listen to you," he was not actively listening. As James and Jongeward state, Happihour was using his psychic energy to form a question, create a diversion, or plan a counterattack in his head." [19]

Listening is not the only communication behavior with parallels in both Theory X-Y and TA; written communication behaviors can also be discussed by both theories. James and Jongeward discuss the use of certain words to indicate the Parent ego state: "should," "have to," or "must" convey the idea of "oughtness." [20] One might hypothesize that the presence of these words in extremes may indicate the presence of the Parent ego state.

The senior author conducted a content analysis of two employment manuals, one belonging to a Theory X company and one to a Theory Y company. [21] The major finding of this study was that the Theory X employment manual contained significantly more negatives (cannot, can't, don't, never, won't, etc.) and commands (should, must, have to, will, required, forbidden, always, impossible, etc.) than the Theory Y manual. The contrast between the two manuals illustrates not only the difference between X and Y but also the difference between the "constant Parent" and the "integrated Adult":

(Theory X)   Do not operate any machine which is not in your regular line of duty — or with which you are not familiar — unless you are instructed by your foreman.

(Theory Y)   Before operating an unfamiliar machine, be sure that you receive instructions from your foreman.

(Theory X)   Do not talk to any fellow-worker while he is operating a machine. His life will cost you your job!

(Theory Y)   Try to limit your talk with others to the breaks. By talking with a neighbor while operating a machine, you and/or he might become distracted and get hurt.

Besides differing on the use of commands and negatives, the above examples contrast the critical Parent and the Adult (in the first pair) and the critical Parent with the nurturing Parent (in the second pair).

CONCLUSIONS

An analysis of McGregor's Theory X-Y and TA have revealed that certain parallels exist between the two; it would appear that the former could be explained or understood better in terms of the latter:

1. When a Theory X manager is operating from the assumption of authority and control, he is apparently behaving through his "constant Parent"; the Theory Y manager who attempts to integrate management and employee objectives is operating through his "integrated Adult" or with the Adult as executive.

2. Theory X managers do not listen as much or as well as Theory Y managers; the latter appear to be the better "strokers."

3. Theory X managers use more commands and negatives than Theory Y managers; in other words, the vocabulary of the X-manager is more Parent-oriented than that of the Y-manager (which appears to be more Adult-oriented).

The above conclusions would indicate that McGregor's and Berne's theories have a lot in common. With the increasing popularity of TA applications to business, industry, and other organizations, it would be beneficial, if not crucial, for managers, trainers, consultants, etc., to familiarize themselves with both theories. Once this happens, it will be easier for managers to recognize when they play *See What You Made Me Do* and consultants to be aware if they play *I'm Only Trying to Help You.*

FOOTNOTES AND REFERENCES

1. Douglas McGregor, *The Professional Manager* (New York: McGraw-Hill, 1967), p. 79.

2. Douglas McGregor, *The Human Side of Enterprise* (New York: McGraw-Hill, 1960), p. 12.

3. Abraham H. Maslow, *Motivation and Personality* (New York: Harper & Row, 1954), p. 33.

4. Rensis Likert, *New Patterns of Management* (New York: McGraw-Hill, 1961), pp. 14-24.

5. Frederick Herzberg, F.B. Mausner, Barbara Synderman, *The Motivation to Work* (New York: John Wiley, 1959), p. 52.

6. Edwin A. Fleishman and Edwin Harris, "Patterns of Leadership Behavior Related to Employee Grievances and Turnover," *Personnel Psychology*, **15** (1962): 43-56.

7. Robert R. Blake and Jane S. Mouton, *The Managerial Grid* (Houston: Gulf Publishing, 1964), p. 10.

8. Paul Hersey and Kenneth H. Blanchard, *Management of Organizational Behavior* (Englewood Cliffs, New Jersey: Prentice-Hall, 1969), p. 3.

9. McGregor, *Human Side of Enterprise*, pp. 33-34.

10. *Ibid.*, pp. 34-43.

11. *Ibid.*, pp. 47-49.

12. Muriel James and Dorothy Jongeward, *Born To Win: Transactional Analysis with Gestalt Experiments* (Reading, Massachusetts: Addison-Wesley, 1971), p. 229.

13. McGregor, *Human Side of Enterprise*, p. 34.

14. Eric Berne, *Principles of Group Treatment* (New York: Oxford University Press, 1964), p. 220.

15. Abraham Maslow, *op. cit.*, pp. 211-214.

16. James and Jongeward, *op. cit.*, p. 271.

17. W. Charles Redding and George Sanborn, *Readings in Business and Industrial Communication* (New York: Harper and Row, 1964), pp. 294-348.

18. James and Jongeward, *op. cit.*, p. 48.

19. *Ibid.*, p. 264.

20. *Ibid.*, p. 104.

21. Gerald Goldhaber, "A Content Analysis of Two Employment Manuals — With Implications for Theory X – Theory Y Management Assumptions," *EPS*, 11MS No. 426-1, April, 1971.

14

THE TRANS(A)CTIONAL MANAGER: AN ANALYSIS OF TWO CONTEMPORARY MANAGEMENT THEORIES

by Lyman K. Randall*

INTRODUCTION

Within the last 15 years considerable research and writing has appeared regarding the question, "What kinds of management approaches seem to lead to the best short- and long-term results for organizations?" Among those writing have been Robert Blake and Jane Mouton who have written about the 9,9 Managerial Grid Style and Rensis Likert who has written about System IV, or Participative Management. The theories of each of these have described a more desirable approach to managing organizations than the more commonly found management practices. Although these theories have been widely read and discussed in both universities and work organizations, they have not been widely used and implemented into the daily management practices of organizations. Why?

Some individuals claim that the theories simply are not valid. This claim, however, ignores the research which each author cites in support of his theory. Other individuals claim that their organizations are significantly different from those used in the research and are therefore unsuitable for the more desirable management system approach described by the researchers. Still others are attracted to the theories but are frustrated by the large number of occasions when realities of organization life seem to contradict a given theory. If you are among those in the latter group, this paper is written for you.

The ideas expressed in this paper are tentative. Don't accept them on faith. Test them against your own experience. The author encourages any additional points or modifications you may want to suggest.

---

*   See Chapter 7, page 131, for biographical notes.

WHAT CAUSES 9,9 MANAGERIAL STYLE BEHAVIORS?

Introduction

Several years ago Drs. Robert Blake and Jane Mouton integrated a large amount of leadership research that had been previously conducted by other investigators. They called their new conceptual framework "The Managerial Grid." This name was derived from the following two-axis diagram which they created to identify differing managerial leadership styles.

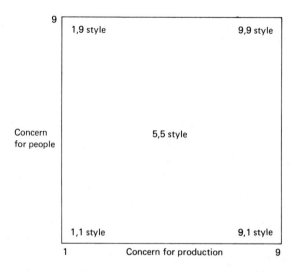

In their conceptualization, the vertical axis represents a manager's concern for people (or how much attention and energy he spends on individuals as they work). The horizontal axis represents a manager's concern for production (or how much attention and energy he gives to getting work tasks accomplished). Each axis is divided into nine units with 1 representing the lowest degree and 9 standing for the highest degree of concern on each scale.

Although it is theoretically possible to plot 81 points on such a 9 by 9 grid, Blake and Mouton identified five points on it as symbolizing different basic managerial styles. A 9,1 leadership style is typical of a manager who has an extremely high concern for accomplishing production tasks but a very low concern for his people who must achieve them. A manager using this style explicitly or implicitly assumes that efficiency in work results from arranging the procedures and conditions of work in such a way that human elements can interfere, at most, to a minimum degree. Conflicts between work requirements and people's needs are nearly always resolved in favor of work, with no effort to integrate the desires of individuals.

A 1,9 leadership style is typical of a manager who has an extremely high concern for the people he works with but a low concern for the productive work which they achieve. An individual who manages with this style assumes that thoughtful attention to the needs that people have for satisfying relationships will lead to a comfortable and friendly organizational climate. This style is perhaps identical to the old "human relations" school of thought, i.e., "If you're kind to people, they will be happy and have high morale. This, in turn, will cause them to produce more." Interpersonal conflict is seen as negative and harmful to relationships, so it is ignored if at all possible.

The 1,1 leadership style is typical of a manager who has a low concern for both people and production. An individual who manages with this style assumes that the exertion of minimum effort to get required work done is appropriate for sustaining organizational leadership. He may philosophize, "People work best when you leave them alone!" Conflict is largely ignored.

The 9,9 leadership style is typical of a manager who has a high concern for both his people and the work they do. An individual managing with this style assumes that giving high priority to solving both people problems and work or task problems results in committed and trusting workers and also high productivity results.

The 5,5 leadership style is typical of a manager who attempts to compromise his moderate concern for his people with his equally moderate concern for production results. An individual who manages with this style assumes that adequate organizational performance is possible only through trading-off the need to get work out with the need to maintain satisfactory morale. His behavior often fluctuates between "being tough on people to increase productivity" and "being nice to people to increase their sagging morale." Conflicts are usually negotiated, with compromises being sought to resolve most situations.

A Transactional Analysis

It is possible to analyze the five basic managerial grid styles using the following concepts from transactional analysis theory*:

1. Dominant life positions

2. Types of time structuring used

3. Types of transactions aimed at problem solving

---

*   For the reader's information, P = Parent ego state; A = Adult ego state; C = Child ego state.

The 9,1 grid style

9 9

Concern for people

1. *Life position.* The manager sees himself in a I'm OK – You're not-OK life position. Many of his activities with workers can be classified as "getting rid of actions," i.e. firing, disciplining, efficiency time studies, etc.
2. *Time structuring.* Task activities (work) are the only overt time structuring legitimized by the manager. Rituals are therefore built around task activities, i.e "washing-up," coffee breaks, punching-out, etc. Games are frequently used by workers and the manager to handle not-OK feelings and satisfy stroking needs, and as ineffective strategies for problem-solving. The manager often plays "getting rid of" games such as *Now I've Got You, You S.O.B.*, *Uproar*, and *If It Weren't For Them*. Workers covertly play these same games against management, but overtly often play persecuted games such as *Ain't It Awful* and *Why Does This Always Happen To Me?* Neither the manager nor the workers have many authentic encounters since this requires a shift in life positions to I'm OK – You're OK.
3. *Problem solving.* As long as the manager is working on a task problem, he is able to use his Ⓐ and to resolve it effectively. He probably was promoted to his job based on this kind of Ⓐ expertise. However, he is much less effective in solving interpersonal problems. With these, both his Ⓟ and Ⓒ usually get involved. If he realizes this at all, he rationalizes to justify his Ⓟ reaction: "Workers should take care of their problems off the job. They get paid well for producing!"
4. *Transactions and ego states.* In dealing with his people the manager often uses Ⓟ→Ⓒ kinds of transactions. This results in Ⓟ→Ⓒ parallel transactions, Ⓟ→Ⓒ crossed transactions, and Ⓟ→Ⓒ duplex transactions.
5. *Stroking.* The manager gives very few strokes to others and when he does, it is usually through criticism. Workers get their strokes mostly through game-playing and through rituals and pastimes with each other.

9,1

Concern for production

The 1,9 grid style

1,9 ─── 9

Concern for people

1. *Life position.* The manager sees himself in an I'm not-OK — You're OK life position. Because of his existential stance, his Ⓒ is expecting a magical shift to I'm OK by strong emphasis on everybody liking everybody else. Until his Ⓒ tapes are updated, however, his not-OK feelings will still dominate. Many of his actions with others can be classified as "getting away from others" behaviors. This is usually accomplished by keeping superficially friendly relations with everyone, never admitting any not-OK feelings, and denying that conflict (crossed transactions) exist.

2. *Time structuring.* Rituals and pastimes receive more attention than any other time structuring. A heavy amount of these are essential for producing the amount of marshmallow-strokes (nonsolid) required by the manager, who is magically trying to transform his not-OK Ⓒ by pleasing everyone. Withdrawal is used to handle not-OK feelings since expressing them directly is frowned upon. Games which are often played are concerned with helping others, e.g., *Why Don't You? — Yes, But, I'm Only Trying to Help You*, and with getting strokes, e.g., *Wooden Leg* and *Schlemiel.* He is largely incapable of engaging in authentic encounters.

3. *Problem solving.* The manager is ineffective at solving both task problems and interpersonal problems. He tends to spend little time concentrating on task activities, and he doesn't have the updated Ⓟ and Ⓒ to enable him to use authentic encounters. His attempts at problem solving are often games which prove to be ineffective.

4. *Transactions and ego states.* The manager's Ⓐ is used infrequently to solve task or people problems. Usually it is used to create rituals and pastimes (recreation clubs, recognition banquets, etc.) to keep his workers feeling like one big happy family. His Ⓒ covertly dominates by its wish to be magically made OK. His Ⓟ enforces a management climate which prohibits crossed transactions and "getting rid of others" games.

5. *Stroking.* The manager creates a work situation in which he is surrounded by strokes. Unfortunately they are of low nutritional value since none are given in authentic encounters, and he continues to feel not-OK.

9

Concern for production

The 1,1 grid style

Concern for people

9

1. *Life position.* The manager sees himself in an I'm not-OK — You're not-OK life position. In his despair he is only trying to hang on till he retires or gets a job that pays him well and requires nothing of him. His actions with others are characterized by "getting nowhere with them."

2. *Time structuring.* On the job, the manager uses a large amount of withdrawal. The less contact with others, the better. He also uses pastimes and rituals if forced by circumstances to have contact with others. If he engages in activities (task), they will usually be solo endeavors, i.e., working by himself or pursuing solitary recreation. He plays only a few games and rarely has an authentic encounter.

3. *Problem solving.* The manager is an ineffective problem solver when working with others, although he may apply his (A) to solve task problems when forced to (usually alone rather than with others).

4. *Transactions and ego states.* He has a very low volume of transactions. His not-OK (C) is in charge of most of them. He may be seen as a loner and a loser.

5. *Stroking.* Because of his minimal transactions, he gives only rare strokes and receives even fewer strokes. He locks himself into his not-OK position.

1,1   9

Concern for production

The 9,9 grid style

9   9,9

	1. *Life position.* The manager is in an I'm OK — You're OK life position. He is aware that most not-OK situations (which may also cause not-OK feelings) can be reasonably figured out and resolved by his Ⓐ. He also has experienced that this is often true in his relationships with others. Therefore, he gives them opportunities to figure things out, estimate probabilities, and make decisions which affect them directly, because he knows that others can usually employ their Ⓐ's when given the opportunity.

Concern for people

2. *Time structuring.* Withdrawal (on the job and in life) receives minimal attention from the manager. He knows the stroking value of rituals and pastimes, so he engages in them and gives others the choice to do the same. He is not reluctant, however, to interrupt them if they are being used to avoid coping with a priority task problem or interpersonal problem. He is able to use his Ⓐ to put activities (tasks) into sharp focus (problem definition and objective-setting). He feels OK about himself and others so he respects Ⓐ expertise which others may have regarding a problem. He often uses others as resources. He is aware of the games he plays and for what reasons (to get strokes or to handle not-OK feelings). He generally, however, does not save "dirty stamps."* He gives others the choice of engaging in games or not and interrupts them only if they are beginning to create serious task and/or interpersonal problems. He often uses authentic encounters to figure out joint solutions to interpersonal problems.

3. *Problem solving.* The manager is an exceptionally effective problem solver — for both task and interpersonal problems. He uses his emancipated Ⓐ skillfully when working on problems.

4. *Transactions and ego states.* Although he often uses his Ⓐ in transactions, he also is free to use both his Ⓟ and Ⓒ since they have been updated by his Ⓐ. He therefore engages in a rich mix of transactions but with executive authority and protection provided by his Ⓐ. He is not fearful of crossed transactions (conflict) because he knows most of them can be resolved. He often uses duplex transactions as the basis for his humor. His Natural Ⓒ often shines through his transactions.

5. *Stroking.* He gives and receives many strokes — through humor, through authentic encounters, through rituals and pastimes, and through his OK regard for others with whom he is transacting.

1   9

Concern for production

---

* Referred to in TA literature as gray stamps or brown stamps.

4. Other kinds of frequently used transactions and ego state dominance

5. Kinds and amounts of stroking

Grid Back-Up Styles and the 5,5 Grid Position

In their managerial grid leadership theory, Blake and Mouton establish a concept which they call "a manager's back-up style." This refers to their observation that a manager will often use one managerial grid style when initially confronting a given problem or situation. However, if this approach does not resolve things satisfactorily for him, the manager will shift to a second grid style. This secondary grid style is called the "back-up style."

In TA terms, the manager operates from a single dominant life position more than 50% of the time. All life positions, except I'm OK — You're OK (grid 9,9), are based either directly or indirectly on the manager's not-OK feelings (in his ©) which often dominate both his transactions with others and the manner in which he structures his time. What Blake and Mouton refer to as a shift in grid styles can also be viewed as a shift in ego states being used by the manager as the executive ego state. For example, in the I'm not-OK — You're OK position (1,9 grid style), the not-OK © is in executive control of most transactions and is trying to please the ℗ in others so they will like him and magically stroke him into being OK. However, when a manager shifts to an I'm not-OK — You're not-OK position (1,1 grid style), the not-OK © is still in control but has given up in despair that it can ever feel OK. If a manager is in a dominant I'm OK — You're OK position (9,9 grid style) but shifts temporarily to another position, his Ⓐ has temporarily lost the executive authority in his behavior and his not-OK © begins to dominate for that situation.

In their theory, Blake and Mouton establish the 5,5 grid style as a kind of "middle of the road" position for those who do not primarily function in one of the other four grid styles. A person who appears to swing frequently from one grid style to another is sometimes called "a statistical 5,5 style" in management grid theory.

It is highly probable that no "pure managerial grid style" individuals exist, i.e., no person *always* transacts in a single grid style. TA theory seems to postulate that an individual's managerial grid style will be largely the result of specific behavior outcomes of his own unique personality (℗ · Ⓐ · ©) functioning at any given time and in any given situation. In grid theory, the "statistical 5,5 style" and the "back-up style" concepts are used to explain shifts in behavior style. In

TA theory, these behavior shifts are explained as the result of changes in the executive ego state and the related life position.

WHAT MAKES LIKERT'S SYSTEM IV WORK?

As a young man Rensis Likert worked as a laborer for the Southern Pacific Railroad. From this early work experience he observed that the manner in which the employees were supervised often seemed to influence work outcomes more than quality standards or statements issued by those with formal authority. Dr. Likert has spent much of his professional life conducting research on this early personal observation.

This research has included studies of numerous organizations with various locations, sizes, purposes, and degrees of effectiveness. Until his retirement in 1970, Dr. Likert was the Director of the Institute for Social Research (ISR) at the University of Michigan, a position which he held from 1946. With Likert's leadership, ISR invested 25 years in investigating why some organizations are able to accomplish the end results which they set out to achieve, whereas others fail to do so. Using a multiple choice survey technique in which Likert had played a prominent role in developing in the early 1930's, ISR staff members continuously refined their investigations and conclusions. The following concepts are among the current results of this research.

Causal, Intervening, and End-Result Variables

Through their studies, Likert and his colleagues tried to find cause and effect relationships between their measurements of management actions and the end results achieved by management. From their efforts they concluded that all organizations are significantly influenced by three different kinds of variables. These are causal variables, intervening variables, and end-result variables.

Causal Variables

These are described as the most important ones, since they begin a series of actions which greatly influence later events. Likert confines his definition of causal variables to those things which management can *directly* influence and change. He excludes influences such as national economy and government regulation which management cannot directly modify.

Likert's causal variables include the following:

1. Available technology and competence of individuals in this technology

2. Facilities

3. Organizational policies

4. Organizational structure

5. Organizational climate that is established by the actions of top management in the following areas:

   a)   Management's willingness to be influenced by the ideas and perceptions of individuals at lower levels in the organization

   b)   The process management uses in making decisions

   c)   Its assumptions and actions regarding lateral coordination and collaboration with peers in other functions

The variable of organizational climate greatly influences two other equally important causal variables:

6. Supervisory leadership

7. Peer leadership

Likert describes effective supervisory leadership as being comprised of four factors:

   a)   *Supportive leadership style.* To use Likert's words ". . . The relationship between the superior and subordinate is crucial. This relationship. . .should be one which is supportive and ego building. The more often the superior's behavior is ego-building rather than ego-deflating, the better will be the effect of his behavior on organizational performance. It is essential to keep in mind that the interactions between the leader and the subordinate must be viewed in the light of the subordinate's background, values, and expectations. The subordinate's perception of the situation, rather than the supervisor's, determines whether or not the experience is supportive." [1]

   b)   *Emphasis on high performance aspiration and goals.* Likert describes this factor in the following way: "A firm must succeed and grow to provide its employees with what they want from a job: pride in the job and company, job security, adequate pay, and opportunities for promotion. Economic success is a situational requirement which can be met only if the organization, its departments and its members have high performance goals. Superiors consequently should have high performance aspirations, but this is not enough. Every member should have high performance aspirations as well. Since these high performance goals should not be imposed on employees, there must be a mechanism through which employees can help set the high-level goals which the satisfaction of their own needs requires." [2]

c) *Time and effort spent on team building.* Team building concentrates on behaviors between work group members which will first create and then maintain healthy and productive interpersonal relationships.

d) *Work facilitation.* Accomplishing work through the efforts of group members is, of course, a primary function of supervisory leadership. Supervisory behaviors which serve to develop or provide effective work methods, facilities, equipment, and know-how for accomplishing the group's work goals are described as work facilitation. The amount of work facilitation which a supervisor does is perhaps also an indication of how much commitment he has to the work team, its goals, and his supportive feelings toward its members.

Peer leadership, or leadership executed by work group members of the same level on each other, is made up of the same four factors which comprise supervisory leadership: (a) supportiveness, (b) high-performance aspirations and goals, (c) team building, and (d) work facilitation. Research evidence seems to indicate the following conclusions about peer leadership.

a) In work groups the total amount of peer leadership is at least as great as the total amount of supervisory leadership.

b) Peer leadership is at least as important as supervisory leadership, and possibly more so, in accomplishing work group goals.

c) Supervisory leadership will often influence the amount of peer leadership found within a work group.

Of the seven causal variables described, Likert and his associates have developed survey tools for measuring only the last three: organizational climate, supervisory leadership, and peer leadership.

Intervening Variables

Likert describes intervening variables as those factors which reflect the internal state and health of the organization. They are directly influenced by the causal variables described earlier and have a major impact on end-result variables. They include the following collective aspects of a group's working processes:

1. Motivation of individuals

2. Individual and group problem solving

3. Decision making

4. Coordination

5. Communication

End-Result Variables

In Likert's theoretical framework, end-result variables are always dependent on both the causal and intervening variables and reflect the observable achievements of the organization. They include such organizational outcomes as productivity, costs, earnings, scrap loss, and quality performance.

Several other "costs of doing business" are also end-result variables and reflect in somewhat different terms the effectiveness and efficiency of the total management system. These include employee turnover, grievances, employee attendance, and employee satisfactions.

In addition to the three causal factors mentioned earlier, Likert and his associates have also developed survey tools to measure the intervening variables and the end-result employee satisfactions.

How A Management System Works

Each of the variables described above influences at least one or more of the other variables. Collectively they tend to operate somewhat like a closed-loop system as diagrammed on the next page.

The causal variables of organizational policies, structure, and climate (I-C, I-D, and I-E) are determined by the behavior of a few key individuals in top management. As shown in the diagram, these causal variables, in turn, greatly influence supervisory leadership behaviors (I-F). And supervisory leadership behaviors are critical in determining peer leadership behaviors (I-G). Collectively these variables largely determine the kind of behaviors occurring within the work group in relation to the intervening variables of motivation, problem solving, decision making, coordination, and communication (II-A, II-B, II-C, II-D, and II-E). This entire sequence of behaviors determines the kind of end results that the organization is able to achieve (III-A through III-G).

Since top management executives usually monitor the end-result variables very closely, they tend to take action whenever the end results fall short of their expectations. This action is normally in the form of executive behavior which either modifies or reinforces the causal variables of organizational policies, structure, and climate (I-C, I-D, and

Exhibit 1. Likert's Management System Conceptual Sequence

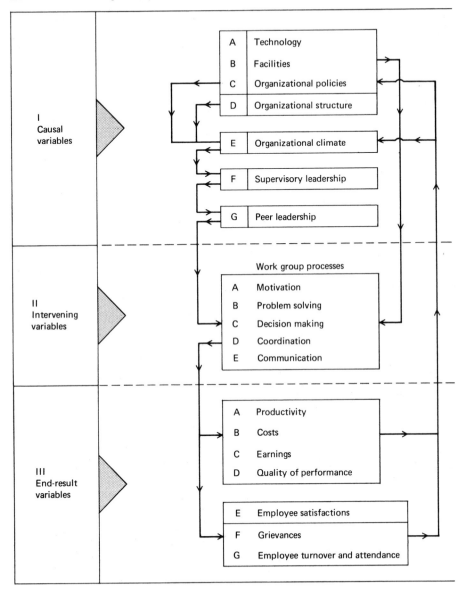

I-E). These variables, in turn, influence supervisory leadership behaviors (I-F), etc. Thus, the chain of management behaviors becomes cyclical.

Measuring and Creating Differences in Management Systems

If management systems tend to operate in the cyclical manner described above, how are significant changes in a management system accomplished? It is not sufficient to say that improvement can be achieved by simply changing organizational policy and climate, supervisory leadership, and peer leadership. The questions still remain, "How can these critical causal behaviors be modified? Who does the modifying?" Before these questions can be answered, let's take a brief look at the method Likert uses to measure the causal and intervening variables of a management system.

Likert and his associates have constructed questionnaires to obtain employee perceptions of causal and intervening variables of the management system in which they work. Each item on the questionnaire is constructed as a continuum. At one of the continuum, the described behavior is of an exploitive authoritarian nature. A management system which is characterized by a series of behaviors at this end of the measurement continuum is labeled System I by Likert.

At the opposite end of the continuum on each questionnaire item, the described behavior is characterized by a high degree of individual participation. A management system which is characterized by a series of behaviors at this end of the measurement continuum is called System IV. Likert has also identified two intermediate kinds of management behaviors which fall between the two extremes of exploitive authoritarian management and highly participative management. He calls these System II (benevolent authoritarianism) and System III (consultative). In summary, each item on a Likert questionnaire is constructed as a continuum which measures four types of management behavior.

System I	System II	System III	System IV
Exploitive authoritarian	Benevolent authoritarian	Consultative	Participative

In Exhibit 1 an analysis was made of the relationships between causal variables, intervening variables, and end-result variables as they function within Likert's management system framework. In Exhibit 2 which follows, a series of items from Likert's questionnaires is examined. Only System I and System IV management behaviors are listed since they represent opposite extremes on each question's continuum. After each description of System I and System IV behavior characteristics, the transactional analysis characteristics of the same behavior are described.

Exhibit 2

**Comparing Likert System I and System IV
Management Characteristics within a
Transactional Analysis Framework**

Exhibit 2 appears on the following twenty-two pages. The text will continue on page 310.

Exhibit 2. Comparing Likert System I and System IV Management Characteristics within a Transactional Analysis Framework

MANAGEMENT CHARACTERISTICS	LIKERT SYSTEM I CHARACTERISTICS (EXPLOITIVE AUTHORITARIAN)	TRANSACTIONAL ANALYSIS CHARACTERISTICS	LIKERT SYSTEM IV CHARACTERISTICS (PARTICIPATIVE)	TRANSACTIONAL ANALYSIS CHARACTERISTICS
Attitudes towards other members of the organization	Subservient attitudes toward superiors, coupled with hostility; hostility toward peers and contempt for subordinates; widespread distrust.	Top management's assumption about itself and lower level employees (I'm OK - You're not-OK) results in many (P)→(C) kinds of transactions (either parallel or duplex). This management approach hooks a high amount of not-OK (C) tapes in lower-level employees which are expended through either rebellious (C) actions or games designed to cash in collected dirty stamps. Since trust resides in the (C) of employees, it has turned to distrust since the (C) has been clobbered so many times by the (P) of higher levels and the not-OK (C) of fellow workers.	Favorable, cooperative attitudes throughout the organization, with mutual trust and confidence.	Top management's assumption about itself and lower-level employees (I'm OK - You're OK) provides many opportunities for people to use (A) at all levels. Through this progressive building of (A) s in all employees, the (C) s in employees are protected from frequent and arbitrary clobbering by (P) s of people above them. With this kind of (A) protection of (C) s, a high level of trust develops in the (C) which, in turn, makes more effective team problem solving by (A) s in the organization more probable.

ORGANIZATIONAL CLIMATE
CAUSAL VARIABLES

| *Adequacy of upward communication via line organization* | Very little. | Higher management levels often use $P \rightarrow C$ transactions. Thereby lower levels are treated as not-OK people. This creates high probability that information communicated upward by these lower levels will be discounted, since it comes from not-OK people. Being discounted by higher management makes lower levels feel even more not-OK and thereby limits even more the upward communication. The result is probably either withdrawal or game playing. | A great deal. | The OK feelings that exist at all levels of the organization minimize the need to defend and protect through game playing or withdrawal. People are accustomed to using their (A)s for problem solving and data inputs. |

Exhibit 2 (continued)

MANAGEMENT CHARACTERISTICS	LIKERT SYSTEM I CHARACTERISTICS (EXPLOITIVE AUTHORITARIAN)	TRANSACTIONAL ANALYSIS CHARACTERISTICS	LIKERT SYSTEM IV CHARACTERISTICS (PARTICIPATIVE)	TRANSACTIONAL ANALYSIS CHARACTERISTICS
Subordinates' feeling of responsibility for initiating accurate upward communication	None at all.	Management is seen as (P) and subordinates feel themselves to be (C) with large amount of not-OK feelings experienced. Within this context management is seen by subordinates as a deserving recipient of numerous dirty stamps.	Considerable responsibility felt and much initiative. Group communicates all relevant communication.	Assuming responsibility for individual action and initiating these actions occurs in persons who have strengthened their (A)s by updating both (C) and (P) tapes. In an organization characterized by a high degree of I'm OK - You're OK, this has higher probability of occurring. In addition, since data is stored in the (A), there is greater likelihood of data being communicated in organizations where (A)→(A) transactions occur most of the time.

ORGANIZATIONAL CLIMATE
CAUSAL VARIABLES

| *Need for supplementary upward communication system* | Need to supplement upward communication by spy system, suggestion system, or some similar devices. | Because so little Ⓐ is used in upward communication, minimal task data gets communicated upward. (Most upward communication is about not-OK feelings). Therefore other data sources are essential. This type of action is, in fact, an attempt to correct the symptoms without changing the causes of the symptom. The solution only uses more Ⓟ oriented devices which is what helped to create the problem in the first place. | No need for any supplementary system. | (See above.) |

Exhibit 2 (continued)

MANAGEMENT CHARACTERISTICS	LIKERT SYSTEM I CHARACTERISTICS (EXPLOITIVE AUTHORITARIAN)	TRANSACTIONAL ANALYSIS CHARACTERISTICS	LIKERT SYSTEM IV CHARACTERISTICS (PARTICIPATIVE)	TRANSACTIONAL ANALYSIS CHARACTERISTICS
Amount and character of interaction	Little interaction and always with fear and distrust.	The strong I'm not-OK - You're OK position of most employees leads to a set of "get away from others" behaviors. Among the strongest not-OK feelings generated in the (C) of employees are fear and distrust.	Extensive, friendly interaction with high degree of confidence and trust.	The strong I'm OK - You're OK position of most employees leads to a set of "getting on with others" behaviors. This high motivation to have interaction with others whenever desired or appropriate is, in part, caused by the (C) s of employees having so much trust and confidence in their own and others (A) s to figure things out satisfactorily.
Extent to which subordinates can influence the goals, methods, and activities of	None.	Superiors see subordinates as not-OK, so why bother to contaminate decisions with their ideas and thoughts.	A great deal.	Superiors see subordinates as also OK people who have (A) s capable of figuring things out.

their units and departments as seen by superiors	None except through informal organization or via unionization.	Top management often concludes that the more often data can be generated and used by people close to the problem, the more likely workable and optimal solutions will be figured out.
Extent to which subordinates can influence the goals, methods, and activities of their units and departments as seen by subordinates	In organizational relationships characterized by high amounts of $P \longrightarrow C$ transactions, the two basic options available to subordinates to influence upward are: (1) games, and (2) the creation of a counter-organization in which equally strong P behavior is possible, i.e., a union.	Substantial amount, both directly and via unionization.

(See above.) |

Exhibit 2 (continued)

MANAGEMENT CHARACTERISTICS	LIKERT SYSTEM I CHARACTERISTICS (EXPLOITIVE AUTHORITARIAN)	TRANSACTIONAL ANALYSIS CHARACTERISTICS	LIKERT SYSTEM IV CHARACTERISTICS (PARTICIPATIVE)	TRANSACTIONAL ANALYSIS CHARACTERISTICS
Amount of actual influence which superiors can exercise over the goals, activity, and methods of their units and departments	Believed to be substantial but actually moderate, *unless* capacity to exercise severe punishment is present.	The Ⓟ s in top management see themselves as powerful influences over the not-OK Ⓒ s in subordinates. This underestimates, however, the potency of Ⓒ s games which Ⓟ s in management cannot figure out but can only react to. This gives subordinates strong "ulterior power."	Substantial but often done indirectly, as for example, by superior building effective interaction — influence system.	Superior builds strong interaction influence systems by his own I'm OK - You're OK position. This in turn translates to "getting on with others" motivation regarding his methods of time structuring, stroking, and leadership. He has learned to be a winner, i.e., get what he wants without hurting or undermining others.
Extent to which an adequate structure exists for the flow of information from one part of the	Downward only.	Information to be communicated is limited to only OK information. Therefore, OK information can only come from OK people (bosses)	Capacity for information to flow in all directions from all levels and for influence to be exerted by all units on all units.	In employee groups where Ⓐ s are in control most of the time, people do not need Ⓟ permission to get or give information to levels or

ORGANIZATIONAL CLIMATE
CAUSAL VARIABLES

organization to another, there- by enabling influence to be exerted

who then pass it down to the not-OK people (subordinates).

units of the organ- ization which are outside "normal organization chan- nels" (which is a (P)-oriented con- cept). Emphasis instead is on (A)- oriented problem solving, and the organizational norm ((P) permission) is that it's OK to get information needed to solve problems.

Exhibit 2 (continued)

MANAGEMENT CHARACTERISTICS	LIKERT SYSTEM I CHARACTERISTICS (EXPLOITIVE AUTHORITARIAN)	TRANSACTIONAL ANALYSIS CHARACTERISTICS	LIKERT SYSTEM IV CHARACTERISTICS (PARTICIPATIVE)	TRANSACTIONAL ANALYSIS CHARACTERISTICS
At what levels of the organization are decisions formally made?	Bulk of decisions at top of organization.	The top of the organization is where the OK people are. Subordinates are seen as not-OK Ⓒ . Ⓒ should be seen and not heard!	Decision making widely done throughout the organization, although well integrated through linking process provided by overlapping groups.	Employees at all levels seen as OK people with Ⓐ s capable of figuring things out and making decisions. The main problem becomes one of coordinating individual and group efforts so decisions will be integrated into organization wholes. This is achieved more easily since each person operates most of the time in Ⓐ rather than behaving as Ⓒ when he is in subordinate role and then as Ⓟ when he is in superior role.

ORGANIZATIONAL CLIMATE
CAUSAL VARIABLES

| *How adequate and accurate is the information available for decision making at the place where the decisions are made?* | Partial and often inaccurate information only is available. | For the reasons outlined in sections above regarding communication and interaction influence, information at the top is incomplete and/or distorted. | Relatively complete and accurate information available based on measurements and efficient flow of information in organization. | For the reasons outlined above regarding communication and interaction influence, information is complete and accurate. |

Exhibit 2 (continued)

MANAGEMENT CHARACTERISTICS	LIKERT SYSTEM I CHARACTERISTICS (EXPLOITIVE AUTHORITARIAN)	TRANSACTIONAL ANALYSIS CHARACTERISTICS	LIKERT SYSTEM IV CHARACTERISTICS (PARTICIPATIVE)	TRANSACTIONAL ANALYSIS CHARACTERISTICS
Extent to which technical and professional knowledge is used in decision making	Used only if possessed at higher levels.	High Ⓟ orientation of top management does not, for several reasons, facilitate subordinates using professional knowledge and experience which is largely stored in their Ⓐ s. • Lower levels seen as not-OK and therefore top management has low trust in their professional expertise. • High Ⓟ orientation creates organizational norms (going strictly through channels) which makes it difficult to draw directly on expertise.	Most of what is available anywhere within the organization is used.	Top management's I'm OK - You're OK orientation creates situations in which relatively free access to Ⓐ data throughout the organization is possible.

ORGANIZATIONAL CLIMATE
CAUSAL VARIABLES

SUPERVISORY LEADERSHIP CAUSAL VARIABLES	Far apart.	Usually very close.
Psychological closeness of superiors to subordinates (i.e., how well does superior know and understand problems faced by subordinates?)	• Lower levels are also suspicious (lots of not-OK ☺) about what top management *really* has up its sleeve if it does attempt to draw on its professional expertise. Strong orientation by management toward subordinates of I'm OK - You're not-OK results in considerable "get rid of" types of behavior (firing, punishing, threatening, using fear, etc.). Subordinates' orientation toward superiors of I'm not-OK - You're OK generates large amounts of "getting away from" types of behavior (games, union security actions, sabotage, avoidance, withdrawal, etc.)	The strong I'm OK - You're OK orientation of employees at all levels results in dominance of "getting on with others" kinds of behavior. Stroking needs are met directly and naturally rather than through subterfuge.

Exhibit 2 (continued)

MANAGEMENT CHARACTERISTICS	LIKERT SYSTEM I CHARACTERISTICS (EXPLOITIVE AUTHORITARIAN)	TRANSACTIONAL ANALYSIS CHARACTERISTICS	LIKERT SYSTEM IV CHARACTERISTICS (PARTICIPATIVE)	TRANSACTIONAL ANALYSIS CHARACTERISTICS
Accuracy of perceptions by superiors and subordinates	Often in error.	The situation described above produces high frequency of game playing or withdrawal in which the purpose of the transaction is *not* the communication of accurate feelings or information but is, instead, the coping with not-OK feelings.	Usually quite accurate.	The situation described above allows each person more choices in how to use his Ⓐ in transacting with others. Because Ⓐ is stronger in employees, fewer occasions arise when not-OK feelings are dealt with through games and withdrawal. Instead, problems are dealt with more directly in authentic encounter.
Manner in which goal setting or ordering is usually done	Orders issued from the top.	The I'm OK - You're not OK position assumed by top management and their resulting Ⓟ⟶Ⓒ orientation toward lower level employees	Except in emergencies, goals are usually established by means of group participation.	Widespread I'm OK - You're OK orientation leads to logical consequence of utilizing as much Ⓐ-generated data as possible for

SUPERVISORY LEADERSHIP
CAUSAL VARIABLES

problem-solving, decision making, and goal setting. Group participation seen as economical device for tapping large amount of Ⓐ data in short period of time – plus insuring accuracy since distortions are more likely to be corrected.

leads to logical consequence of *telling* subordinates what to do and not do.

Exhibit 2 (continued)

MANAGEMENT CHARACTERISTICS	LIKERT SYSTEM I CHARACTERISTICS (EXPLOITIVE AUTHORITARIAN)	TRANSACTIONAL ANALYSIS CHARACTERISTICS	LIKERT SYSTEM IV CHARACTERISTICS (PARTICIPATIVE)	TRANSACTIONAL ANALYSIS CHARACTERISTICS
To what extent do the different hierarchical levels tend to strive for high performance goals?	High goals pressed by top management but resisted by subordinates.	With it's I'm OK - You're not-OK orientation, top management has a tendency to set high goals. However, its perception of lower levels may cause some ulterior setting of *extra*-high goals for lower levels since they are seen as "foot draggers" on any goal (Ⓒ resistance). This anticipation of game playing by lower levels leads top management to play games by asking for more performance than they expect to get. Both top management and lower levels can accurately point to the ulterior transactions of the other — thus a self-fulfilling prophecy is perpetuated.	High goals sought by all levels, with lower levels sometimes pressing for higher goals than top levels.	Lower level employees have more Ⓐ data about themselves, their capabilities, and their work situations than does top management. With strong I'm OK - You're OK orientation, employees are motivated to behave in "getting on with others" directions. This increases likelihood that they decide what they want, then *do* it. The personal satisfactions come more from *doing* than from winning games over others or cashing in dirty stamps with others.

SUPERVISORY LEADERSHIP
CAUSAL VARIABLES

INTERVENING VARIABLES

Are there forces to accept, resist, or reject goals?	Goals are overtly accepted but are covertly resisted strongly.	The not-OK Ⓒ (or complaint Ⓒ) in most employees causes them to outwardly go along with the goals for fear of getting into trouble if they don't; however, because the not-OK feelings in the Ⓒ are reinforced, more intense versions of games result which are the covert resistance.	Goals are fully accepted, both overtly and covertly.	Since most employees have an opportunity to explore and test goals with their Ⓐ s, there is a lower probability that their Ⓒ s will be fearful or resentful, or that their Ⓟ s will be reacting to the inappropriateness of goals.
At what hierarchical levels in the organization does primary concern exist with regard to the performance of the control function?	At the very top only.	This is the logical consequence of all the other System I casual variables. Control *must* be at the top (which is saying that System I management has now become a self-fulfilling prophecy.)	Concern for performance of control responsibility is likely to be felt throughout the entire organization.	This is the logical consequence of all other System IV casual variables. It could not be any other way without the preceding processes appearing to be a grand duplex game.

Exhibit 2 (continued)

MANAGEMENT CHARACTERISTICS	LIKERT SYSTEM I CHARACTERISTICS (EXPLOITIVE AUTHORITARIAN)	TRANSACTIONAL ANALYSIS CHARACTERISTICS	LIKERT SYSTEM IV CHARACTERISTICS (PARTICIPATIVE)	TRANSACTIONAL ANALYSIS CHARACTERISTICS
How accurate are the measurements and information used to guide the control function, and to what extent do forces exist in the organization to distort and falsify this information?	Very strong forces exist to distort and falsify; as a consequence, measurements and information are usually incomplete and often inaccurate.	In a system characterized by strong not-OK feelings, people use duplex transactions (games) to protect themselves (their not-OK Ⓒ s) and their life positions. Data is therefore often distorted in the playing of these games. Probably the distortion of measurement data becomes a major game itself. Other distortions occur in the process of cashing in dirty stamps (where often the prize is a free bum steer).	Strong pressures to obtain complete and accurate information to guide one's own behavior and behavior of own and related work groups; therefore, information and measurements tend to be complete and accurate.	I'm OK - You're OK relationships are recognized as interdependent. If one person switches to a different life position, it becomes more difficult to maintain I'm OK - You're OK. Since intense game playing is not necessary to protect the Ⓒ in people, their Ⓐ s are free to do problem-solving for which accurate and adequate data is needed.
Extent to which there is an informal organization present that supports	Informal organization present that opposes goals of formal organization.	"It's us against them!" Since top management behaves in "getting rid of others" manner	Informal and formal organization are the same; therefore, all social forces support	This can be true only if the formal organization is seen as a much loser network of work relationships

or opposes goals of formal organization	(from I'm OK - You're not-OK position), there is understandable fear and anxiety in the © of people at lower levels. It is reasonable for them, therefore, to protect their © s by maneuvers initiated by Ⓟ s (unions), by © (through game-playing), and by Ⓐ s, figuring ways to beat the system. Probably the opposition is not so much directed toward goals as it is toward coercion and manipulation used by management implementing them.	efforts to achieve organizational goals.	than appears on organization charts. It is doubtful that *all* social forces *directly* support efforts to achieve organizational goals, since some of the social forces are directed toward stroking and maintaining OKness which are individual goals. However, if these individual goals are met, more energy is available to spend on organization goals.
What is the manner in which motivational forces are used?	Fear, threats, punishment, and occasional rewards are used.	Negative strokes used frequently to hook not-OK © which enables the Ⓟ in supervisor to maintain control.	Lots of rewards in addition to economic ones. Group participation and involvement in goal setting, improving methods, appraising progress toward goals, etc.

Heavy stroking occurs in group participation. The dominate orientation of I'm OK - You're OK becomes a powerful motivational force. The Ⓐ s of people are used to protect and feed the natural © in themselves and others.

Exhibit 2 (continued)

MANAGEMENT CHARACTERISTICS	LIKERT SYSTEM I CHARACTERISTICS (EXPLOITIVE AUTHORITARIAN)	TRANSACTIONAL ANALYSIS CHARACTERISTICS	LIKERT SYSTEM IV CHARACTERISTICS (PARTICIPATIVE)	TRANSACTIONAL ANALYSIS CHARACTERISTICS
What kinds of attitudes are developed toward the organization and its goals?	People's attitudes are usually hostile and counter to the organizational goals.	Not-OK feelings in ©s of employees are a natural response to management's ℗ approach. This creates a high frequency of duplex, crossed, and ℗→© parallel transactions, all of which reduce opportunities for the (A)s of employees to work on solutions to the organization's problems.	People's attitudes generally are strongly favorable and provide powerful stimulation to behavior implementing organization's goals.	The above situation also frees people's (A)s to spend time and energy on working toward goals of organization.
What is the amount of interaction and communication aimed at achieving the organization's objectives?	Very little.	Most time structuring is spent on things other than work (activities). Withdrawal, rituals, pastimes, and games consume most of the time because of the	Much with both individuals and groups.	Because of dominant I'm OK - You're OK life positions in the organization, considerable one-to-one and group time structuring are spent on tasks (activities) and

INTERVENING VARIABLES

What is the direction of information flow?	Downward.	Down, up, and with peers.
Extent to which communications are accepted by subordinates	Viewed with great suspicion.	Generally accepted, but if not, openly and candidly questioned.

not-OK in the life positions perpetuated by people in the organization.

Superiors   Subordinates

The © s in people have learned to distrust what is said since their Ⓐ s have figured out that communications have a low probability of working out the way the words imply they will.

resolving work-related interpersonal problems (authentic encounters.)

People at all levels

With dominant I'm OK - You're OK orientation, the © s in people trust the others who are doing the communicating. This results in the listener either accepting what is said or openly questioning it if it doesn't make sense.

Exhibit 2 (continued)

MANAGEMENT CHARACTERISTICS	LIKERT SYSTEM I CHARACTERISTICS (EXPLOITIVE AUTHORITARIAN)	TRANSACTIONAL ANALYSIS CHARACTERISTICS	LIKERT SYSTEM IV CHARACTERISTICS (PARTICIPATIVE)	TRANSACTIONAL ANALYSIS CHARACTERISTICS
Productivity	Mediocre productivity.	This is the only possible consequence of all the above not-OKness, game playing, withdrawal, and emphasis on (P) → (C) behavior.	Excellent productivity.	When people have updated their old (P) and (C) recordings, this frees their (A) s to figure out how to accomplish things they want without hurting themselves or others. An organization which encourages each person to do this benefits by getting its needs met, since they are so interdependent with each person achieving his own wants.
Excessive absenteeism and turnover	Tends to be high when people are free to move to other jobs.	Widespread I'm not-OK assumptions about themselves cause employees to use frequently "getting away from others" behaviors.	Low.	If people are fortunate enough to find themselves working in an organization characterized by I'm OK - You're OK

	Relatively high unless carefully policed.	Both calling in sick and changing jobs are common ways to get away from others.	life positions, who wants to leave?
Scrap loss and waste		Frequent use of Ⓒ behaviors by lower levels causes high waste for several reasons: 1. Waste is free prize for cashing in dirty stamps against top management. 2. Top management seen in Ⓟ framework; therefore, it's their responsibility to catch waste. 3. Low use of Ⓐ s by employees to figure out solutions to waste problems.	
	Members themselves will use measurements and other steps to keep losses to a minimum.		Scrap and waste are just two more problems that employees are accustomed to using their own Ⓐ s to figure out and resolve.

Making Likert's System IV Work

As seen in the analysis described in Exhibit 2, certain preconditions exist which determine the causal variables of organizational climate and supervisory leadership. These preconditions pertain to the personal and interpersonal orientation of employees in the organization, especially the management employees. In Exhibit 2 transactional analysis has been used to differentiate these preconditions in a System I management orientation from those in a System IV management orientation.

It is perhaps appropriate to regard these preconditions referred to above as precausal variables. Before the causal variables of organizational climate, supervisory leadership, and peer leadership can be modified, a change must first occur in these precausal variables. It is possible to describe precausal variables with a behavior framework other than transactional analysis. However, within the TA framework used in Exhibit 2, precausal variables include the following:

- The degree to which the I'm OK – You're OK life position orientation is acted on by the majority of employees, particularly managers and key executives.
- The factor above requires many individuals to have updated Ⓟ and Ⓒ tapes. This is accomplished by strong Ⓐ 's.
- The proportion of Ⓟ◄─►Ⓒ transactions compared with Ⓐ◄─►Ⓐ transactions.
- The amount of not-OK feelings generated in individual employees by crossed transactions and duplex transactions.
- The degree to which employees save up their not-OK feelings for later use by cashing in dirty stamps.
- The proportion of time structuring spent on task problem solving (activities) and interpersonal problem solving (authentic encounters) versus withdrawal, pastimes, and games.
- The degree to which stroking naturally occurs based on OKness versus the degree to which stroking does not occur or is based on not-OK feelings.

In summary, the precausal variables described above were derived from the transactional analysis description in Exhibit 2. These precausal variables influence the causal variables in the following manner.

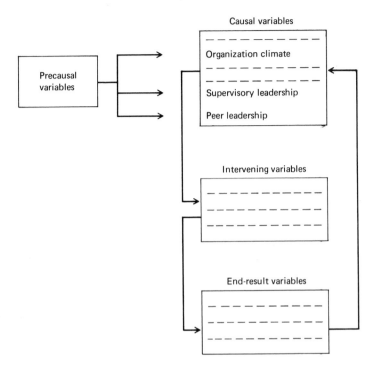

Causal variables

Organization climate

Supervisory leadership

Peer leadership

Precausal variables

Intervening variables

End-result variables

FOOTNOTES AND REFERENCES

1. Rensis Likert, *The Human Organization: Its Management and Value* (New York: McGraw-Hill, 1967), p. 51.

2. *Ibid.*, p. 51.

EPILOGUE

It is my hope that TA will be used in organizations
to liberate people and institutions from past bondages
that inhibit growth, healthy adaptations, and the
self-actualization of people. What are organizations
for if they do not in some way meet the needs of
people?

APPENDIX A: BIBLIOGRAPHY

The following bibliography is given for the person who wishes to be aware of other books and materials about transactional analysis. Most of these items can be ordered through:

International Transactional Analysis Association
3155 College Avenue
Berkeley, California 94705

This association also publishes a *Directory of Affiliates and Geographical List of Members* and has available other publications not mentioned below.

Information concerning training in TA should also be directed to this address.

For information regarding TA training and programs for organizations, write:

Transactional Analysis Management Institute
487 Malaga Way
Pleasant Hill, California 94523

BIBLIOGRAPHY

Berne, Eric, *Games People Play* (New York: Grove Press, 1964).

Berne, Eric, *Layman's Guide to Psychiatry and Psychoanalysis* (New York: Simon & Schuster, 1957).

Berne, Eric, *Principles of Group Treatment* (New York: Oxford University Press, 1964).

Berne, Eric, *Sex in Human Loving* (New York: Simon & Schuster, 1971).

Berne, Eric, *The Structure and Dynamics of Organizations and Groups* (Philadelphia: J.B. Lippincott, 1963).

Berne, Eric, *Transactional Analysis in Psychotherapy* (New York: Grove Press, 1961).

Berne, Eric, *What Do You Say After You Say Hello?* (New York: Grove Press, 1972).

Harris, Thomas, *I'm OK-You're OK: A Practical Guide to Transactional Analysis* (New York: Harper & Row, 1969).

James, Muriel, *Born to Love: Transactional Analysis in the Church* (Reading, Massachusetts: Addison-Wesley, 1973).

James, Muriel and Jongeward, Dorothy, *Born to Win: Transactional Analysis with Gestalt Experiments* (Reading, Massachusetts: Addison-Wesley, 1971).

Jongeward, Dorothy, cassette recording, "An Overview of Transactional Analysis," professionally narrated (send for through Addison-Wesley, Reading, Massachusetts, or the International Transactional Analysis Association).

Jongeward, Dorothy, and Scott, Dru, *Affirmative Action for Women: A Practical Guide* (to be published by Addison-Wesley, 1974).

McCormick, Paul and Campos, Leonard, *Introduce Yourself to Transactional Analysis* (Stockton, California: San Joaquin Transactional Analysis Study Group, 1969).

Schiff, Jacqui Lee with Day, Beth, *All My Children* (New York: M. Evans, 1971).

Steiner, Claude M., *Games Alcoholics Play* (New York: Grove Press, 1971).

Transactional Analysis Bulletin (back issues) now the *Transactional Analysis Journal*. (Write International Transactional Analysis Association, address above.)

APPENDIX B: ORGANIZATIONAL GAME

Your project now is to diagram a game played in your organization.*

1. Describe plausible reason for transaction.

2. What are the secret messages?

3. Diagram the transaction.

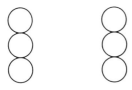

4. What is the feeling payoff for the players?

5. Name the game.

6. How can the game be stopped?

---

*   Prepared by Thomas C. Clary

APPENDIX C: THE GAMES PEOPLE PLAY

Games are played from the manipulative roles of Victim, Persecutor, and Rescuer. These roles switch as the game progresses. Also, these games can be played from different roles. This is a guide only.*

Victim games usually reinforce a psychological position of I'm not-OK. Inadequacy and/or depression stamps† may be collected.

Kick Me
Wooden Leg
Harried Executive
Lunch Bag
Why Does This Always Happen to Me?
Poor Me

Ain't It Awful (about me)
Love Me No Matter What I Do
 (Schlemiel)
See How Hard I Try
Stupid

Blaming games reinforce an I'm not-OK position by acting out a You're not-OK drama. Purity and self-righteous stamps may be collected, often covering up fear.

If It Weren't for You
See What You Made Me Do?

Persecutor games usually reinforce a psychological position of You're not-OK. Anger and/or purity stamps may be collected.

Blemish
Corner
Now I've Got You, You S.O.B.
Rapo
Bear Trapper
Let's You and Him Fight
Yes, But
I Told You So

Making Someone Sorry
Uproar
Why Do You Always . . .
Ain't It Awful (about you)
Mine is Better Than Yours
Putting Someone Down
Psychiatry

Rescuer games usually reinforce the You're not-OK position. Purity, anger, inadequacy, and/or depression stamps may be collected.

I'm Only Trying to Help You
Let Me Do It for You

Games are played to avoid or regulate intimacy, to get strokes, to collect stamps, to reinforce psychological positions, or to reinforce psychosomatic illness. They are a bad habit and can be given up in favor of more honest, authentic, intimate human encounter based on the present rather than on what happened in the past. Winners try their best to give up destructive or hurtful games.

---

*   Prepared by Dorothy Jongeward

†   Stamps represent feelings that are collected, saved up, and then cashed in, similar to the way we collect and redeem S&H green stamps.

APPENDIX D: "WHAT DO YOU DO WHEN YOUR SCRIPT RUNS OUT?"

Dorothy Jongeward, M. Ed.

Many hundreds of students go through my TA courses designed especially for women.* Nearly two-thirds of these women (primarily suburban housewives) exhibit what I've analyzed as the Sleeping Beauty Script. [1]

A typical Sleeping Beauty is one who bases her script identity and destiny almost exclusively on feminine identification and Parent-programmed, traditional female roles. She lacks a strong dual identity as described by Virginia Satir, [2] negating her sense of personhood and strengthening her sense of femaleness.

Script messages are sent through her first toys which are likely to be baby dolls and play household-gadgets at the exclusion of other possibilities. Parents' strokes determine her adaptations. They frown, discounting aggressive or scientific play, and smile when she is clean, quiet, and motherly. Her feminine scripting may be reinforced with verbalizations such as: "Isn't she the cute little mother." "See how sweet she is with her baby doll." The little girl begins to think of herself as "little mother," and her other possibilities are discounted.

She generally achieves well in grade school. Teachers like her. Her main adaptive pattern is compliance, which gains her much approval.

As she reaches age 12-14, her interests begin to center around her appearance to an *extreme* degree, often to the detriment of having fun, competing, or achieving. For example, she may not swim with the gang because her hair and eye make-up would be spoiled.

By age 14-16, she adapts her infantile script to adult life and firms up her script destiny as "I'm going to get married and have children" (often the sequence is reversed). When this script goal firms up, she "goes to sleep." Sleeping Beauty sleeps instead of developing her own unique talents and intellect. She sleeps instead of self-actualizing her full potential. In fact, she may play *Stupid* or practice martyrdom, playing the Victim role.

Her sleeping state is easily diagnosed when she makes such statements as:

"I don't need to know math. I'm just going to be a housewife."

From *Transactional Analysis Journal*, 2 (April 1972):2. Reprinted by permission from the International Transactional Analysis Association.

Dorothy Jongeward, M. Ed. is a consultant and lecturer in business, education, psychology of women, sex education.

* Since 1962 such classes as: Psychology of Women, The Nature of Women, Seminar for Career Women, Transactional Analysis of Women.

"Why should I struggle in college? I'm just going to get married."

At this point marriage and children are the goal, the end in life, not a beginning. She thinks ahead to marriage but is deluded about the realities of marriage and child rearing. These delusions are reinforced by the mass media, which eagerly offers her help to reach her goal. She is encouraged to clean up her breath, sweeten her arm pits, remove the hair from her legs, and to spray away offensive feminine odors. Her script compulsion contaminates her Adult reality-testing function; her Parent contaminates her Adult with prejudicial messages about male/female roles and goal expectations.

If she goes to college, she takes the easy course and/or drops out when Mr. Right, her script complement, comes along with a kiss. (He may want her to help him fulfill his vocational scripting.) He is likely to come on authoritarian and prejudicial, reinforcing her Parental messages about a woman's place and function. She may play *If It Weren't For Him* and/or *See What He Makes Me Do?* As one Sleeping Beauty complained, "Why, Edward would have a fit if I went to night school!"

Sleeping Beauty maintains a sense of OKness as long as she follows her script compulsion and is caring for children. However, as her last child approaches age 15-16, she begins to feel lonely, her time is less structured, and depression becomes her main negative stamp collection. By the time her last child leaves, she is around forty years old and may have been to a doctor who prescribes anti-depressants or tranquilizers. If not tranquilizers, she may turn to alcohol.

At this point, her Open End script [3] runs out. She has completed her script and now faces an existential vacuum. No scripting messages come to her rescue to tell her what to do with her time. Some women, in desperation, have another baby to fill up the next ten years. This kind of temporary solution only structures time until the script runs out again and the Script Vacuum re-occurs. Then there is only death to wait for. I see many cases in which an authority figure — doctor, nurse, parent, counselor — has suggested another baby as a solution, perhaps not realizing that in the long run this will not solve the problem. As Eric Berne advises, "The moral of this is that a script should not have a time limit on it, but should be designed to last a whole lifetime, no matter how long that lifetime may be." [4]

It is interesting to compare how the Script Vacuum has evolved as more of a problem for contemporary women than for women at the turn of the century. Compare the pie diagram of Mrs. Average today (which follows) to what it would have been in 1900.

Mrs. Average today marries by age 19, has 2.7 children (this continues to drop), gives birth to her last child at age 26, and has a life expectancy of 74 years.

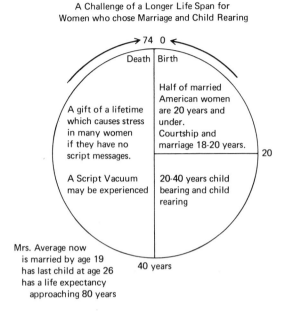

A Challenge of a Longer Life Span for
Women who chose Marriage and Child Rearing

74 0

Death | Birth

A gift of a lifetime
which causes stress
in many women
if they have no
script messages.

Half of married
American women
are 20 years and
under.
Courtship and
marriage 18-20 years.

20

A Script Vacuum
may be experienced

20-40 years child
bearing and child
rearing

Mrs. Average now
is married by age 19
has last child at age 26
has a life expectancy
approaching 80 years

40 years

Mrs. Average at the turn of the century married at age 22, had a large number of children, gave birth up to her menopause, and had a life expectancy of only 48 years! She had no time for her script to run out and might be hard put to understand what the fuss is all about with many women today.

When a modern woman suffers a Script Vacuum, she is likely to feel lost, finished, depressed, and useless in what is actually the prime of her life. Her drama is over and a new lifetime stretches before her that nobody told her about or prepared her for. As one woman put it, revealing the power of her delusions, "When my last kid went out the door, my whole sense of self went with him and a terrible feeling of not knowing what to do fell over me. I guess I expected babies to last forever. Here I am 43 and finished. I've never even thought of doing anything else."

Important to the treatment of Sleeping Beauty is the Adult in-put on the Open End script. She needs to become aware of the physical and mental symptoms of having no script and of the futility she faces waiting for inner messages to tell her what to do. I have had the best results with this if her previous roles of housewife and mother are not discounted. Otherwise, her resentments may be displaced as her children take the blame for her having "sacrificed" her personal development for them. Resentment toward husband and children is common when Sleeping Beauty "wakes up" and realizes where she is in her life. Her energy is better used if it is directed toward solving the problem. At this point, she can begin to understand and better cope with her uncomfortable, sometimes depressive feelings. Often a woman will start helping other women.

Eventually, to effect a cure she must begin to examine new life styles and set goals. Constructive goals are essential for developing a winner script for her remaining life's time.

Goals are more likely to be winner goals if they are based on the reality of talents and potentials of the woman. Vocational and educational counseling are often necessary to help establish these data. She needs to work hard gathering realistic, Adult information about herself and her possibilities. Her therapy "homework" is centered around gathering this information and setting and reaching goals.

To effect a cure, social changes may be necessary. [5] The commitment of the counselor may be directed toward seeking this change, as was mine. When I first became aware of the high number of women who had Sleeping Beauty or some other Open End script, there were few places available for them to fulfill the educational goals they set. As a result, I was able to develop curriculum for the local Adult School District which was picked up by other school districts, begin courses for women at the university level, instruct high-school counselors on how to break up this script earlier in life through my Family Life Education courses for educators, and testify before the California Status of Women Commission on behalf of continuing education for women.

An exercise that is useful is to have the client set goals for specific periods of time. For example, the first six months she may set goals monthly. (For some, daily goals may be necessary.) She deals with the questions: "Where do I expect to be one month from today?" and, "What do I expect to be doing?" Gradually, the time is extended until she learns to think in these terms. It is important to have this second script go well into old age planning for realistic and satisfying activities for late life. (This is very similar to the kinds of programs that are developing for men whose scripts end at retirement.)

I have seen hundreds of women begin to take responsibility for their own life direction: Some by returning to school, some by developing a community project, getting a job, or developing a talent they were aware of at 10 years old. These are the women who choose getting on with life over waiting for the final curtain, or, as Berne wrote, "waiting for the Promised Land." [6]

REFERENCES

1. Cf Hogie Wycoff, "The Stroke Economy in Women's Scripts," *Transactional Analysis Journal*, Vol. 1, No. 3, July 1971, pp. 16-20. See also, Hogie Wycoff, "Radical Psychiatry and Transactional Analysis in Women's Groups," *Transactional Analysis Bulletin*, Oct. 1970, Vol. 9, No. 36. pp. 128-133.

2. Virginia Satir, *Conjoint Family Therapy*, Science and Behavior Books, Palo Alto, 1964, pp. 19, 48-53.

3. Eric Berne, *Sex in Human Loving*, Simon and Schuster, 1970, pp. 167-170.

4. Ibid., p. 170.

5. Cf Eric Berne, "Editor's Page." *Transactional Analysis Bulletin*, Vol. 8. No. 29. Jan. 1969, pp. 7-8.

6. Berne, *Sex in Human Loving*, p. 167.